T0256720

Explainable AI for Practitioners

*Designing and Implementing
Explainable ML Solutions*

Michael Munn and David Pitman

Foreword by Ankur Taly

Beijing · Boston · Farnham · Sebastopol · Tokyo

Explainable AI for Practitioners

by Michael Munn and David Pitman

Copyright © 2023 Michael Munn, David Pitman, and O'Reilly Media, Inc. All rights reserved.

Published by O'Reilly Media, Inc., 1005 Gravenstein Highway North, Sebastopol, CA 95472.

O'Reilly books may be purchased for educational, business, or sales promotional use. Online editions are also available for most titles (*http://oreilly.com*). For more information, contact our corporate/institutional sales department: 800-998-9938 or *corporate@oreilly.com*.

Acquisitions Editor: Nicole Butterfield
Development Editor: Rita Fernando
Production Editor: Jonathon Owen
Copyeditor: nSight, Inc.
Proofreader: Piper Editorial Consulting, LLC

Indexer: nSight, Inc.
Interior Designer: David Futato
Cover Designer: Karen Montgomery
Illustrator: Kate Dullea

November 2022:   First Edition

Revision History for the First Edition

2022-11-28:   First Release

See *https://oreil.ly/explainable-ai* for release details.

The O'Reilly logo is a registered trademark of O'Reilly Media, Inc. *Explainable AI for Practitioners*, the cover image, and related trade dress are trademarks of O'Reilly Media, Inc.

The views expressed in this work are those of the authors, and do not represent the publisher's views. While the publisher and the authors have used good faith efforts to ensure that the information and instructions contained in this work are accurate, the publisher and the authors disclaim all responsibility for errors or omissions, including without limitation responsibility for damages resulting from the use of or reliance on this work. Use of the information and instructions contained in this work is at your own risk. If any code samples or other technology this work contains or describes is subject to open source licenses or the intellectual property rights of others, it is your responsibility to ensure that your use thereof complies with such licenses and/or rights.

978-1-098-11913-3

[LSI]

Table of Contents

Foreword

When developing machine learning (ML) models, I am sure all of you have asked the questions: *Oh, how did it get that right?* or *That's weird, why would it predict that?* As software engineers, our first instinct is to trace through the code to find the answers. Unfortunately, this does not get us very far with ML models because their "code" is automatically generated, not human-readable, and may span a vast number (sometimes billions!) of parameters. One needs a special set of tools to understand ML models. Explainable AI (XAI) is a field of machine learning focused on developing and analyzing such tools.

Model explanations are not just a nice-to-have feature to satisfy our curiosities about how a model works. For practitioners, it is a must-have to ensure that they are not flying blind. Machine learning models are notorious for being right for the wrong reason. A classic example of this, discussed in this book, is that of a medical imaging model where explanations revealed that the model relied on "pen marks" on X-ray images to make disease predictions.

The rise of ML models in high-stakes decision-making has sparked a surge in the field of XAI with a plethora of techniques proposed across a variety of data modalities. The vast number of available techniques has been both a blessing and a curse for practitioners. At the heart of this issue is that there is no such thing as a perfect explanation. A good explanation must balance faithfulness to the model with human intelligibility and must offer meaningful insights. Achieving this is nontrivial. For instance, an explanation that translates the model into a giant mathematical formula is faithful but not intelligible, and hence not useful. Different explanation methods strike a different trade-off between faithfulness, human intelligibility, and computational efficiency. Furthermore, for any ML-based decision-making system, there are several stakeholders interested in explanations from different perspectives. For instance, end users may seek explanations to understand the factors behind the decisions they receive, while regulators may seek explanations to assess whether the model's reasoning is sound and unbiased. All these nuances leave practitioners struggling to set up the appropriate explanation framework for their system. This book fills that gap.

This book first equips the reader with the landscape and taxonomy of explainability methods and all the involved stakeholders. Michael and David then tap into their extensive experience in developing, productionizing, and applying explainability techniques at Google, and present some of the key battle-tested methods. The techniques are organized by the data modalities that they are best suited to. For each technique, they convey the intuition for how the technique works, and walk through how it is implemented and applied. Through a number of sidebars sprinkled across the book, they also elegantly convey a number of complex and nuanced aspects of each technique, e.g., the importance of the sampling Kernel for LIME, the importance of choosing the right baseline for Integrated Gradients.

A distinguishing aspect of this book is its emphasis on the human factors in XAI. Explanations are not a silver bullet to making models more transparent or to improve them. Appropriate visualization of explanation and human interpretation play an equally important (if not larger) role. To that end, instead of assessing explanations in isolation, one must assess the effectiveness of the model + explanation + human trio. Human involvement naturally brings with it a suite of biases. I have witnessed this firsthand in my own research, where in a clinical study on assessing the impact of explanations for a diabetic retinopathy model, we noticed how doctors were prone to "over-relying" on explanations, and accepting inaccurate model predictions. Michael and David devote an entire chapter to discuss such issues, and the various pitfalls that come with human involvement.

Explainability is an indispensable requirement for all ML models, and therefore, this book is a must-read for all ML practitioners. This book helps practitioners unpack what explainability means in practice, and build a toolkit of explainability methods. My advice to readers is to not be discouraged by the lack of a single "magic method," and instead appreciate the unique strengths of different methods. I am confident that this book will help you identify the right explainability approach for your model and stakeholders.

— Ankur Taly
Staff Research Scientist, Google
August 2022
Sunnyvale, California

Preface

The use of AI as a tool to solve real-world challenges has experienced rapid growth, making these systems ubiquitous in our lives. More and more, machine learning (ML) is being used to support high-stakes decisions and being used in applications from healthcare to autonomous driving. With this growth, the need to be able to explain these opaque AI systems has become even more urgent and, in many cases, the lack of explainability is a barrier for applications where interpretability is essential.

This book is a collection of some of the most effective and commonly used techniques for explaining why an ML model makes the predictions it does. We discuss the many aspects of Explainable AI (XAI), including the challenges, metrics for success, and use case studies to guide best practices. Ultimately, the goal of this book is to bridge the gap between the vast amount of work that has been done in XAI and provide a quick reference for practitioners that aim to implement XAI into their ML workflow.

Who Should Read This Book?

Modern ML and AI have been used to solve very complex real-world problems, and model explainability is important for anyone who interacts with or develops those models, from the engineers and the product owners that build these systems to the business stakeholders and the individuals that use them. This book is for anyone wishing to incorporate the best practices of Explainable AI into their ML solutions. Anyone with an interest in model explainability and model interpretability will benefit from the discussions in this book.

That being said, our primary focus is on practitioners; that is, engineers and data scientists who are tasked with building ML models and methods for incorporating explainability into their current workflows. This book will introduce you to a catalog of ideas concerning model explainability and enable users to quickly get up to speed on this increasingly important and quickly evolving field of AI. We will discuss best practices for implementing these techniques and help you make informed decisions about which technique to use and when. We'll also look at the big picture and discuss how XAI can be used throughout the entire ML workflow to assist you in building more robust ML solutions.

This book is not meant to be a foundational reference on machine learning, and as such, we won't spend time discussing specific model architectures or details of model building. We assume that you are already somewhat familiar with the basics of ML and data processing. We'll review these concepts as they arise, but refer you to the plethora of other resources to fill in any remaining gaps.

What Is and What Is Not in This Book?

Explainability is one of the core tenets of Responsible AI. Responsible AI is a broad and emerging field encompassing topics such as ML fairness, AI ethics, governance, and privacy and security. We won't go into these other areas in this book, although they may come up in context. Explainability has become increasingly important in recent years, with a deep and very active area of academic research focused on model explainability and advancing cutting-edge techniques. While we will at times reference some of this research, that is not the goal of this book, and we will not dive deep into active research topics. All of the techniques discussed here are grounded in some mathematical theory, be it game theory or mathematical optimization, and while it's helpful at times to understand these theoretical underpinnings, that is not the focus of this book. Furthermore, although these methods may have sound theoretical groundings, their application and benefits are far from well understood. Our goal is to help you, the practitioner, quickly get up to speed in the field, learn common techniques of XAI, and get some insight into this tricky gray area of how to apply these tools in your ML systems.

This is a book for ML engineers working in the industry with a focus on practical implementation intended for real-world applications. The book is not intended for research scientists in industry labs or academia, though early researchers may find it to be a valuable reference. In general, we do not explore the theory behind different techniques but do detail the mathematics and reference papers so you can investigate further if you desire.

For example, in Chapter 4, when discussing Integrated Gradients, we don't spend any time reviewing how line integrals are defined and mathematically computed, but try to lend some intuition that explains how the formulas are being used. In doing so, we'll see how this intuition can help guide the best practices for the implementation of Integrated Gradients, such as how varying the number of subintervals when approximating the integral affects the outcome.

In this book, we show you how to effectively implement and use explainability as an ML practitioner—an individual who is already familiar with machine learning, perhaps as a data scientist or ML engineer. We assume you are familiar with common ML architectures, but may not know the exact implementation details, and are comfortable with a moderate degree of coding, as some explainability techniques do not have a good off-the-shelf implementation. Our goal in this book is to give you the ability in your day-to-day ML work to generate explanations of why a model behaves and how a dataset influences that model. To accomplish this, we will teach you three concepts:

- Understand the field of Explainable AI so you have the necessary background to make decisions about how, why, and where to use explainability, along with how to tailor explanations for different audiences (Chapters 2 and 7).

- Give you a toolbox of well-proven explainability techniques for different situations (Chapters 3 through 5). Although many explainability techniques can be used in a variety of ways, we find it is easiest to organize these tools by the model modality (e.g., structured data, image, text).

- Understand where Explainable AI is heading in the future and what to keep in mind as you start to reach the edge of the map of known explainability (Chapters 6 and 8).

This book is pragmatic. Our goal is not to give rigorous proofs for a given technique. Instead, we try to lend some intuition as to how a specific technique works, with a focus on the hands-on implementation considerations that you, as an ML practitioner, may have. So, there may be formulas but only insofar as they help in illustrating an idea or justifying why one might choose a specific set of hyperparameters for a specific technique over another. Where possible, we reference well-established implementations for techniques. If that is not possible, we provide a reference implementation you can reuse or adapt to your situation, along with a GitHub repository (*https://github.com/munnm/XAI-for-practitioners*) for code and notebook samples.

Pragmatism requires distinguishing between what is best for a given scenario, so we are also opinionated on the techniques we have chosen for your toolbox. Our selection does not represent the entire set of options available in Explainable AI. In choosing techniques for this toolbox, we used the following heuristics in deciding what to cover:

- Has this technique been sufficiently used in industry that we understand its benefits and shortcomings? We give priority to techniques that have been in use for at least a few years and for which there are many case studies available to demonstrate their utility.

- How much expertise in Explainable AI is required to correctly use or implement this technique? Generally, we favor techniques that require less expertise, as we assume you are reading this book to understand how to use explainability rather than building up a deep expertise in explainability (for which many other excellent books exist already).

- How brittle and/or resilient is the technique? We place an emphasis on techniques that can be used in more situations and are less prone to easily breaking if not configured correctly.

As you read this book, you may notice that we also cover many techniques that explain how the dataset and its structure influenced the behavior of the model. This can seem counterintuitive: why are we concerned with datasets, and aren't models what we want to better understand? There are two reasons for this approach. The first is what is under the control of the ML practitioner and can be easily changed: it is usually far easier to manipulate a dataset than rebuild or change a model architecture. The second is that we find many of the techniques that focus on the model itself to generate explanations; while intriguing, these are ultimately not actionable. For example, some explainability techniques seek to explain the behavior of CNN image classification models by creating artificial images that show how the model is perceiving an image at different layers. While this type of technique creates fascinating explanations that lead to a vigorous discussion about the way CNNs may work, we have yet to see the technique be consistently applied in industry to achieve one of the goals of explainability we listed above.

Code Samples

In this book, ML practitioners will learn techniques and best practices for incorporating explainability into their models and ML solutions. To aid in this pursuit, we provide code examples for many of the techniques we discuss in the book. Models are built using common machine learning libraries, like Keras/TensorFlow, PyTorch or scikit-learn, and when possible we'll use open source libraries to show how these techniques are implemented in practice. All the code that is referenced in the book is part of our GitHub repository (*https://github.com/munnm/XAI-for-practitioners*). We strongly encourage you to try out those code samples.

The code is secondary in importance to the concepts and techniques being covered. Our aim has been that the topic and principles should remain relevant regardless of changes to TensorFlow or Keras or any specific library. Some of the libraries we use may be newer than others and thus be updated or improved in the future.

If you have a technical question or a problem using the code examples, please send email to *bookquestions@oreilly.com*.

This book is here to help you get your job done. In general, if example code is offered with this book, you may use it in your programs and documentation. You do not need to contact us for permission unless you're reproducing a significant portion of the code. For example, writing a program that uses several chunks of code from this book does not require permission. Selling or distributing examples from O'Reilly books does require permission. Answering a question by citing this book and quoting example code does not require permission. Incorporating a significant amount of example code from this book into your product's documentation does require permission.

We appreciate, but generally do not require, attribution. An attribution usually includes the title, author, publisher, and ISBN. For example: *"Explainable AI for Practitioners* by Michael Munn and David Pitman (O'Reilly). Copyright 2023 Michael Munn, David Pitman, and O'Reilly Media, Inc., 978-1-098-11913-3."

If you feel your use of code examples falls outside fair use or the permission given above, feel free to contact us at *permissions@oreilly.com*.

Navigating This Book

The initial chapters of the book give a high-level overview of the principles concerning model explainability, setting up the framework for the following chapters. The middle chapters focus more on specific techniques and implementations. The later chapters focus on how to interact with explainability, keeping in mind stakeholders, end users, and others; and how explainability can be used to enhance the entire ML workflow. We've arranged these middle technical chapters according to model data type or use case. So, one chapter focuses on explainability techniques for tabular data (Chapter 3) while another focuses on techniques for computer vision (Chapter 4) or natural language (Chapter 5).

The reason for this data modality-focused structure is not because the techniques in these chapters can only be applied in that setting. Although some of the techniques do lend themselves more to a specific data type (e.g., XRAI for image data models or individual conditional expectation plots for tabular data models), many of the techniques can work as is or with some slight modification for all different data modalities (e.g., LIME and Integrated Gradients). Instead, we've chosen this structure because we anticipate that most readers will approach this book with a use case–driven mindset. That is, you likely have a problem and dataset already in mind that you have been working with and know well; and the easiest and quickest entry point into this potentially new domain is via that context.

This way, you can easily jump right to a technique for a specific use case in which you are interested. Of course, not all techniques align themselves with a single use case, and when possible we'll indicate cross-references between the chapters for where and how that technique could be used for a different type of data modality or to provide an alternate perspective.

This is all to say that we encourage the reader to explore other techniques in other chapters, even if they do not directly relate to the problem you currently have in mind. You'll likely still find some useful and relevant information. XAI is a rapidly developing field with new techniques constantly being introduced. Our goal is that after reading this book you'll be able to take part in that ongoing conversation and, at the same time, be equipped to apply these ideas in your current or future ML projects.

This book is organized as follows:

- Chapter 1 provides an introduction to the main concepts and principles surrounding explainability in machine learning. We'll discuss the motivations behind explainability and how different people benefit from explainability, from the engineers and developers to the business stakeholders and end users.

- Chapter 2 gives a high-level taxonomy of various explainability techniques to act as a mental road map for how these methods can be categorized and understood.

- Chapters 3 through 6 focus on specific explainability techniques and are arranged according to a specific use case, from tabular data to computer vision and natural language. In particular, Chapter 6 focuses on advanced techniques and new and emerging perspectives on XAI. Each chapter covers a handful of techniques, their pros and cons, and implementation considerations.

- Chapter 7 focuses on human interaction aspects of explainability, such as common pitfalls and how best to create actionable outcomes from an explainability technique.

- In Chapter 8, we give a summary and road map for how to apply this XAI toolkit of the various techniques covered in the book throughout the entire ML workflow.

The GitHub repository (*https://github.com/munnm/XAI-for-practitioners*) for this book also contains all of the figures in full color for readers of the print version.

Conventions Used in This Book

The following typographical conventions are used in this book:

Italic
: Indicates new terms, URLs, email addresses, filenames, and file extensions.

`Constant width`
: Used for program listings, as well as within paragraphs to refer to program elements such as variable or function names, databases, data types, environment variables, statements, and keywords.

 This element signifies a general note.

This element indicates a warning or caution.

O'Reilly Online Learning

 For more than 40 years, *O'Reilly Media* has provided technology and business training, knowledge, and insight to help companies succeed.

Our unique network of experts and innovators share their knowledge and expertise through books, articles, and our online learning platform. O'Reilly's online learning platform gives you on-demand access to live training courses, in-depth learning paths, interactive coding environments, and a vast collection of text and video from O'Reilly and 200+ other publishers. For more information, visit *https://oreilly.com*.

How to Contact Us

Please address comments and questions concerning this book to the publisher:

O'Reilly Media, Inc.
1005 Gravenstein Highway North
Sebastopol, CA 95472
800-998-9938 (in the United States or Canada)
707-829-0515 (international or local)
707-829-0104 (fax)

We have a web page for this book, where we list errata, examples, and any additional information. You can access this page at *https://oreil.ly/explainable-ai*.

Email *bookquestions@oreilly.com* to comment or ask technical questions about this book.

For news and information about our books and courses, visit *https://oreilly.com*.

Find us on LinkedIn: *https://linkedin.com/company/oreilly-media*

Follow us on Twitter: *https://twitter.com/oreillymedia*

Watch us on YouTube: *https://www.youtube.com/oreillymedia*

Acknowledgments

A book like this would not be possible without the generosity of our fellow Googlers. We are especially thankful to Takumi Ohiyama, Michael Abel, and Xi Cheng for their thoughtful and detailed review. Their eye for detail and knack for exposition greatly improved the entire book. Thanks also to Sheeraz Ahmad, Parker Barnes, Sal Haykal, Ankur Taly, Besim Avci, and Mukund Sundararajan for their invaluable feedback and input both on early versions of this manuscript and throughout. Of course, any errors that remain are fully ours. Thanks to the Cloud AI Professional Services, PAIR, Responsible AI teams, and the Google Cloud Advanced Solutions Lab for being thoughtful partners. Thanks to our managers, Xavi Gonzalvo, Michael Riley, and Chenyu Zhao for giving us the freedom to work on and publish this book.

Thanks also to the O'Reilly team for their inimitable guidance and feedback. In particular, we'd like to thank Laura Uzcátegui and Nura Kawa for their detailed technical review and Carol Keller for her thorough attention to detail during copyediting. Special thanks to Rita Fernando for shepherding us through the process from start to finish. Thanks also to Rebecca Novak, who advised on an early proposal for this book, and our copyeditors. Thanks for all your help!

David would like to thank Emily for reams of great support and motivation, including lucid explanations of what makes for compelling writing.

Michael: Phil, thank you, yet again, for bearing with my less-than-ideal schedule. Thanks always to my parents and my family for your constant support in all my endeavors, and especially to my brother Rudy, who kept me motivated when it was difficult to find motivation.

We are donating 100% of the royalties from this book to the Sentencing Project, an organization dedicated to promoting effective and humane responses to crime that minimize imprisonment and criminalization of youth and adults by promoting racial, ethnic, economic, and gender justice.

## CHAPTER 1

Introduction

Explainable AI, also known as *XAI*, is a field of machine learning (ML) consisting of techniques that aim to give a better understanding of model behavior by providing explanations as to how a model made a prediction. Knowing how a model behaves, and how it is influenced by its training dataset, gives anyone who builds or uses ML powerful new abilities to improve models, build confidence in their predictions, and understand when things go awry. Explainable AI techniques are especially useful because they do not rely on a particular model—once you know an Explainable AI method, you can use it in many scenarios. This book is designed to give you the ability to understand how Explainable AI techniques work so you can build an intuition for when to use one approach over another, how to apply these techniques, and how to evaluate these explanations so you understand their benefits and limitations, as well as communicate them to your stakeholders. Explanations can be very powerful and are easily able to convey a new understanding of why a model makes a certain prediction, as Figure 1-1 demonstrates, but they also require skill and nuance to use correctly.

Figure 1-1. An explanation using Blur-IG (described in Chapter 4) that shows what pixels influenced an image classification model to predict that the animal on the cover of this book is a parrot.

Why Explainable AI

In 2018, data scientists built a machine learning (ML) model to identify diseases from chest X-rays. The goal was to allow radiologists to be able to review more X-rays per day with the help of AI. In testing, the model achieved very high, but not perfect, accuracy with a validation dataset. There was just one problem: the model performed terribly in real-world settings. For months, the researchers tried to find why there was a discrepancy. The model had been trained on the same type of chest X-rays shown in Figure 1-2, and the X-rays had any identifying information removed. Even with new data, they kept encountering the same problem: fantastic performance in training, only to be followed by terrible results in a hospital setting. Why was this happening?

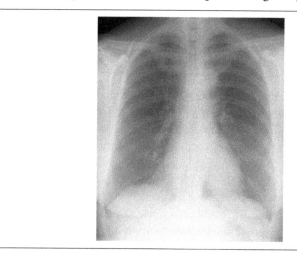

Figure 1-2. An example of the chest X-rays used to train the model to recognize diseases. Can you identify what led the model astray?[1]

A few years later, another research group, this time eye doctors in the UK, embarked on a mission to train a model to identify diseases from retinal scans of a patient's eye (see Figure 1-3). After they had trained the model, they encountered an equally surprising, but very different result. While the model was very good at identifying diseases, it was uncannily accurate at also predicting the sex of the patient.

---

1 The authors thank the National Cancer Institute (NCI) for access to their data collected by the Prostate, Lung, Colorectal and Ovarian (PLCO) Cancer Screening Trial. The statements contained herein are solely those of the authors and do not represent or imply concurrence or endorsement by NCI.

Figure 1-3. An example of retinal fundus images, which show the interior of an eye and can be used to predict diseases such as diabetes.

There were two fascinating aspects of this prediction. First, the doctors had not designed the ML to predict the patient's sex; this was an inadvertent output of their model architecture and ML experiments. Second, if these predictions were accurate, this correlation between the interior of our eyes and our sex was a completely new discovery in ophthalmology. Had the ML made a brand-new discovery, or was something flawed in the model or dataset such that information about a patient's sex was leaking into the model's inference?

In both cases of the chest X-ray and the retinal images, the opaque nature of machine learning had turned on its users. Modern machine learning has succeeded precisely because computers could teach themselves how to perform many tasks using an approach of consuming vast amounts of information to iteratively tune a large number of parameters. However, the large quantities of data involved in training these models have made it pragmatically impossible for a human to directly examine and understand the behavior of a model or how a dataset influenced the model. While any machine learning model can be inspected by looking at individual weights or specific data samples used to train the model, this examination rarely yields useful insights.

In the first example we gave, the X-ray model that performed well in testing and was useless in practice, the data scientists who built the model did all the right things. They removed text labels from the images to prevent the model from learning how to read and predict a disease based on ancillary information. They properly divided their training, testing, and validation datasets, and used a reasonable model architecture that built upon an existing process (radiologists examining X-rays) that already proved it was feasible to identify diseases from a patient's X-ray. And yet, even with these precautions and expertise, their model was still a failure. The eye doctors who built an ML model for classifying eye disease were world-class experts in their own field who understood ophthalmology but were not machine learning experts. If their discovery that our eyes, which have been exhaustively studied for hundreds of years, still held secrets about human biology, how could they perform a rigorous analysis of the machine learning model to be certain their discovery was real? Fortunately, Explainable AI provides new ways for ML practitioners, stakeholders, and end users to answer these types of questions.

What Is Explainable AI?

At Explainable AI's core is the creation of explanations, or to create explainability for a model. Explainability is the concept that a model's actions can be described in terms that are comprehensible to whoever is consuming the predictions of the ML model. This explainability serves a variety of purposes, from improving model quality to building confidence, and even providing a pathway for remediation when a prediction is not one you were expecting. As we have built increasingly complex models, we have discovered that a high-performing model is not sufficient to be acceptable in the real world. It is necessary that a prediction also has a reasonable explanation and, overall, the model behaves in the way its creators intended.

Imagine an AI who is your coworker on a project. Regardless of how well your AI coworker performs any task you give them, it would be incredibly frustrating if your entire collaboration with the AI consisted of them vanishing after taking on a task, suddenly reappearing with the finished work, and then vanishing again as soon as they delivered it to you. If their work was superb, perhaps you would be accepting of this transactional relationship, but the quality of your AI coworker's results can vary considerably. Unfortunately, the AI never answers your questions or even tells you how they arrived at the result.

As AI becomes our coworkers, colleagues, and more responsible for decisions affecting many aspects of our life, the feedback is clear that having AI as a silent partner is unsatisfying. We want (and in the future, will have a right) to expect we can have a two-way dialogue with our machine learning model to understand why it performed the way it did. Explainable AI represents the beginning of this dialogue, by opening up a new way for an ML system to convey how it works instead of simply delivering the results of a task.

Who Needs Explainability?

To understand how explainability aided the researchers in our two examples of where conventional ML workflows failed to address the issues encountered, it is also necessary to talk about who uses explainability and why. In our work on Explainable AI for Google Cloud, we have engaged with many companies, data scientists, ML engineers, and business executives who have sought to understand how a model works and why. From these interactions, we have found that there are three distinct groups of people who are seeking explanations, and each group has distinct but overlapping motivations and needs. Throughout the book, we will refer to all of these groups as *explainability consumers* because they are the recipient of an explanation and act upon that explanation. Our consumers can be divided into three roles:

Practitioners
> Data scientists and engineers who are familiar with machine learning

Observers
> Business stakeholders and regulators who have some familiarity with machine learning but are primarily concerned with the function and overall performance of the ML system

End users
> Domain experts and affected users who may have little-to-no knowledge of ML and are also recipients of the ML system's output

A person can simultaneously assume multiple roles as an ML consumer. For example, a common pattern we see is that data scientists start as ML practitioners, but over time build up an understanding of the field they are serving and eventually become domain experts themselves, allowing them to act as an end user in evaluating a prediction and explanation.

In our chest X-ray case study, the ML practitioners built the model but did not have domain expertise in radiology. They understood how the ML system works and how it was trained but did not have a deep understanding of the practice of radiology. In contrast, in the retina images case study, the ophthalmologist researchers with domain expertise who built the model found the ML had discovered a new correlation between the appearance of the interior of our eyes and our sex, but they lacked the expertise of ML practitioners to be confident the model was functioning correctly.

Each group had very different needs for explaining why the model acted the way it did. The ML practitioners were looking for precise and accurate explanations that could expose the step at which the ML had failed. The ophthalmologists, as end users, were looking for an explanation that was more conceptual and would help them construct a hypothesis for why the classification occurred and also allow them to build trust in the model's predictions.

Challenges in Explainability

How we use Explainable AI for a model depends on the goals of those consuming the explanations. Suppose, based on just the information we have given about these individuals, their ML, and their challenges, we asked you to implement an Explainable AI technique that will generate explanations of how the model arrived at its predictions. You toil away and implement a way to generate what you think are good explanations for these ML models by using Integrated Gradients (Chapter 4) to highlight pixels that were influential in the prediction. You excitedly deliver a set of predictions with relevant pixels highlighted in the image, but rather than being celebrated as the person who saved the day, you immediately get questions like:

- How do I know this explanation is accurate?
- What does it mean that one pixel is highlighted more than another?
- What happens if we remove these pixels?
- Why did it highlight these pixels instead of what we think is important over here?
- Could you do this for the entire dataset?

In trying to answer one question, you inadvertently caused five more questions to be asked! Each of these questions are valid and worth asking, but may not help your audience in their original goal to understand the model's behavior. However, as explainability is a relatively new field in AI, it is likely you will encounter these questions, for which there are no easy answers. In Explainable AI, there are several outstanding challenges:

- Demonstrating the semantic correctness of explanation techniques above and beyond the theoretical soundness of the underlying mathematics
- Combining different explanation techniques in an easy and safe way that enhances understanding rather than generating more confusion
- Building tools that allow consumers to easily explore, probe, and build richer explanations
- Generating explanations that are computationally efficient
- Building a strong framework for determining the robustness of explanation techniques

Promising research is being conducted in all of these areas; however, none have yet achieved acceptance within the explainability community to the level that we would feel confident in recommending them. Additionally, many of these questions have led to research papers that investigate how explanation techniques may be fundamentally broken. This is a very promising line of research but, as we discuss in Chapter 7, may be better viewed as research that probes how susceptible XAI techniques are to adversarial attacks or are brittle and unable to generate good explanations outside of their original design parameters. Many of these questions are sufficiently interesting that we recommend caution when using explanations for high-risk or safety-critical AIs.

Evaluating Explainability

Let's return to our two case studies to see how they fared after using explainability. For the chest X-ray, the ML practitioners had been unable to discover why the model performed very well in training and testing, but poorly in the real world. One of the researchers used an explainability technique, Integrated Gradients, to highlight pixels in the chest X-ray that were influential in the prediction. Integrated Gradients (covered in more depth in Chapter 4) evaluates the prediction by starting with a baseline image—for example, one that is all black, and progressively generating new images with pixels that are closer to the original input. These intermediate images are then fed to the model to create new predictions. The predictions are consolidated into a new version of the input image where pixels that were influential to the model's original prediction are shown in a new color, which is known as a saliency map. The intensity of the coloring reflects how strong the pixels influenced the model. At first glance, the explanations were as baffling as the original problem.

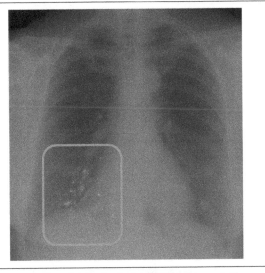

Figure 1-4. The explanation for which pixels, highlighted in red, the model thought indicated a disease in the chest X-ray. For readability, the area of the image containing the most attributed pixels is outlined by the blue box. (Print readers can see the color image at https://oreil.ly/xai-fig-1-4.)

An example of one of these images is shown in Figure 1-4, and it may appear that no pixels were used in the prediction. However, if you look at the lower left of this image, you will notice a smattering of red pixels among the black and white of the chest X-ray. These appear to be quite random as well. It's not until one closely looks at this area of the image that you can barely perceive what appear to be scratch marks on the X-ray. However, these are not random scratches, but the pen marks of a radiologist who had drawn where the disease was in the X-ray, as we can see in Figure 1-5. The model then became trained to associate pen markings with a disease being present. However, in the real-world setting, the X-rays had no pen markings on them because the raw X-ray images were fed to the model before being shown to a radiologist who could have marked them up.

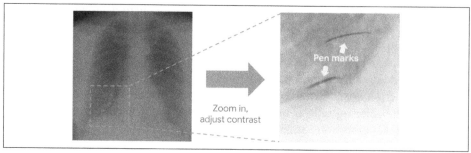

Figure 1-5. Example of the pen markings in a chest X-ray within the training dataset.

Once the researchers figured out the cause of their performance mismatch, that pen markings had leaked information to the model about whether to classify the X-ray as showing disease or not, they could build a new dataset that had not been annotated by radiologists. The model's subsequent performance was not noticeably worse in training than the original model and performed better in the real-world setting.

Let's turn to the retina ¡study. How did ophthalmologists use Explainable AI to become confident that their ML model could predict the sex of a patient based on their retinal fundus images? The researchers used a technique known as XRAI (discussed in Chapter 4; no relation to X-rays) to highlight regions of the eye image that influenced the model's prediction. The explanations, seen in Figure 1-6, showed that the model was attentive to the optic nerve (the large blob to one side of the retina) and the blood vessels radiating out from the optic nerve.

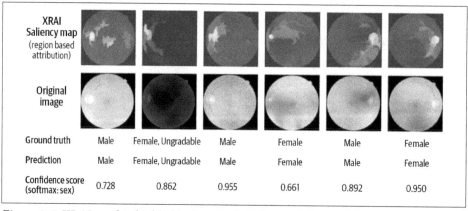

Figure 1-6. XRAI used to highlight what pixels influenced the model's prediction of a patient's sex based on a photograph of the interior of their eye, from an article by Korot et al.[2]

---

2 Edward Korot et al., "Predicting Sex from Retinal Fundus Photographs Using Automated Deep Learning," *Scientific Reports* 11, article no. 10286 (May 2021), *https://oreil.ly/Le50t*.

By seeing that the model had become influenced by such specific parts of the eye's anatomy, the researchers were convinced that the model was indeed making correct predictions. This work was also sufficient to convince the broader scientific community, as the results were eventually published as a paper in *Scientific Reports*.

How Has Explainability Been Used?

The two examples we gave focused on explainability for image models in medical research and healthcare. You may often find that examples of explainability involve an image model because it is easier to understand the explanation for an image than the relative importance of different features in structured data or the mapping of influential tokens in a language model. In this section, we look at some other case studies of how Explainable AI has been used beyond image models.

How LinkedIn Uses Explainable AI

Since 2018, LinkedIn has successfully used Explainable AI across many areas of its business, from recruiting to sales, and ML engineering. For example, in 2022 LinkedIn revealed that Explainable AI was key to the adoption of a ranking and recommendation ML system used by their sales team to prioritize which customers to engage with based on the ML's prediction of how likely it was that the customer would stop using existing products (also known as *churn*), or their potential to be sold new ones (known as *upselling*). While the ML performed well, the AI team at LinkedIn quickly discovered that the system was not going to be used by their sales teams unless it included a rationale for the predictions:

> While this ML-based approach was very useful, we found from focus group studies that ML-based model scores alone weren't the most helpful tool for our sales representatives. Rather, they wanted to understand the underlying reasons behind the scores—such as why the model score was higher for Customer A but lower for Customer B—and they also wanted to be able to double-check the reasoning with their domain knowledge.[3]

Similar to our chest X-ray example, LinkedIn has also used Explainable AI to improve the quality of their ML models. In this case, their ML team productionized the use of explainability across many models by building a tool that allows LinkedIn data scientists and engineers to perturb features (see Chapter 3) to generate alternative scenarios for predictions to understand how a model may behave with a slightly different set of inputs.[4]

---

3 Jilei Yang et al., "The Journey to Build an Explainable AI-Driven Recommendation System to Help Scale Sales Efficiency Across LinkedIn," LinkedIn, April 6, 2022, *https://oreil.ly/JJPj9*.

4 Daniel Qiu and Yucheng Qian, "Relevance Debugging and Explaining at LinkedIn," LinkedIn, 2019, *https://oreil.ly/cSFhj*.

LinkedIn has gone a step further to create an app, CrystalCandle,[5] that translates raw explanations for structured data, which are often just numbers, into narrative explanations (we discuss narrative explanations further in Chapter 7). An example of the narrative explanations they have built are shown in Table 1-1.

Table 1-1. LinkedIn's CrystalCandle comparison of raw explanations versus the corresponding narrative explanations

Model prediction and interpretation (nonintuitive)	Narrative insights (user-friendly)
Propensity score: 0.85 (top 2%) Top important features (with importance score):	This account is extremely likely to upsell. Its upsell likelihood is larger than 98% of all accounts, which is driven by:
• paid_job_s4: 0.030 • job_view_s4: 0.013 • hire_cntr_s3: 0.011 • conn_cmp_s4: 0.009	• Paid job posts changed from 10 to 15 (+50%) in the last month. • Views per job changed from 200 to 300 (+50%) in the last month.

PwC Uses Explainable AI for Auto Insurance Claims

Working with a large auto insurer, PricewaterhouseCoopers (PwC) built an ML system to estimate the amount of an insurance claim. In building the system, PwC clearly highlights how Explainable AI was not an optional addition to their core project, but a necessary requirement for the ML to be adopted by the insurance company, their claims adjusters, and customers. They call out four different benefits from using explainability in their ML solution:

> The company's explainable AI model was a game changer as it enabled the following:
>
> - empowered auto claim estimators to identify where to focus attention during an assessment
> - provided approaches for sharing knowledge among the estimator team to accurately determine which group should handle specific estimates
> - identified 29% efficiency savings possible with full implementation of proof of concept models across the estimator team
> - reduced rework and improved customer experience through reduced cycle times[6]

In our work with customers at Google Cloud, we have also seen similar benefits to many customers who have built explainability into their AI.

---

5 Jilei Yang et al., "CrystalCandle: A User-Facing Model Explainer for Narrative Explanations," arXiv, 2021, *https://arxiv.org/abs/2105.12941*.

6 See PwC, "Insurance Claims Estimator Uses AI for Efficiency," (*https://oreil.ly/3vMUr*) for more information.

Accenture Labs Explains Loan Decisions

The experience of receiving a loan from a bank can be a confusing experience. The loan applicant is asked to fill in many forms and provide evidence of their financial situation and history in order to apply for a loan, often only asking for approval for the broad terms of the loan and the amount. In response, consumers are either approved, often with an interest rate decided by the bank, or they are denied with no further information. Accenture Labs demonstrated how even a common loan, the Home Equity Line of Credit (HELOC), could benefit from providing positive counterfactual explanations (covered in Chapter 2) as part of an ML's prediction for whether to approve or deny a loan application. These counterfactual explanations focused on creating a "what-if" scenario for what aspects of the applicant's credit history and financial situation would have resulted in the loan being approved or denied. In this case study, Accenture focused on understanding how explainability could be used across different ML systems,[7] demonstrating the value of how using Explainable AI allowed for explanations to still be generated, while the underlying model was changed to different model architectures.

DARPA Uses Explainable AI to Build "Third-Wave AI"

The Defense Advanced Research Projects Agency (DARPA), an arm of the US Department of Defense, conducted a five-year program (*https://oreil.ly/xAbXI*)[8] with many projects to investigate the use of Explainable AI. DARPA's goals in using Explainable AI are to "produce more explainable models, while maintaining a high level of learning performance" and "enable human users to understand, appropriately trust, and effectively manage the emerging generation of artificially intelligent part-ners." DARPA believes explainability is a key component of the next generation of AI systems, where "machines understand the context and environment in which they operate, and over time build underlying explanatory models that allow them to characterize real-world phenomena." Over the past few years, the program has had several annual workshops demonstrating the feasibility of building explainability into many different types of ML, from data analysis to autonomous systems and assistive decision-making tools.

Summary

In this chapter, we introduced the concept of Explainable AI, a set of techniques that can be applied to ML models, after they have been built, to explain their

---

7 Roy McGrath et al., "Interpretable Credit Application Predictions with Counterfactual Explanations," arXiv, 2018, *https://arxiv.org/abs/1811.05245*.

8 Dr. Matt Turek, "Explainable Artificial Intelligence (XAI)," DARPA.

behavior for one or more predictions made by the model. We also explored why Explainable AI is needed by different groups who work with ML models, such as ML practitioners, observers, and end users. Each of these types of users has different needs for explainability, ranging from improving the quality of a model to building confidence in the model's effectiveness. To demonstrate this, we looked at several case studies of how explainability has been used. We started by contrasting two real-world examples in medicine, where one set of ML practitioners was trying to debug a poorly performing model used for classifying diseases from chest X-rays, while another group, ophthalmologists, needed to understand why their model had made a novel discovery about the inside of our eyes. To provide an introduction to other ways Explainable AI has been used, we also looked at other use cases across sales, fintech, and the defense industry. This introduction should help show you the variety of ways that explainability can be used, from different types of data and explanations, to the universal need for explainability regardless of the specific domain you are working in and the problem that ML is solving for your business.

In the rest of this book, we will discuss in more detail the tools and frameworks you need to effectively use Explainable AI as part of your day-to-day work in building and deploying ML models. We will also give you a background in explainability so you can reason about the trade-offs between different types of techniques and give you a guide to developing responsible, beneficial interactions with explainability for other ML users. Our toolbox covers the three most popular data modalities in ML: tabular, image, and text, with an additional survey of more advanced techniques, including example- and concept-based approaches to XAI and how to frame XAI for time-series models. Throughout this book, we try to give an opinionated perspective on which tools are best suited for different use cases, and why, so you can be more pragmatic in your choices about how to employ explainability.

In Chapter 2, we give you a framework for how different explainability methods can be categorized and evaluated, along with a taxonomy of how to describe who is ultimately using an explanation to help clarify the goals you will have in developing an Explainable AI for your ML model.

## CHAPTER 2

An Overview of Explainability

Explainability has been a part of machine learning since the inception of AI. The very first AIs, rule-based chain systems, were specifically constructed to provide a clear understanding of what led to a prediction. The field continued to pursue explainability as a key part of models, partly due to a focus on general AI but also to justify that the research was sane and on the right track, for many decades until the complexity of model architectures outpaced our ability to explain what was happening. After the introduction of ML neurons and neural nets in the 1980s,[1] research into explainability waned as researchers focused on surviving the first AI winter by turning to techniques that were "explainable" because they relied solely on statistical techniques, such as Bayesian inference, that were well-proven in other fields. Explainability in its modern form (and what we largely focus on in this book) was revived, now as a distinct field of research, in the mid-2010s in response to the persistent question of *This model works really well…but how?*

In just a few years, the field has gone from obscurity to one of intense interest and investigation. Remarkably, many powerful explainability techniques have been invented, or repurposed from other fields, in the short time since. However, the rapid transition from theory to practice, and the increasing need for explainability from users who interact with ML, such as end users and business stakeholders, has led to growing confusion about the capability and extent of different methods. Many fundamental terms of explainability are routinely used to represent different, even contradictory, ideas; it is easy for explanations to be misunderstood due to practitioners rushing to provide assurance that ML is working as expected. Even

---

1 Ironically, the use of neurons and neural nets was inspired by trying to explain how our brain's vision system was able to accomplish seemingly impossible tasks, like performing edge detection and pattern classification before an object was classified by our conscious mind.

the terms explainability and interpretability are routinely swapped, despite having very different focuses. For example, while writing this book, we were asked by a knowledgeable industry organization to describe explainable and interpretable capabilities of a system, but the definitions of explainability and interpretability were flipped in comparison to how the rest of industry defines the terms! Recognizing the confusion over explainability, the purpose of this chapter is to provide a background and common language for future chapters.

What Are Explanations?

When a model makes a prediction, Explainable AI (XAI) methods generate an explanation that gives insight into the model's behavior as to how it arrived at that prediction. When we seek explanations, we are trying to understand, *Why* did X happen? As an example, if we had a weather model that predicted when it rains, and we wanted to know *why* the model suddenly gave a 90% chance of precipitation, a useful explanation would be, 90% precipitation was predicted because the sky was overcast. Figuring out this *why* can help us build a better comprehension of what influences a model, how that influence occurs, and where the model performs (or fails). As part of building our own mental models, we often find a pure explanation to be unsatisfactory, so we are also interested in explanations that provide a *counterfactual*, or *foil*, to the original situation. Counterfactuals are scenarios that seek to provide an opposing, plausible, scenario of why X did not happen. If we are seeking to explain, Why did it rain today? we may also try to find the counterfactual explanation for, Why did it *not* rain today [in a hypothetical world]? While our primary explanation for why it rained might include temperature, barometric pressure, and humidity, it may be easier to explain that it did not rain because there were no clouds in the sky, implying that clouds are part of an explanation for why it does rain.

We also often seek explanations that are causal, or in the form of "X was predicted because of Y." These explanations are attractive because they give an immediate sense of what a counterfactual prediction would be: remove X and presumably the prediction will no longer be Y. It certainly sounds more definitive to say, "It rains because there are clouds in the sky." However, this is not always true; rain can occur even with clear skies in some circumstances. Establishing causality with data-focused explanations is extremely difficult (even for time-series data), and no causal techniques have been proposed that are both useful in practice and have a high level of guarantee in their analysis. Instead, if you want to establish causal relationships within your model or data, we recommend you explore the field of interpretable, causal models.

Interpretability and Explainability

As one begins discussing XAI, a common question to ask is, *What is the difference between explainability and interpretability?* There is not yet an official definition for either term, although a draft standard from the International Organization for Standardization (ISO) is in the early stages (which we will discuss more in "AI Regulations and Explainability" on page 237). As we show in Figure 2-1, think of interpretability and explainability as two ends of a spectrum of explanation techniques for ML.

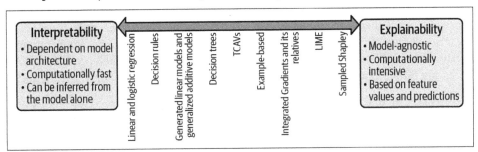

Figure 2-1. Explainability and interpretability are two ends of a spectrum. Here we show key characteristics of techniques at each end of the spectrum, and show some examples of where techniques fall along this spectrum.

At one end is interpretability, and interpretable techniques are inherently part of the model's architecture; removing the parts from the model that generate the interpretable explanations would result in the breaking of the model (either its predictive power or even its ability to generate a prediction at all). The raw results of interpretability methods can also be thought of as side outputs of the model, and they are often calculated as part of the inference process, so they account for little additional computation overhead. Interpretability is powerful because the techniques rely directly on the inner workings of the model, and as such, are supposed to provide explanations that more faithfully describe the behavior of the model.

However, these techniques may not result in explanations that are more understandable and may only be a narrow window into a single aspect of a complex system.[2] Another downside of interpretable models is that they are unique to each model architecture, and interpretability results cannot be compared between different architectures. One significant benefit of interpretable techniques is that they can be used in absence of inputs and predictions. This means that one can use interpretability techniques to gain an understanding of a model's behavior before it is deployed and used by others.

In contrast and at the other end of the spectrum, XAI techniques are designed to be used independently of the model itself. The techniques are often derived from observing how the ML model behaves in use, and then deriving an explanation from

---

2 For further reading on this topic, we suggest the arXiv 2019 article "Attention Is Not Explanation" (*https://oreil.ly/OAz3E*) by Sarthak Jain and Byron Wallace as an example of how interpretability does not necessarily result in explanations.

those observed predictions. This approach allows the most robust XAI techniques (those at the farthest along the XAI end of the spectrum) to be derived from the theory that is independent of a particular model architecture, giving them a stronger argument that the technique generates a meaningful and accurate description of the model's behavior, rather than just exposing a single aspect of the model's internal processes. Since these techniques also rely on actual data and predicted values, they are also derived from the actual execution of the model (and its environment), meaning that XAI explanations have a basis in a set of feature values, prediction, and execution rather than being a conjecture about the supposed behavior of the model.

A downside of XAI techniques is that because they rely on predictions (and often calculate many variations of a prediction), they are almost always computationally more intensive than interpretability. However, one of the most attractive aspects of XAI techniques is their independence from a particular model architecture. As long as your model satisfies the prerequisites for a technique, you can almost always compare the explanations (from the same technique) between different model architectures. This is an incredibly powerful trait because it allows you to swap out different models without having to rework your explanations. You can then compare explanations from the previous model to the current one, or even to a completely different model in the field.

As we have said, interpretability and explainability are two ends of a spectrum, and the techniques are not mutually exclusive, nor is one approach always better than the other. As we present techniques in Chapters 3 through 6, you will see that some fall closer to the middle of the spectrum (for example, TCAVs discussed in Chapter 6), while others, such as sampled Shapley (discussed in Chapter 3), are at the XAI end of the spectrum.

Explainability Consumers

Understanding and using the results of XAI can look very different depending on who is receiving the explanation. As a practitioner, for example, your needs from an explanation are very different from those of a nontechnical individual who may be receiving an explanation as part of an ML system in production that they may not even know exists!

Understanding the primary types of users, or personas, will be helpful as you learn about different techniques so you can assess which will best suit your audience's needs. In Chapter 7, we will go into more detail about how to build good experiences for these different audiences with explainability.

More broadly, we can think of anyone as a consumer of an explanation. The ML system is presenting additional information to help a human perceive what is unique about the circumstances of a prediction, comprehend how the ML system behaves, and, ultimately, be able to extrapolate to what could influence a future prediction.

Currently, a key limitation of XAI is that most techniques are a one-way description; the ML system communicates an explanation to the human, with no ability to respond to any follow-on requests by the user. Put another way, many XAI methods are talking *at* users rather than *conversing with* users. However, while these techniques are explaining an ML system, none would be considered to be machine learning algorithms. Although very sophisticated, these techniques are all "dumb" in the sense that we cannot interact with them in a two-way dialogue. A smart explainability technique could adapt to our queries, learning how to guide us toward the best explanation, or answer the question we didn't know we were asking. For now, if we want to try and obtain more information about a prediction, the best we can do is to change the parameters of our explanation request, or try a different explainability technique. In Chapter 8, we outline how this will change in the future, but in the meantime, most explainability techniques represent a process closer to submitting a requisition form to an opaque bureaucracy to get information rather than going to your doctor and engaging in a conversation to understand why you have a headache. In our work with Explainable AI, we have found that it is useful to group explainability consumers into three broad groups based on their needs: practitioners, observers, and end users.

Practitioners—Data Scientists and ML Engineers

ML *practitioners* predominantly use explainability as they are building and tuning a model. Their primary goal is to map an explanation to actionable steps that can be taken to improve the model's performance, such as changing the model architecture, training data, or even the structure of the dataset itself before the model is deployed. The goal of this process is often to improve the training loss and validation set performance, but there are times when accuracy may not be the primary concern. For example, a data scientist may be concerned that the model has become influenced by data artifacts not present in the real-world data (for example, a doctor's pen marks on an X-ray for a diagnosis model, as discussed in Chapter 1) or that the model is generating outcomes that are unfairly biased toward certain individuals.

However, an ML engineer may be asking, How can we improve the performance of our data pipeline? Certain features may be costly to obtain, or computationally expensive to transform into a usable form. If we find that the model rarely uses those features in practice, then it is an easy decision to remove them to improve the system overall. Practitioners may also be interested in explainability once the system is deployed, but their interest still remains in understanding the underlying mechanisms and performance. Explainability has proven to be a robust and powerful tool for monitoring deployed models for drift and skew in their predictions, indicating when a model should be retrained (see also the discussion on how XAI can be incorporated in the entire ML workflow in Chapter 8). And of course, you may simply be interested in an explanation because, like any practitioner, you've encountered a situation when the model made you squint and say "What the...?"

Observers—Business Stakeholders and Regulators

Another group of explainability consumers is *observers*. These are individuals, committees, or organizations who are not involved in the research, design, and engineering of the model, but also are not using the model in deployment. They often fall into two categories: stakeholders, who are within the organization building the model, and regulators, who are outside the organization.

Stakeholders often prefer a nontechnical explanation, instead seeking information that will allow them to build trust that the model is behaving as is expected, and in the situation it was designed for. Stakeholders often come to an explanation with a broader, business-focused question they are trying to answer: Do we need to invest in more training data? or How can I trust that this new model has learned to focus on the right things so we're not surprised later?

Regulators are often from a public organization or industry body, but they may also come from another part of a company, (i.e., Model Risk Management) or be an auditor from another company, such as an insurance company. Regulators seek to validate and verify that a model adheres to a specific set of criteria, and will continue to do so in the future. Unlike stakeholders, a regulator's explainability needs can range from quite technical to vague, depending on the regulation. A common example of this conundrum is in the needs of many regulators to assess evidence that a model is not biased toward a specific category of individuals (e.g., race, gender, socioeconomic status) while also determining that the model behaves fairly in practice, with no further definition given for what entails fairness. Since regulators may routinely audit a model, explanations that require less human effort to produce or understand, and can be generated efficiently and reliably, are often more useful.

End Users—Domain Experts and Affected Users

Individuals or groups who use, or are impacted by, a model's predictions are known as *end users*. *Domain experts* have a sophisticated understanding of the environment the model is operating in, but may have little to no expertise in machine learning, or even the features used by the model if they are derived, or new to the profession. Domain experts often use explanations as part of a decision support tool. For example, if an image model predicts manufacturing defects in parts on an assembly line, a quality control inspector may use an explanation highlighting where the model found the defect in the machined part to help make a decision about which part of the manufacturing process is broken.

Affected users often have little or no understanding of how the model works, the data it uses, or what that data represents. We refer to these users as affected because they may not directly use the model, but the model prediction results in a tangible impact on them. Examples of affected individuals include people receiving credit offers, where a model has predicted their ability to repay loans, or a community receiving increased funding for road maintenance. In either case, the affected users primarily want to understand and assess if the prediction was fair and that it was based on correct information. As a follow-up, these users seek explanations that can give them the ability to understand how they could alter factors within their control to meaningfully change a future prediction. You may be unhappy that you were given a loan with a very, very high interest rate, but understand that it is fair because you have a poor history of repaying loans on time. After understanding the current situation, you might reasonably ask, How long of a history of on-time loan payments would I need to establish in order to get a lower interest rate?

Types of Explanations

Modern-day machine learning solutions are often complex systems incorporating many components from data processing and feature engineering pipelines, to model training and development to model serving, monitoring, and updating. As a result, there are many factors that contribute to explaining why and how a machine learning system makes the predictions it does, and explainability methods can be applied at each step of the ML development pipeline. In addition, the format of an explanation can depend on the data modality of the model (e.g., whether it is a tabular, image, or text model). Explanations can also range from being very specific by being generated for a single prediction or based upon a set of predictions to give a broader insight into the model's overall behavior. In the following sections, we'll give a high-level description of the various types of explanations that can be used to better understand how ML solutions work.

Premodeling Explainability

Machine learning models rely on data and although many Explainable AI techniques rely on interacting with a model, the insights they create are often focused on the dataset and features. Thus, one of the most critical stages of developing model explanations begins before any modeling takes place and is purely data focused. Premodeling explainability[3] is focused on understanding the data or any feature engineering that is used to train the ML model.

As an example, consider a machine learning model that takes current and past atmospheric information (like humidity, temperature, cloud cover, etc.) and predicts the likelihood of rain. An example of an explainable prediction that is model dependent would be, "The model predicted a 90% chance of rain because, among the data inputs, humidity is 80% and cloud cover is 100%." This type of explanation relies on feature attribution for that model prediction. On the other hand, premodeling

---

3 In industry, these techniques may also be referred to as feature-based explainability.

explanations focus only on the properties of a dataset and are independent of any model, such as "The standard deviation of the chance of rain is +/− 18%, with an average of 38%." Inherently explainable models, such as linear and statistical models, may blur this distinction, with explanations such as "For each 10% increase in the cloud cover, there is a 5% increase in the chance of rain." Given the extensive availability of resources available on more "classical" statistical and linear modeling, we will only briefly discuss here commonly used premodeling explainability techniques.

Explanations that focus solely on the dataset are often referred to as exploratory data analysis (EDA). EDA is a collection of statistical techniques and visualizations that are used to gain more insight into a dataset. There are many techniques for summarizing and visualizing datasets, and there are quite a few useful tools that are commonly used such as Know Your Data (*https://oreil.ly/AQvC1*), Pandas Profiling (*https://oreil.ly/iJJ8C*), and Facets (*https://oreil.ly/IsaSk*). These tools allow you to quickly get a sense of the statistical properties of the features in your dataset such as the mean, standard deviation, range, and percentage of missing samples as well as the feature dimensionality and presence of any outliers. From the perspective of explainability, this knowledge of the data distribution and data quality is important for understanding model behavior, interpreting model predictions, and exposing any biases that might exist within the dataset.

In addition to these summary univariate statistics, explanations in the form of EDA can also take the form of multivariate statistics that describe the relationship between two or more variables or features in your dataset. Multivariate analysis is a useful tool to compute statistics that show the interaction between features and the target. This type of correlation analysis is useful not just for helping to explain model behavior but can also be beneficial for improving model performance. If two features are highly correlated, this could indicate an opportunity to simplify the feature space, which can improve interpretability of the machine learning model. Also, knowledge of these interdependencies is important when analyzing your model using other explainability techniques; for example, see in Chapter 3 where we discuss the effect highly correlated features have on interpreting the results of techniques like partial dependence plots or related techniques for tabular datasets. There are a number of visualization tools that can assist in this type of correlation analysis such as pair plots, heatmaps, biplots, projection plots (t-SNE, MDS, etc.), and parallel coordinate plots.

Intrinsic Versus Post Hoc Explainability

When and how do we receive an explanation for a prediction? Explanations that are part of the model's prediction itself are known as *intrinsic* explanations, while explanations that are performed after the model has been trained and rely on the prediction to create the explanation are called *post hoc* explanations. Most of the techniques we discuss in this book are post hoc explanations because they are more portable and can be decoupled from the model itself. By contrast, generating intrinsic explanations often requires modifications to the model or an inherently interpretable model. Often, intrinsic explanations are based on inherent properties of the model or are by-products of the model's internal calculations for generating a prediction.

To make this more concrete, let's look at the difference between an intrinsic explanation and a post hoc explanation of how much a linear regression model relied on three different features in a dataset for making its prediction:

$$\text{Pred}(y) = 0.1 \cdot \text{feature}_A + 0.7 \cdot \text{feature}_B + 0.4 \cdot \text{feature}_C$$

Given an input example where $\text{feature}_A = 10$, $\text{feature}_B = 20$, $\text{feature}_C = 40$, the model will predict ($\text{Pred}(y)$) a value of 31. If we wanted an explanation of how the model worked, we could create an explanation that describes which feature most influenced the model's prediction. For a linear model, an intrinsic explanation for this would simply be the coefficients, or weights, for each feature, with the largest coefficient 0.7 being for Feature B. So, our intrinsic explanation is "Feature B had the greatest influence on the model's prediction." In this case, we relied on the fact that linear regressions are inherently interpretable models, so we could use that interpretable trait to easily generate the explanation.

However, most ML models are not inherently interpretable and, based on the complexity of the model, it may be very difficult to generate an intrinsic explanation. We could still generate a post hoc explanation for our linear regression model in a variety of ways. However, since post hoc explanations have little or no visibility into the internal workings of the model, we will use Shapley values (covered later in the chapter and in depth in Chapter 3) to simulate many predictions by the model, but with various combinations of the features (A, B, C) for the given inputs (10, 20, 40) and predicted value (31). Combining the results from these simulations leads us to the same explanation: that Feature B most influenced the model's behavior.

 You may notice that some libraries are set up to provide an explanation with the prediction—this does not necessarily mean the explanation is intrinsic, as it may be that the service first generates the prediction, then the explanation, before returning both together.

Within the group of post hoc explainability techniques, another factor to group techniques is whether the method is *model agnostic* or *model specific*. A model-agnostic technique does not rely on the model's architecture, or some inherent property of the model, so it can be used universally across many different types of models, datasets, and scenarios. As you might imagine, it is also more useful to become more familiar with these techniques because you will have more opportunities to reuse them than a technique that only works on a specific type of model architecture.

How can a technique not know anything about the model, and yet still generate useful explanations? Most of these techniques rely on changing inputs to the model, correlating similar predictions, or running multiple simulations of a model. By comparison, a technique that relies on the model itself will leverage some internal aspect of the model's architecture to aid in generating the explanation. For example, an explanation for tree-based models may look at the weights of specific nodes within the tree to extract the most influential decision points within the tree to explain a prediction.

Does this mean that *opaque*, or black box, models[4] always use model-agnostic techniques, while explainability for transparent, or interpretable, models is always model specific? Not necessarily; there are many unique explanation techniques for deep neural networks (DNNs) that are considered opaque models, and a linear regression model could be explained using Shapley values, a model-agnostic technique.

Local, Cohort, and Global Explanations

Explanations themselves can cover a wide variety of topics, but one of the most fundamental is whether the explanation is *local*, *cohort*, or *global* with respect to the range of predictions the explanation covers. A local explanation seeks to provide context and understanding for a single prediction. A global explanation provides information about the overall behavior of the model across all predictions. Cohort explanations lie in between, providing an understanding for a subset of predictions made by the model.

Local explanations may be similar for comparable inferences, but this is not an absolute and depends on the technique, model, and dataset. Put another way, it is rarely safe to assume that an explanation for one set of inputs and inference is blindly applicable to a similar set of inputs and/or prediction. Consider, for example, a decision tree model that predicts expected rainfall with a decision node that strictly checks whether the humidity is greater than 80%. Such a model can lead to very different predictions and explanations for two days when the humidity is 80% versus 81%.

Global explanations can come in many forms, and because they are not directly representative of any individual prediction, they likely represent more of a survey, or summary statistic, about the model's behavior. How global explanations are generated is highly dependent on the technique, but most approaches rely either on generating explanations for all predictions (usually in the training or validation dataset) and then aggregating these explanations together, or on perturbing the inputs or weights of the model across a wide range of values.

---

4 Following Google developer guidelines, we avoid the use of the phrase "black box" in this book. See *https:// developers.google.com/style/word-list#black-box* for more details.

Global explanations are typically useful for business stakeholders, regulators, or for serving as a guide to compare the deployed model's behavior against its original performance.

 Global explanations are not a set of rules describing the boundaries of a model's behavior, but instead only what has been observed based on the original training data. Once a model is deployed and is exposed to new data examples not seen during training, it is possible that during inference local explanations can differ from or even directly contradict global explanations.

Explainable methods for cohorts are usually the same techniques as what is used to calculate global explanations, just applied to a smaller set of data. One powerful aspect of cohort explanations is that one cohort can be compared against another cohort to provide insights about the global behavior of the model that may not be apparent if we just sought a global explanation. These comparisons are useful enough in their own right to serve as the underpinnings for another pillar of responsible AI: testing and evaluating the fairness of a model.

Fairness techniques seek to evaluate how a model performs for one cohort of predictions compared to another, with the goal of ensuring that the model generates similar predictions based on relevant factors rather than discriminating on characteristics that are deemed to be unimportant or may not even be desirable to use in the first place. A classic example is how an AI that seeks to determine whether an individual should be approved for a loan may be trained on historical data in the US, which contains prevalent discrimination against people of different races. Scrutinizing the ML for fairness would tell us whether the model learned this racial discrimination, or whether it is basing its decisions solely on the relevant financial background of the individual, such as their income and history of on-time loan payments. Although explainability and fairness share many of the same underpinnings, how to apply and understand fairness, as well as the techniques themselves, are sufficiently distinct from explainability and we do not cover them in this book.

Attributions, Counterfactual, and Example-Based Explanations

Explanations can come in many forms depending on the type of information they use to convey an understanding of the model. When asked, many of us think of *attribution-based* explanations that are focused on highlighting relevant properties of the system, e.g., "It is raining because there are clouds in the sky." In this case, the sky's contents are a feature in our weather model, and clouds are an attribute of that feature.

In Explainable AI, *example-based*, or *similarity*, explanations are those that focus on providing a different scenario that is analogous to the prediction being explained. For example, in our previous explanation, we could have also said, "It is raining because the weather is mostly like the conditions when it rains in Rome." To ease the burden of understanding why similar predictions are relevant, example-based explanation techniques typically include secondary information to help highlight the similarities and differences in the dataset and/or how the model acted between the two predictions. We will cover example-based explanations in more depth in Chapter 6.

Earlier when we said it was raining because of clouds, we could have also explained this by providing a *counterfactual* explanation: "It does not rain when it is sunny." Proponents and opponents are part of counterfactual explanations, which humans often find more satisfying than pure attribution-based explanations because they rely on offering other examples of inputs and predictions to compare and contrast model behavior. Following our weather-based example, "clouds" would be the *proponent* of our counterfactual explanation, while "sunny" is the *opponent* to our explanation.[5] Counterfactuals are often portrayed as negations (e.g., "It does *not* rain when it is sunny."), but this is not a requirement of counterfactual explanations. We could have just as easily found a counterfactual to a weather prediction for cold weather with the counterfactual "It is hot when it is sunny." Finding and understanding the causes behind proponents and opponents can be difficult depending on the modality of the dataset. An opponent value that is negative in a structured dataset is much easier to comprehend than why a texture in an image is considered an opponent by the model.

Next we will look at most common types of explanations that are used today, providing a general overview of each type, so you can understand, broadly, your options for explainability techniques.

Themes Throughout Explainability

Explainability is a broad and multidisciplinary area of machine learning that brings together ideas in various fields from game theory to social sciences. As a result, there is a large and continually growing number of explainability methods and techniques that have been introduced. In this section, we'll give an overview of some common themes that have been introduced and further developed in the field.

Feature Attributions

Methods based on attributing model behavior to features in the dataset are common throughout XAI. What does it mean to attribute a prediction to an individual feature in your dataset? Formally, a feature attribution represents the influence of that feature (and its value for a local explanation) on the prediction. Feature attributions can be

---

5 Counterfactual explanations are often defined by differing values to the inputs rather than features. In this example, for an actual model, the input feature would be a categorical value representing cloud cover as (clouds, overcast, scattered clouds, sunny).

absolute, for example, if a predicted temperature is 24°C, a feature could be attributed 8°C of that predicted value, or even a negative value like –12°C, meaning it lowered the final predicted value.

 In this book, we describe features as influencing a model, while the specific amount of influence is the attribution. In practice, "feature influence" and "feature attribution" are often used interchangeably.

If the idea of a feature having influence that is relative seems strange to you, then you're in good company. Understanding what feature attributions convey as explanations, and what they don't, is rife with confusion and it is often difficult for end users to build an understanding of feature attributions' true mechanism. For a more intuitive feel of how feature attributions work, let's walk through an imaginary scenario of an orchestra playing music. Within this orchestra, there are a variety of musicians (which we will treat as features) that contribute to the overall performance of how well the orchestra plays a musical composition. For Explainable AI, let's imagine that the orchestra is going to participate in ExplainableVision, a competition where a judge (the ML model) tries to predict how well an orchestra performs music by listening to the music played by each individual musician in the orchestra. In our analogy, we can use feature attributions to understand how each musician influenced the overall rating of the orchestra given by the judge.

Each feature attribution represents how a musician sways the judge toward the most accurate prediction of the overall musical talent of the orchestra. Some musicians may be useful to the judge in determining an accurate score of the overall orchestra's performance, so we would assign them a high value for their feature attribution. Perhaps it is because they are close to the average talent of the orchestra, or the amount of time they spend playing in any given performance is very high. However, other musicians may not be as helpful and cause the judge to give an inaccurate score, in which case we would give them a small feature attribution. This low score could be for a number of reasons. For example, it could be because those musicians are just bad at playing music, which is distracting to the judge. Or perhaps, they're fine musicians but they play out of harmony with the rest of the orchestra. Or maybe they're fantastic musicians and cause the judge to give a very positive assessment of the orchestra's talent, even though the rest of the orchestra is really bad. In any of these cases, the feature attribution of that musician should be given a smaller value because their contribution negatively affects the judge's ability to provide an accurate score of the orchestra's overall skill. For either high- or low-feature attribution scores, the assessment to determine the attribution of a single musician to the judge's overall prediction of the orchestra's talent is still "How much did that musician influence the judge's rating?"

Choosing an appropriate feature attribution technique is not just a matter of finding the latest or most accurate state-of-the-art method. Techniques can vary wildly, or even be completely opposed in the attribution they give to different features. Figure 2-2 shows an example of this by comparing seven different feature attribution techniques for the same dataset and model.

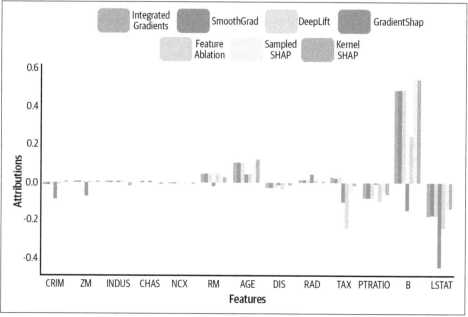

Figure 2-2. Feature attributions across seven different techniques for a PyTorch model trained on the Boston Housing dataset. (Print readers can see the color image at https:// oreil.ly/xai-fig-2-2.)

In this example, the Integrated Gradients (IG), SmoothGrad, and DeepLIFT techniques closely agree in their feature attribution values, even though DeepLIFT is conceptually a different approach from IG and SmoothGrad. Conversely, the GradientSHAP technique strongly diverges from its sibling techniques, Sampled SHAP and Kernel SHAP, despite all three using the same underlying theory. Finally, we can see how feature ablation, which is not similar to any of the other methods, sometimes has very similar attributions to other techniques (i.e., for the features RM and PTRATIO), but has attributed influence to the features B and TAX, unlike any other method.

Feature attributions can also be relative, representing a percentage of influence compared to other features used by the model. For our temperature prediction model, instead of attributing absolute values like 8°C of the predicted value of 24°C, we could instead say that a feature was responsible for 21% of the predicted value, with other features being responsible for 18%, 42%, and more. However, many of the assumptions usually held about working with relative values and percentages do not necessarily hold for these types of feature attributions: percentages may not sum up to 100%, and negative percentages are equally difficult to reason about. We discuss more about how to avoid confusion when working with feature attributions in Chapter 7.

Feature attributions may still seem abstract, which is okay because they rely on the modality of the dataset. For example, in Chapter 3, "Explainability for Tabular Data," we will discuss feature attributions as numerical values because the inputs are scalar. By comparison, in Chapter 4, "Explainability for Image Data," feature attributions are the contribution by individual pixels in the image to the prediction. In Chapter 5, which is focused on natural language processing (NLP), the feature attributions are typically prescribed to tokenized words.

Shapley values

One commonly used method to determine feature attribution is Shapley values. Shapley values use game theory to determine a feature's influence on a prediction. Unlike a technique such as feature permutation (see Chapter 3 where we discuss permutation feature importance), which relies on changing the values of features to estimate their impact, Shapley values are purely observational, instead inferring feature attributions through testing combinations with different groups of features.

A Shapley value is calculated using cooperative game theory; Lloyd Shapley published the technique in 1951, and it contributed to his 2012 Nobel Prize in Economics. It is useful to understand the core idea behind Shapley values in order to decide if they're worth it for your use case and be able to use them effectively with your ML model. Shapley values rely on examining how each feature influences the predicted value of a model by generating many predictions based on a partial set of the features used by the model and comparing the results of the predicted values.

We can describe how Shapley values are computed in two ways: coalitions and paths. With coalitions, Shapley values are represented by grouping the features of a dataset into multiple, overlapping subsets, which are the coalitions. For each coalition, a prediction value is generated using only the features in that coalition and compared against the prediction for a coalition that includes one additional feature. With paths, calculating Shapley values can also be framed as a dynamic programming problem, where a series of steps, or paths, are generated. Each step in a path represents incrementally, including another feature from the dataset to generate the prediction. We generate many different paths to represent the different permutations of the order in which features could be included.

More concretely, imagine we had a weather dataset, and we wanted to predict the amount of rain (in inches). In this example, we'll refer to this prediction function as P(), which takes any subset of features, e.g., {feature_1, feature_2, …} as its input. For the purposes of explaining how Shapley values are calculated, it is not important to understand how P() determined the predicted values.[6] The ability to explain an opaque model, while not knowing how it works internally, is one of the advantages of many explainability techniques.

The Math of Shapley Values

Originally, Shapley values were formulated as a way to divide up the value of some payoff fairly across all players using cooperative game theory. In the context of ML, we think of the payoff as the output of the learned model function v and the set of all model input features N as the players.[7] Calculating the Shapley value relies on examining the value of v for coalitions of features, which are essentially subsets of N denoted as S. Within a cohort S, we denote the Shapley value attributed to a feature i as s_i. The formula for calculating an individual Shapley value of i via coalitions is:

$$s_i = \frac{1}{|N|!} \sum_{S \subseteq N \setminus i} |S|! \cdot (|N| - |S| - 1)! [v(S \cup i) - v(S)]$$

To demystify this formula a bit, the Shapley value is a marginal calculation of the contribution of a coalition with i and without i (i.e., $v(S \cup i) - v(S)$) summed up over all coalitions that don't have i (i.e., $S \subseteq N \setminus i$). Each of those marginal calculations is weighted by all the possible ways that we could have gotten that marginal calculation (i.e., $|S|!(|N| - |S| - 1)!$) divided by all the possible coalitions (i.e., $|N|!$). In total, the sum of all feature attributions, $s_{1...N}$, will be equal to $v(N)$.

Alternatively, we can also calculate the Shapley values using a path formulation, which is more common for Explainability, by defining an ordering of features (the path) as R, and P_i^R, which is the set of features in N, or partial path, that precedes i in the order of R. We then use this formula to calculate the Shapley value of i via paths:

$$s_i = \frac{1}{|N|!} \sum_R \left[v\left(P_i^R \cup i\right) - v\left(P_i^R\right) \right]$$

Implementations of Shapley values differ in how $v(S)$ is defined, with the most basic implementation, but highly inefficient, version being $v(S) = f(x_S)$ where $f(x_S)$ is the function for a model to calculate a prediction for an individual feature input.

---

6 Also, P() is not a probability function, so you may encounter combinations of inputs that violate assumptions about probability function notation.

7 To make this equation easier to use as you compare different implementations of Shapley values, we use the same notation as this 2020 article in arXiv, "The Many Shapley Values for Model Explanation" (*https://arxiv.org/abs/1908.08474*) by Mukund Sundararajan and Amir Najmi, although we have moved the denominator out of the summation to make it easier to compare with the path formulation.

In the simplest version of our weather dataset, we just have two features, `temperature` and `cloud_cover`. To calculate the Shapley values for each of the individual features `temperature` and `cloud_cover`, we first compute four individual predictions for different combinations of features in the dataset:

- `P({})` = 0 // initially no features, also known as a null baseline
- `P(temperature) = 2 inches`
- `P(cloud_cover) = 5 inches`
- `P({temperature, cloud_cover}) = 6 inches`

For now, don't worry about how we arrived at these predicted values using only a subset of features—we'll discuss that later in this chapter, as well as in Chapter 3 where we talk about baselines.

Our prediction that uses all of the features in the dataset is `P({temperature, cloud_cover})`, which gives us an estimated 6 (inches) of rain. To determine the Shapley value individually for `temperature`, we first remove our `P(cloud_cover)` prediction (5) from the overall `P({temperature, cloud_cover})` (6), leading to a contribution of 1. However, this is only part of the Shapley value; to compute the entire path, we also need to move backward from `P(temperature)` to `P({})`, leading to a contribution of 2. We then average the contributions from each step on the path to arrive at a Shapley value of 1.5 for `temperature`.[8] Using the same approach, we can calculate that the Shapley value for `cloud_cover` is 4.5 (by averaging 6 – 2 and 5 – 0).

This reveals a useful property of Shapley values, *efficiency*, meaning that the entire prediction is equal to the sum of the Shapley values of individual features. In our preceding example, our combined contributions (Shapley values) of 1.5 (`temperature`) and 4.5 (`cloud_cover`) summed to 6 (our original prediction, which included all of the features).

In this example, we have two paths, one to calculate the contribution of temperature and another to calculate the contribution of `cloud_cover`:

- `P({})` → `P({temperature})` → `P({temperature, cloud_cover})`
- `P({})` → `P({cloud_cover})` → `P({temperature, cloud_cover})`

What happens if we have more than two features? To accomplish this, we begin computing the Shapley paths, or unordered, incremental groupings of features. A path represents a way to go from no features in our prediction to the full set of

---

8 For larger coalition sizes, the average is weighed by the number of coalitions of that size. See the formal definition of Shapley values for details.

features we used in our model. Each step in the path represents an additional feature in our coalition.

Let's expand our weather dataset to include a humidity feature, for an overall prediction that is P({temperature, cloud_cover, humidity}).

Our Shapley paths, shown in Figure 2-3, are now:

- P({}) → P({temperature}) → P({temperature, cloud_cover}) → P({cloud_cover, temperature, humidity})

- P({}) → P({temperature}) → P({humidity, temperature}) → P({cloud_cover, temperature, humidity})

- P({}) → P({cloud_cover}) → P({temperature, cloud_cover}) → P({cloud_cover, temperature, humidity})

- P({}) → P({cloud_cover}) → P({cloud_cover, humidity}) → P({cloud_cover, temperature, humidity})

- P({}) → P({humidity}) → P({humidity, temperature}) → P({cloud_cover, temperature, humidity})

- P({}) → P({humidity}) → P({cloud_cover, humidity}) → P({cloud_cover, temperature, humidity})

You may have noticed that we have repeated parts in our paths, such as P({humidity, temperature}) or P({cloud_cover, humidity}). The ordering of the features does not matter for how Shapley values are computed either using the paths or the coalitions frameworks. In fact, the computation can be sped up by saving the values along the path to avoid recomputation. This is an important property, and the one most misunderstood, as we'll discuss in further detail later regarding a common misconception with Shapley values and causality.

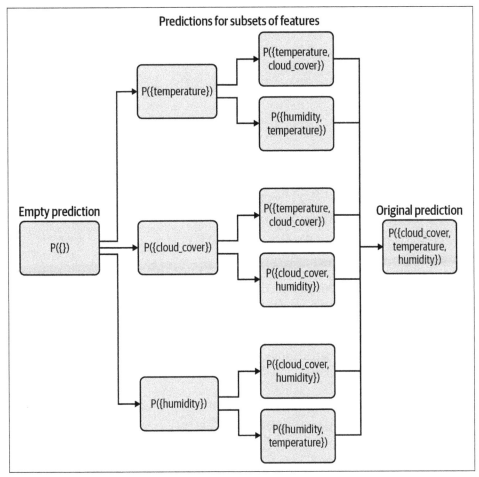

Figure 2-3. The Shapley paths for constructing Shapley values for our weather model using the features `temperature, cloud_cover,` *and* `humidity`.

Returning to our weather dataset, how would we calculate the Shapley value for our humidity feature? First, we need to know the predicted value for our different combinations of features:

- `P({}) = 3`
- `P(temperature) = 2`
- `P(cloud_cover) = 4`
- `P(humidity) = 5`
- `P({temperature, cloud_cover}) = 6`
- `P({temperature, humidity}) = 8`
- `P({cloud_cover, humidity}) = 10`
- `P({cloud_cover, temperature, humidity}) = 15`

In our earlier example when we only considered temperature and cloud cover, we did not need to calculate the indirect contribution of any feature. Now with multiple intermediate steps in our path, we need to determine how much each feature contributed along the path to the final predicted value. For the first path, we expand each step in the path to include the contribution made by the new feature added to the coalition. To calculate the attributions, we take the difference of the predicted value before and after the step occurs:

- Step 1 (base case): `P({})` → `P({temperature}`

    `Intermediate_Attribution_temperature = P({temperature}) - P({})`
    `= 2 - 3 = -1`

- Step 2: `P({temperature})` → `P({temperature, cloud_cover})`

    `Intermediate_Attribution_cloud_cover = P({temperature, cloud_cover}) -`
    `P({temperature}) = 6 - 2 = 4`

- Step 3: `P({temperature, cloud_cover})` → `P({cloud_cover, temperature, humidity})`

    `Intermediate_Attribution_humidity = P({cloud_cover, temperature,`
    `humidity}) - P({temperature, cloud_cover}) = 15 - 6 = 9`

Why are these intermediate attributions? We have more than one Shapley path, so we must continue to compute the partial attributions across all paths. To obtain the final feature attribution, we take the average of all of the intermediate attributions for that feature.

What About Classification Models?

Although it is not immediately obvious, using Shapley values with classification models is perfectly okay, and not as hard as it seems. This is because almost all modern classification models represent classes not as a set of labels, but in some vector form (for example, either through embeddings, or one-hot encoding). In this case, our mental representation of how Shapley values push an inference toward or away from the final prediction value may not be as accurate. Rather than thinking of the Shapley value as pushing toward one class and away from another, envision a Shapley value as strengthening or weakening the predicted score for that individual class. For a multiclass classification model, the Shapley values are doing this strengthening and weakening for each class. A typical way to calculate Shapley values for multiclass classification is to independently calculate the Shapley values for each possible class, rather than just the predicted class.

Sampled Shapley technique

In a world with infinite time, you would calculate intermediate attributions for every possible path, representing every possible coalition of features. However, this quickly becomes computationally infeasible—for a dataset with 10 features, we would need to get predictions for 2^{10} combinations[9] (or 1,023 additional predictions!). So, almost every feature attribution technique you encounter that relies on Shapley values will use an optimized method known as *sampled Shapley*.

The idea behind sampled Shapley is that you can approximate these paths by either skipping steps in the path for some features where there does not appear to be a large contribution, sampling random coalitions and averaging the results using Monte Carlo methods via repeated samplings, or following gradients. The trade-off to using sampling is that we now have an *approximation* of the true attribution values, with an associated *approximation error*. Due to this approximation error, our Shapley values may not sum up to the predicted result. There is no universal way to calculate the approximation error, or a "good" range for the approximation error, but generally you will want to try tuning the number of sampled paths to get the best trade-off between computation performance and error; a higher number of sampled paths will decrease the error but increase runtime, and vice versa.

Baselines

The explanations provided by Shapley values are contrastive, meaning they try to account for deviations from a baseline prediction. In our examples of Shapley paths,

---

9 The actual number of predictions could be even higher if you did not optimize and save the results of predictions to be reused between different paths.

we repeatedly referred to model prediction values using only a subset of the features our model was built for (e.g., P{temperature, cloud_cover} when our model took temperature, cloud_cover, and also humidity as inputs). There are several ways to compute these "partial" predictions, but for the purposes of this book we will focus on Shapley techniques, which use baselines.[10]

The main concept behind baselines is that if one can find a neutral, or *uninformative*, value for a feature, that value will not influence the prediction and therefore not contribute to the Shapley value. We can then use these uninformative values as placeholders in our model input when calculating the Shapley value for different feature coalitions. In our rainfall example, our partial prediction of P({cloud_cover = 0.8, humidity = 0.9}) = 10 may actually be fed to the model with a baseline value for temperature of temperature = 22 (Celsius), or P({cloud_cover = 0.8, humidity = 0.9, temperature = 22}) = 10

Baselines can vary; there may be an uninformative baseline that is best for different groups of predictions, or a carefully crafted baseline that is uninformative across your entire training dataset. We discuss the best way to craft baselines in Chapter 3 through Chapter 6, which are focused on explanations for different modalities.

Which Way to Calculate Shapley Values?

Calculating Shapley values as originally intended (by entirely removing features and observing the result) is rarely feasible in ML because most datasets are historical—it is not feasible to "rerun" or re-create the environment of the dataset without a certain feature, or combination of features, and observe what a new predicted value would be. Due to this, a variety of techniques have been invented over time to overcome these limitations by addressing how to treat the removed features and combinations in intermediate steps of the path. Many involve creating a synthetic value for the removed feature(s) that allows the model to be used as is with minimal contribution from the removed features, rather than trying to alter the model architecture or final predicted value, and often assuming that the ordering of features in the intermediate path steps does not matter. For example, the open source SHAP library (*https://oreil.ly/DpuJO*) has four different implementations for efficiently calculating Shapley values based on the model architecture. For a deeper discussion of the different Shapley value techniques, see the very well-written "The Many Shapley Values for Model Explanation" (*https://oreil.ly/pLHjm*) by Sundararajan and Najmi.

---

10 Other options include conditional expectations and RBShap. See also Mukund Sundararajan and Amir Najmi, "The Many Shapley Values for Model Explanation," (*https://oreil.ly/NmhJI*) *PMLR*, 2020, which provides an excellent breakdown of these different approaches, including trade-offs and real-world examples.

You will often see Shapley values referenced as a method for explanations or forming the basis behind others. As they have seen many decades of use across a variety of fields, and been very well studied in academia, they represent one of the most proven techniques for explainability. However, as we saw in discussing sampled Shapley, true Shapley values are computationally infeasible for most datasets, so there are trade-offs to this technique due to the lack of precision. Likewise, although superficially it is easier to understand feature attributions based on Shapley values, it can be quite difficult to explain the game theory concepts to stakeholders to build trust in the use of these techniques.

Gradient-based techniques

Gradient-based approaches toward explainability are some of the most powerful and commonly used techniques in the field. Deep learning models are differentiable by construction, and the derivative of a function contains important information about the local behavior of the function. Furthermore, since gradients are needed to fuel the gradient descent process that most machine learning models are trained upon, the tools of autodifferentiation for computing gradients are robust and well established in computing libraries.

A gradient is a high-dimensional analog of the derivative of a function in one variable. Just as the derivative measures the rate of change of a function at a point, the gradient of a real-valued function is a vector indicating the direction of the steepest ascent. Gradient descent relies on the gradient in the parameter space to find the parameters that minimize the loss. Similarly, measuring the gradient of a model function with respect to its inputs gives valuable information as to how the model predictions may change if the inputs change as well. This, in turn, is very useful for explainability. The gradient contains exactly the information we need to say, "If the input changed this much in this way, the model's prediction would change (or not) as well." Many of the explainability techniques we discuss in this book are based on evaluating how the value of predictions change as the values of features are changing as well.

Gradient-based methods are particularly common for image-based models (see Chapter 4), and they provide an intuitive picture of how these methods are typically applied. Given some example input image, to measure the gradient of how the model arrives at its prediction for that example, the image is varied along a path in feature space from some baseline to the values of the original input image.

But what exactly is a path in feature space? For images, we can think of a picture that is 32 x 32 pixels, like the images in the CIFAR-10 dataset, with three channels for RGB values as a vector in 3,072-dimensional space. Modifying the elements of that vector modifies the picture it represents. For gradient-based techniques, you start with a baseline image (similar in spirit to the role of the baseline in computing

Shapley values) and construct a path in that 3,072-dimensional space that connects the baseline with the vector representing the input image.

Gradient-based techniques for images make a lot of sense because they take advantage of the intrinsic property of an image, namely that it represents an array of uniform features with a fixed, linear scale (e.g., from 0.0 to 1.0 or 0 to 255). This allows these techniques to rapidly evaluate multiple versions, or steps, of an image as they move along the gradient. The technique will then combine its observations from these steps to calculate an attribution value for each pixel,[11] and in some cases, segment these attributions into regions. Gradient-based techniques are also used for tabular (Chapter 3) and text (Chapter 5) models, but the type of baseline you use for those cases will vary.

If this technique of determining attribution values sounds similar to the discussion of Shapley values in this chapter, and sampled Shapley (covered in depth in Chapter 3), that's because it is! Both Integrated Gradients and Shapley values are techniques that measure the individual influence of individual features in the model, and they do that by measuring how the model's prediction changes as new information of the input example is introduced. For Shapley values, this is done combinatorially by adding features individually or in coalitions to determine which features or coalitions have the strongest influence in comparison to a baseline prediction. However, with images, this approach is a bit naive as it rarely makes sense to entirely remove "features" (or substitute with a baseline value) given that a pixel's location in the image is relevant. Furthermore, the pixel's value relative to its neighbors also gives us important information, such as whether it constitutes the edge of an object. The idea of "dropping out" entire regions of an image to understand pixel influence has not yet been well explored and given the computational complexity of exhaustively generating all (or random) regions, it is likely this type of technique will be more used in interpretable models in the future, rather than as a standalone, model-agnostic explainability technique.

Saliency maps and feature attributions

Saliency maps arise in various contexts in machine learning but are probably most familiar in computer vision. Saliency maps, broadly, refer to any technique that aims to determine particular regions or pixels of an image that are somehow more important than others. For example, saliency maps can be used to highlight the regions in an image to better understand where and how a human first focuses their attention by tracking eye movements. The MIT/Tuebingen Saliency Benchmark dataset is a benchmark dataset for eye movement tasks. The saliency maps in this dataset indicate

---

11 As we'll explore further in the chapter, the exact way of calculating how to combine these steps is a key differentiating factor between techniques.

important regions in an image from tracking human eye movements and areas of fixation (see Figure 2-4).

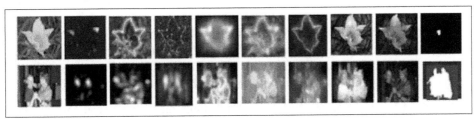

Figure 2-4. Examples from the MIT/Tuebingen Saliency Benchmark dataset.[12]

In the context of explainability and feature attributions, saliency methods serve a similar purpose; that is, they emphasize the regions or pixels of an image that indicate where a trained model focuses its attention to arrive at a given prediction. For example, in Chapter 4 we'll see how the method of Integrated Gradients can be used to produce a mask or overlay highlighting the pixels that contributed most to the model's prediction. We'll see precisely how the mechanics of Integrated Gradients and other gradient-based techniques lead to this kind of attribution mask as well as a host of other saliency-based explainability techniques that can be applied to image models.

Surrogate Models

Another form of explaining a model's behavior is to use a simplified version of the model, the *surrogate*, to give more explanatory power directly from observing the architecture of the model (also known as *model distillation*). In this sense, surrogate models represent a halfway point between post hoc explainability and intrinsic interpretable models. While this may sound like the best of both worlds, the trade-off is that a surrogate model almost always has worse performance than the original model, and usually cannot guarantee that all predictions are accurately explained, particularly in edge cases or areas of the dataset that were underrepresented during training.

Surrogate models usually have a linear, decision tree, or rule-based architecture. Where possible, we try to highlight the ability to use a surrogate model, but the field of automated model distillation still resides more in research labs than industry. What this usually means is that you must build your own techniques, or adapt proofs-of-concept, to make your surrogate models.

---

12 Zoya Bylinskii et al., "MIT Saliency Benchmark," 2015.

Activation

Rather than explaining model behavior by which features influenced the model's prediction, activation methods provide insight into what parts of the model's architecture influenced the prediction. In a DNN, this may be the layers that were most pivotal in the model's classification, or an individual neuron's contribution to the final output. Going even further, some techniques seek to explain through *concepts* learned by the model, driven by what was activated within the architecture for a given input.

Likewise, during training, an individual data point may be active in only certain circumstances, and strongly contribute to a certain set of labels, or range of predicted values. This is typically referred to as *training influence* but is analogous to activations within the model architecture.

Activation methods are among the most recently proposed explainability techniques in machine learning and provide an intriguing approach to leveraging the internal state of a complex model to better understand the model behavior. However, these techniques haven't yet been widely adopted among practitioners in the community, and so you will see less applications of them in this book (although concept activation vectors are discussed in Chapter 6).

Putting It All Together

While we may think of explanations as being primarily about their utility, meaning, and accuracy, understanding the ways in which explanations can vary is the first step in choosing the right tool for the job. By understanding what type of explanation will be most useful to your audience, you can go straight to using the best technique. Choosing an explanation method by simply trying many different techniques until an explanation looks good enough is similar to asking 10 strangers you find on the street for investment advice. You may get a lot of interesting opinions, but it is unlikely most of them will be valid.

Start with asking yourself about who is receiving the explanation, what is it that needs to be explained, and what will happen after the explanation? For example, an end user receiving an explanation about being denied a loan will not find a global explanation focused on understanding the model's architecture to be relevant or actionable. Better to use a technique that is local and focused on the features in order to center the explanation on factors in the user's control. You may even add a technique that provides a counterfactual explanation; for example, that the loan would likely have been approved if their credit score and finances were more similar to other consumers who had requested the same loan amount.

Business stakeholders, on the other hand, want to see the big picture. What types of features are globally influential in this model? Why should this more complex, opaque model be trusted over the previous linear model that's been in use for years?

A global feature attribution technique that is post hoc and model agnostic could be used to compare how both models behave.

Summary

In this chapter, we gave a high-level overview of the main ideas you are likely to consider as a practitioner developing explainable ML solutions. We started by discussing what the explanations are and how an explanation may change depending on the audience (e.g., ML engineers versus business stakeholders versus end users). Each of these groups have distinct needs and thus will interact with explanations in their own way.

We then discussed the different types of common explainability techniques, providing a simple taxonomy that we can use to frame the methods we will discuss in the later chapters of the book. Lastly, we covered some of the recurring themes that arise throughout explainability, like the idea of feature attribution, gradient-based techniques, saliency maps, and more recent developments like surrogate models and activation maps.

In the following chapters, we will dive into explainability for different types of data, starting with tabular datasets in Chapter 3. As you will see in Chapter 3, all the background and terminology in this chapter is immediately put into practice now that we have given you the knowledge to understand and distinguish between different types of techniques.

## CHAPTER 3

Explainability for Tabular Data

Much of the success of deep learning has focused on unstructured data like images, text, audio, and video; however, the vast majority of machine learning models in production are built with tabular data in mind. Think of all the data contained in relational databases and spreadsheets composed of numeric and categorical feature sets. These are examples of structured data and make up the vast majority of real-world AI use cases. In this chapter, we'll examine explainability techniques that are most often used when working with tabular data, like Shapley values, permutation feature importance, tree interpreters, and various versions of partial dependence plots.

Permutation Feature Importance

Here's what you need to know about permutation feature importance:

- Once a model has been fit to the training data, the permutation importance for a single feature measures the decrease in a model score when that feature value is randomly shuffled.

- By shuffling the values of a given feature, you destroy the model's ability to make meaningful predictions using that feature. If the model predictions suffer and the model score is much worse, then the information provided by that feature must have been important to the model when making predictions. On the other hand, if the change in the model score is negligible then that feature isn't as important.

Pros	Cons
• It's easy to implement. Scikit-learn provides a nice, easy-to-use library for computing permutation feature importance.	• Results can be misleading when features are highly correlated. This method has an underlying assumption that features are independent.
• The result is intuitive. The method of permutation feature importance is easy to explain and understand.	• The results of permutation importances do not reflect the intrinsic predictive value of a feature by itself, but instead reflect how important a feature is for a particular model.
• Permutation-based methods work equally well for mixed modes of tabular data (e.g., numeric and categorical features).	• The computation of permutation importances is heavily dependent on the feature shuffling, and different shuffles may produce different results. Multiple runs may be necessary to get a more accurate picture.

Permutation feature importance is a perturbation-based feature attribution technique commonly used for tabular datasets (see Chapter 2 for discussion on feature attributions and perturbation techniques). The common pattern is that the model features are perturbed or modified in some way and then predictions are made on these new examples. Using the model predictions from this collection of new, perturbed examples, you can then determine the impact each feature has on predictions by seeing how the model's predictions vary.

For example, for permutation feature importance, once a model has been fit to the training data, the importance of a feature is determined by measuring the prediction error after permuting the values of a given feature in the validation set. By shuffling the values of a given feature, you destroy the model's ability to make meaningful predictions using that feature.

When you measure the resulting change in the validation error, if the decrease is negligible, then the information provided by that feature wasn't very important or useful in determining the model predictions. That is to say, your model can still do a pretty good job without that feature. If, on the other hand, the model predictions suffer and the validation error is much worse, then the information provided by that feature must have been important to the model when making predictions.

In summary, the permutation feature importance of a model is the decrease in a model score when a single feature value is randomly shuffled. It's particularly helpful for nonlinear or hard-to-interpret models since it only relies on a fitted estimator and the model score could be any evaluation metric that makes sense, such as the mean square error or R^2 for a regression task or accuracy for a classification model. As such, using the taxonomy discussed in Chapter 2, permutation feature importance is a post hoc, global, model-agnostic explainability technique.

Permutation Feature Importance from Scratch

Let's implement permutation feature importance in an example. We'll use the California Housing dataset (*https://oreil.ly/Xdgx3*).[1] This dataset was collected from the 1990 US census and each row represents one census block group (each block group typically has a population of 600 to 3,000 people). Each example contains eight feature attributes like the average number of bedrooms per home or the median income of block residents. The target label for this dataset is MedianHouseVal, the median value of houses within each block expressed in hundreds of thousands of dollars. A small sample of this dataset is shown in Table 3-1, and Table 3-2 gives a description of each of the features and the label.

Table 3-1. The California Housing dataset contains feature attributes of houses at different locations around California suburbs.

MedInc	HouseAge	AveRooms	AveBedrms	Population	AveOccup	Latitude	Longitude	MedianHouseVal
8.3252	41	6.984127	1.02381	322	2.555556	37.88	−122.23	4.526
8.3014	21	6.238137	0.97188	2,401	2.109842	37.86	−122.22	3.585
7.2574	52	8.288136	1.073446	496	2.80226	37.85	−122.24	3.521
5.6431	52	5.817352	1.073059	558	2.547945	37.85	−122.25	3.413
3.8462	52	6.281853	1.081081	565	2.181467	37.85	−122.25	3.422

Table 3-2. The label variable MedianHouseVal represents the median values of the houses within each block, measured in hundreds of thousands of dollars ($100,000).

Feature name	Feature
MedInc	Median income in block group (in $10,000)
HouseAge	Median house age in block group in years
AveRooms	Average number of rooms per household
AveBedrms	Average number of bedrooms per household
Population	Block group population
AveOccup	Average number of household members
Latitude	Block group latitude
Longitude	Block group longitude
MedianHouseVal	Median house value (in $100,00)—target

---

[1] R. Kelley Pace and Ronald Barry, "Sparse Spatial Autoregressions," *Statistics and Probability Letters* 33 (1997): 291–97.

To start, we'll build and train a simple neural network in TensorFlow (the full code for this example can be found in the GitHub repository (*https://oreil.ly/LIfWN*) for this book):

```
model = tf.keras.Sequential([
    tf.keras.layers.Dense(40, activation=tf.nn.relu,
                    input_shape=[len(X_train[0])]),
                    tf.keras.layers.Dense(20, activation=tf.nn.relu),
                    tf.keras.layers.Dense(1)
])

model.compile(optimizer='adam', loss='mse', metrics=['mse'])
model.fit(X_train, y_train, epochs=30)
```

Once the model is trained, we measure the root mean squared error on the holdout test set. For this model the test error is 0.51, which represents an error of about $51,000. To compute the importance score for a given feature, we'll shuffle those feature values in the holdout set and see how much it affects our model performance. For important features, we'd expect the difference in model error to be large, whereas for less important features, shuffling the feature values won't have as much of an effect.

Suppose we want to measure the importance of median income (MedInc). First, we permute the feature values for that feature, then recompute the test error, and compare with the test error 0.51 we measured before (without shuffling MedInc):

```
model_rmse = 0.51
df_perturb['MedInc'] = df_perturb['MedInc'].sample(frac=1.0).values
preds = model.predict(df_perturb.values)
feature_rmse = np.sqrt(compute_mse(preds, y_test))
permutation_feature_importance = model_rmse - feature_rmse
```

This indicates that the importance score for MedInc (median household income) is about –0.44. Repeating this process for each feature in our dataset, we get a table of importance scores for each feature, as shown in Table 3-3.

It's important to note that the scores computed in Table 3-3 are only relative, meaning they can only be interpreted in relation to one another. On their own, the importance score for a single feature doesn't mean much. Even though the permutation importance score is based on the mean squared error loss, it doesn't directly translate to the home's value. For example, we can't say that on average $44,000 of a home's value is determined by the neighborhood's median income. However, we can use these numeric scores to indicate which feature has more or less of an impact on a model's prediction values in relation to each other.

Table 3-3. The importance score of each feature measures how much the model error is affected when those feature values are shuffled and predictions are made against the validation set.

Feature	Score
Latitude	−1.272
Longitude	−1.162
AveRooms	−0.852
AveBedrms	−0.731
MedInc	−0.443
AveOccup	−0.295
HouseAge	−0.079
Population	−0.036

According to Table 3-3, the latitude and longitude are the most important features for determining house value because they have the largest score in absolute value while the median house age and block population are the least important.

> This method of permutation feature importance relies on independence of the different features. If two features, say feature_A and feature_B, are highly correlated, then when we shuffle the values of feature_A, the model may still be able to do well since feature_B essentially contains the same information. Similarly, for shuffling the values of feature_B when we compute its feature importance. So, although these features may individually be very important for the model to make accurate predictions, you wouldn't be able to catch that relationship using permutation feature importance because the two features are highly correlated.
>
> In the example with the California Housing dataset, we could (and should!) examine this kind of multicollinearity in our dataset during our routine data exploration, but this can be particularly tricky to catch when you are working with a large number of features.

Permutation Feature Importance in scikit-learn

In practice, you'd want to shuffle and measure more than once since each shuffling introduces some randomness, which could affect the final result. Here, the shuffling is a kind of sampling without replacement; we're truly just reordering the values for a given feature. However, different shuffles may produce different results. By the law of large numbers (LLN), with repeated samplings we'll ultimately approach the true value of the feature importances, so multiple runs are necessary to get a more accurate picture. When building models in scikit-learn, there is a nice implementation of permutation feature importance that can be used for any fitted estimator.

Let's take another look at the California Housing dataset and fit a neural network in scikit-learn. The features of this dataset include numeric and categorical features, so we'll use the `ColumnTransformer` and `Pipeline` in scikit-learn to create and train our model. The notebook on permutation feature importance (*https://oreil.ly/LIfWN*) in the GitHub repository for this book contains the full code for this example.

Once the model is trained, we can use the `permutation_importance` function in scikit-learn to calculate the feature importance by passing the fitted estimator, the data and targets on which the permutation importance will be computed, the number of times to permute features and calculate the scores, and the scoring metric to use. We'll take n_repeats to be 30 to get a reasonable sample size, and we'll use R^2 as the evaluation metric when scoring the model. The following code block shows how to implement this in the scikit-learn library:

```
r = permutation_importance(mlp_pipeline, X_test, y_test,
                           n_repeats=30,
                           scoring=['r2'],
                           random_state=0)
```

How Many Repeats Is Enough?

Determining the right number of repeats for feature permutation may take a bit of experimentation. In the scikit-learn implementation, the default for the number of times to permute a feature is n_repeats=5. However, you might find that for your dataset, you need more. The larger number of repeats you choose, the more stable the result will be. However, this also increases the computation cost, which can become quite large with larger datasets. It is worth exploring and experimenting a bit with values ranging from 5 to 30 to get an idea of what value works best for your use case and dataset.

In this example, the permutation feature importance is calculated by first evaluating the model baseline using R^2 on the dataset on `X_test`. Then for each feature in the dataset, that feature column is permuted and the R^2 score is computed. The permutation importance is then the difference between the baseline R^2 score and the R^2 score using the permuted features. This process is repeated again and again; in our case, 30 times. The mean and standard deviation of the importance values are returned, so we can inspect the distribution of the importance scores for each feature:

```
for i in r['r2'].importances_mean.argsort()[::-1]:
    print(f'{cal_features[i]:<8}'
          f"{r['r2'].importances_mean[i]:.3f}"
          f" +/- {r['r2'].importances_std[i]:.3f}")
```

which returns:

```
Latitude: 1.842 +/- 0.033
Longitude: 1.758 +/- 0.024
MedInc: 0.673 +/- 0.014
HouseAge: 0.045 +/- 0.003
AveOccup: 0.003 +/- 0.001
AveBedrms: 0.003 +/- 0.001
Population: 0.002 +/- 0.001
AveRooms: 0.002 +/- 0.001
```

Perhaps not surprisingly we (re)learn a basic rule of real estate: house values depend most on location.

Using the Test Set or the Training Set

Permutation feature importances are a global explainability technique and rely on a batch of data to compute feature importances. In the example here, we used the test set X_test but we could easily have substituted the training set X_train instead. By using the test set, it's possible to pinpoint those features that have the greatest importance when generalizing to new data, which is ultimately what we care about in practice. Using the training set to determine importances might cause you to believe that those features are important for unseen data as well at the time of inference. However, it is possible the model was overfitting and those features aren't actually that important. In fact, any features that are deemed important for the training set but not on the test set are precisely those features that are most likely to cause the model to suffer at generalization.

As noted in the documentation for scikit-learn's permutation_importance function, the permutation importance of a feature does not reflect the intrinsic predictive value of a feature by itself but how important this feature is for a particular model. Even though a feature may have low importance for a bad model, that same feature could have high importance for a good model. Thus, you should always evaluate a model using a holdout set *before* computing any feature importances.

Shapley Values

Here's what you need to know about Shapley values:

- Derived from game theory to explain how a feature influences a predicted value
- Commonly implemented explainability technique available in several open source packages as well as cloud-based options

Pros	Cons
• Shapley values can be used for individual predictions, cohorts, and to globally explain the model. • Attributions sum to the total predicted value. • The values provide an intuitive understanding for stakeholders.	• Feature influence is often conflated with causality by practitioners, end users, and stakeholders. • These values are computationally intensive and difficult to use with models with more than ~100 features. • Choosing a good baseline can be difficult.

In Chapter 2, we discussed how Shapley values are computed and, broadly, how they are used in machine learning. In the past several years, Shapley values have become one of the most popular explainability methods for tabular datasets and models. They offer a lucrative way to say "this feature mattered, and this one didn't" with relatively little effort up front given several OSS and cloud-based solutions for computing them. However, this ease of use also hides some of the more difficult implications of incorrectly computing Shapley values.

SHAP (SHapley Additive exPlanations)

The terms *Shapley values* and *SHAP values* are often used interchangeably. However, this is not technically correct. Shapley values represent the theory, and SHAP values are a specific implementation for calculating Shapley values. You may also see reference to *sampled Shapley*, which is an approximation method of an exact Shapley value. Because SHAP values adhere to the four axioms of Shapley values (see the sidebar "The Axioms of Fairness"), it is pragmatically okay to use either term. For continuity, we will continue to use the term Shapley values here to refer to the SHAP values.

The Axioms of Fairness

Shapley values are considered a "favorable and fair" attribution method since they satisfy the four axioms of fairness: efficiency, symmetry, null player, and additivity/linearity:

- The *efficiency* axiom states that the total attribution is distributed in a lossless manner among all the model features. That is to say, the sum of all feature attributions determined when applying Shapley valuesequals the total attribution of the model.

- The *symmetry* axiom says that if two features play equal roles, then their Shapley values must be equal. This means that only the role of a play matters; the labels or specific names are irrelevant. Changing feature names won't change the Shapley value.

- The *null player* axiom says that if the marginal importance of a feature is always zero, then the baseline value of that feature is zero.

- The axiom of *additivity/linearity* ensures consistency among feature attributions with respect to linear combinations of models.

These four axioms provide a unique characterization of the Shapley value. Let's discuss what these axioms state in the context of machine learning explainability. See also the discussion on the axiomatic approach to evaluating explainability techniques in Chapter 6.

SHAP (*https://oreil.ly/5NdmT*) is the most popular OSS implementation of Shapley values. It builds upon the core idea of Shapley values and extends it to support multiple ML frameworks, along with providing a variety of useful visualization methods. SHAP has several implementations for different types of ML models and architectures, as shown in Table 3-4.

Table 3-4. An overview of different implementations within the SHAP library and their uses

SHAP class	ML model /architectures	Notes
TreeExplainer	Tree models, XGBoost, scikit-learn	High performance when computing Shapley values
DeepExplainer	DNNs, TensorFlow	Based on DeepLIFT, approximate Shapley values, difficult to configure
GradientExplainer	Differentiable models, TensorFlow	Slower than DeepExplainers, also approximates Shapley values
LinearExplainer	Linear regression	Computes the exact Shapley value; i.e., weights multiplied by feature values
KernelExplainer	Model agnostic	More difficult to configure, and slowest SHAP Explainer in terms of computation time

SHAP can also be used for other data modalities, such as images and text. See "Explaining Tree-Based Models" on page 63, which is where you'll find more information on how to use TreeExplainer.

Open Source Implementations of Shapley Values

There are other open source implementations of Shapley values that you might find useful. Captum is an OSS framework from Meta for using Explainable AI with PyTorch models. Captum offers a wide range of explainability algorithms, with a flexible approach that makes it easy to swap between different feature attribution techniques by changing only a few lines of code.

Captum supports many feature attribution techniques including sampled Shapley, DeepLIFT, DeepLiftSHAP (SHAP based on DeepLIFT, similar to SHAP's Deep Explainer), feature ablation, feature permutation, Integrated Gradients, SmoothGrad, KernelSHAP, and GradientSHAP. For differences between these implementations, and their limitations, see Captum's excellent Algorithm Comparison Matrix (*https://oreil.ly/qs0Gq*).

Captum does not have any built-in capabilities for visualizing feature attributions for structured data. Instead, attributions are returned as a tensor (or multiple tensors if more than one data sample was provided) of feature attribution (or in this case, Shapley values) that maps to the original organization of the inputs for the model (e.g., the first value in the tensor corresponds to the first feature).

Next, we will see how to use the SHAP library to compute Shapley values for a model trained on the California Housing dataset again. The following code block creates and trains an XGBoost model, then creates an `Explainer` object to compute feature attributions using SHAP. Providing the `Explainer` with an individual prediction returns the calculated Shapley values for that example:

```
model = xgboost.XGBRegressor(objective='reg:squarederror',
                             n_estimators=500)
model.fit(X_train, y_train)

explainer = shap.Explainer(model)
shap_values = explainer(X_test)
```

This approach of creating an explainer by calling `shap.Explainer(model)` works regardless of the model architecture or ML framework used. See the SHAP notebook (*https://oreil.ly/Pft5B*) in the GitHub repository for this book for the full code for this example. There is also an example there using a TensorFlow model.

The `shap_values` is an enumerable corresponding to all the data samples given to `explainer` to predict. In the previous code snippet, we're passing all the examples from the test set `X_test` to `explainer`. The following code block takes an individual value (i.e., the first value) in `shap_values` and extracts the model's prediction for that example, the baseline value, and Shapley values for each feature in the dataset:

```
first_row_shap = shap_values[0]
shapley_values = first_row_shap.values

print(f'Predicted Value: {first_row_shap.base_values + sum(shapley_values)}\n')
print(f'Baseline: {first_row_shap.base_values}\n')

print('Shapley values for features:')
for i, shapley_value in enumerate(shapley_values):
    print(f'{shap_values.feature_names[i]}: {shapley_value}')

print('\nMost to least influential features:')
most_influential_ordering = np.argsort(-np.abs(shapley_values))
for i in range(len(shapley_values)):
    print(f'{shap_values.feature_names[most_influential_ordering[i]]}:
            {shapley_values[most_influential_ordering[i]]}')
```

For the California Housing dataset, this code block returns:

```
Predicted Value: 1.889114398509264

Baseline: 2.063443660736084

Shapley values for features:
MedInc: 0.370290607213974
HouseAge: 0.03518122434616089
AveRooms: 0.15876026451587677
AveBedrms: 0.036185089498758316
Population: -0.06795859336853027
AveOccup: -0.10934144258499146
Latitude: -1.0922733545303345
Longitude: 0.49482694268226624

Most to least influential features:
Latitude: -1.0922733545303345
Longitude: 0.49482694268226624
MedInc: 0.370290607213974
AveRooms: 0.15876026451587677
AveOccup: -0.10934144258499146
Population: -0.06795859336853027
AveBedrms: 0.036185089498758316
HouseAge: 0.03518122434616089
```

Let's unpack this a bit and see how we should interpret this output. For this example instance, i.e., the first example of the test set, the feature values are:

```
MedInc: 3.5625
HouseAge: 43.0
AveRooms: 5.64741641337386
AveBedrms: 1.0486322188449848
Population: 1054.0
AveOccup: 3.2036474164133737
Latitude: 34.11
Longitude: -118.01
```

and the model predicts 1.889, or a median house value of $1,889,000. We also see that the baseline prediction for our model is 2.06, or median house value $2,060,000. The baseline prediction is just the expected value of the model output; that is, the average of the model predictions on all values in the test set. One of the fundamental properties of Shapley values is that the SHAP values of all the input features will sum up to the difference between the baseline model output and the model prediction for that example. This is also demonstrated visually using the waterfall plot in the next section. In fact, this is exactly what we see in the preceding example. If we compute `np.mean(xgb_reg.predict(X_test))`, we see that the average predicted value for the model is 2.06. And summing the baseline value with the Shapley values for each feature in this example gives exactly the model prediction 1.889. The rest of the output lists the individual Shapley values for each feature in this example instance and simply arranges them in increasing order.

Visualizing Local Feature Attributions

To visualize these feature attributions, we can use one of SHAP's many plotting methods. The waterfall plot, shown in Figure 3-1, is one of the most popular. Note that the SHAP values of all the input features sum up to the difference between the baseline model output, in this case 2.063, and the model's prediction for that example, here 1.889:

```
shap.plots.waterfall(shap_values[0])
```

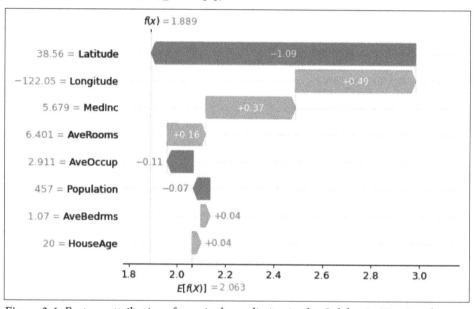

Figure 3-1. Feature attributions for a single prediction in the California Housing dataset using SHAP's waterfall visualization.

The waterfall visualization contains many pieces of information to give context to the feature attributions. The y-axis lists all features, with the feature's value to the left of the feature label (i.e., AveRooms = 6.401 for this example). Each feature attribution is represented as a row in the waterfall, color coded with an arrow for whether the feature contributed positively or negatively toward the final prediction value. Red bars pointing right indicate a positive contribution, while blue bars pointing left indicate a negative contribution. The rows in the visualization are ordered from top to bottom by the greatest to smallest contribution to the predicted score.

As you can imagine, if your model has more than eight features this visualization can become quite unwieldy and hard to read, and likely the less important features have very small attribution values. Shapley feature attributions are *additive*, meaning we can sum them together to represent the overall contribution by a group of features. To make the plot more readable, SHAP aggregates the lowest influence features into a single bar (with the label "4 other features," for example).

 Remember, positive and negative feature attributions simply indicate how the feature contributed to the numerical value of the prediction, not more or less. The feature attribution's magnitude of influence is the absolute value of the attribution.

The visualization also helpfully displays the predicted value with a label of $f(x) = \ldots$ along with a gray line through all rows. Likewise, the baseline predicted value is shown along the x-axis with a label $E[f(X)] = \ldots$ (E is used to indicate this is the expected value of a prediction, although SHAP uses baseline scores internally).

There are two ways to read the waterfall chart. Starting at the top will tell you which features had the greatest influence in the model's prediction. Starting at the bottom and reading toward the top will demonstrate how each feature contribution moved from the baseline toward or away from the predicted value.

 Be careful not to infer causality from how Shapley values are displayed, and to caution your stakeholders to avoid making the same mistake. This is much easier to do than it may seem at first, and we even found ourselves making these associations while writing this book.

Most solutions for displaying Shapley values will use bars to indicate the magnitude of the feature's influence, and stack those bars together to make the chart easier to understand. However, in making these visualizations easier to understand, it is also easy to fall prey to constructing a narrative of "Because of Feature A, Feature B's attribution is…" or "Feature A first contributed to the predicted score, then Feature B built on that…" However, Shapley values simply indicate relative influence by a feature, not a causal relation between features. See Chapter 7 for further discussion on displaying and understanding XAI.

A force plot, like the one in Figure 3-2, is similar to a waterfall plot but puts all the feature attributions displayed on a single axis. It's just a different visual representation of the same information but can be used in conjunction with a waterfall plot to illustrate how features push a prediction value toward (or away) from the baseline prediction. The code snippet that follows shows how to produce such a plot:

```
shap.initjs()
shap.plots.force(shap_values[0])
```

Figure 3-2. The SHAP force plot for an individual prediction showing positive contributions on the left, and negative contributions on the right.

The x-axis of these charts are the range of the values for the feature (with a histogram showing the distribution of values in light gray above the x-axis), while the left y-axis is the feature's Shapley value for each individual prediction of the dataset. SHAP also includes a second measure in these visualizations, which is based on what it determines is the feature with the most cross-interaction with the primary feature you visualized. The values of this secondary feature are shown using a heatmap, coloring each point in the chart according to the value for the secondary feature.

Red and blue colors are used indiscriminately in SHAP's visualizations, and do not necessarily represent a feature's influence on a prediction. SHAP visualizations for individual predictions use red and blue to indicate a positive or negative Shapley value, but other visualizations in SHAP will use red and blue for other purposes, like to distinguish between two feature values. For example, in Figure 3-4, the red and blue colors are used to represent the value of the AveOccup feature across the entire dataset, while in Figure 3-1, the colors represent whether the SHAP value for a particular feature was positive or negative.

Visualizing Global Feature Attributions

There are other ways that SHAP can visualize Shapley values. In our opinion, one of the most useful for explanation analysis is the scatter plots. With the scatter plot, SHAP can also be used to generate visualizations that look at the impact of a feature's contribution as the value of that feature changes in the dataset.

To generate a scatter plot, we provide SHAP with the column of data we'd like to visualize. In the code snippet here, we'll look at the Shapley values for the median income:

```
shap.plots.scatter(shap_values[:,"MedInc"])
```

Figure 3-3 shows the Shapley values for the feature `MedInc` in the plot on the left. We see an upward trend for the feature influence as the value of `MedInc` increases. This suggests that census blocks with higher median income are more likely to positively contribute to the prediction of the median house value away from the baseline, while smaller `MedInc` values influence the model more back toward the baseline prediction score. Compare this with the plot on the right in the figure. The Shapley values for `HouseAge` don't show such a recognizable trend. At the bottom of the plot is a histogram in light gray showing the distribution of data values.

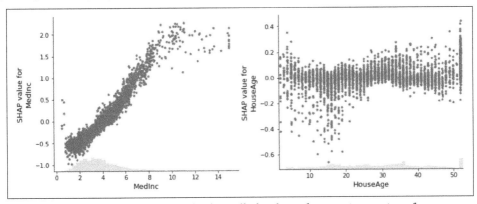

Figure 3-3. The SHAP scatter plot displays all Shapley values against a given feature value. On the left is the feature `MedInc` (the median income of families in the census block) while on the right is the scatter plot for `HouseAge` (the median age of houses in the census block).

Looking at the scatter plot for `HouseAge` in Figure 3-3, notice that there is quite a large vertical dispersion of points for any given value of the median house age. This indicates that there must be a strong nonlinear effect between `HouseAge` and the other model features. Otherwise, we'd see a trend more similar to that for `MedInc`.

By passing the entire `Explanation` object to the scatter plot, we can show which feature is most driving that interaction effect. This is demonstrated in the following code snippet, and the resulting graphic is shown in Figure 3-4. SHAP picks out the feature that has the strongest interaction with `HouseAge`, in this case, for this model, it is `AveOccup` (the average number of households in the census block), and plots the two features together. The points represent `HouseAge` and the color of the points indicate Shapley values for `AveOccup`. If there is an interaction between the two features, it should show up visually and may indicate that there is collinearity between these features in our dataset that influence the model:

```
shap.plots.scatter(shap_values[:,"HouseAge"], color=shap_values)
```

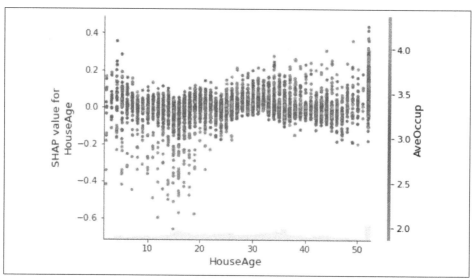

Figure 3-4. SHAP scatter plot for all Shapley values of HouseAge and AveOccup in the California Housing dataset. (Print readers can see the color image at https://oreil.ly/ xai-fig-3-4.)

The scatter plot shown in Figure 3-5 is for the block population feature, denoted by Population in the dataset. For the most part, the Shapley values for this feature hover between 0.2 and negative 0.2.

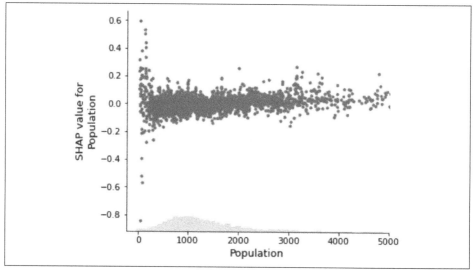

Figure 3-5. SHAP scatter plot for all Shapley values of the Population feature in the California Housing dataset.

However, there are two interesting aspects of the model that are revealed on closer examination:

- `Population` values less than approximately 250 can have a much larger influence on the model's prediction.
- There is a large spread in the Shapley values for a `Population` value near zero.

For the first observation, we could hypothesize that the model has learned an edge case where a very low population within a census block is very informative to the prediction.

Interpreting SHAP Scatter Plots

Recall that Shapley values are additive, so we need to view them in the context of Shapley values for other features to understand their relative contribution to the overall prediction. For example, in the scatter plot in Figure 3-5, it could simply be that the overall predicted value is much larger, or even so large that the relative influence of `Population` at the lower values is even less!

Our second observation reveals an area where the `Population` feature is likely not reliably contributing to the model, or it could be that the overall predicted score varies quite a bit due to other features. A useful technique is to normalize the Shapley values for all features in a prediction to the range of –1 to 1 (relative to the prediction score), which allows one to reliably understand an individual feature's influence without having to constantly reference other features. An important caveat for normalization is that your Shapley values may not cleanly add up to the overall predicted score due to the use of sampled Shapley values, so be sure any code written to handle these normalized values does not assume a strict range or summation to zero. As of writing this chapter, SHAP does not support the ability to normalize Shapley values across predictions.

SHAP can also display global feature attributions. When given all predictions to the `force()` plot function (i.e., `shap.plots.force(shap_values)`), SHAP will render an interactive chart (shown in Figure 3-6) of all attributes across all predictions. This can appear quite intimidating at first.

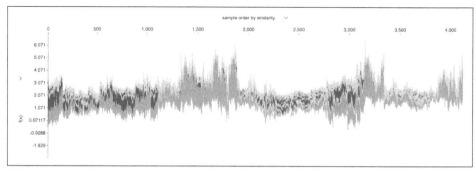

Figure 3-6. An interactive plot of Shapley values across all features and predictions for the test dataset. (Print readers can see the color image at https://oreil.ly/xai-fig-3-6.)

However, the real power in this visualization is to explore the global feature attribution values for an individual feature (as in Figure 3-7), or how two features compare (as shown in Figure 3-8). For Figure 3-7, we chose `MedInc` as the sample selector on the top and specify `MedInc` effects for the y-axis. This shows how various values of the median income push the model predictions toward (or away) from the baseline.

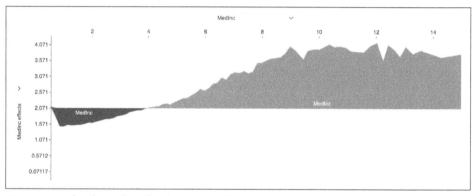

Figure 3-7. Shapley values for the `MedInc` feature across the entire test dataset show how the feature influences the model's prediction as the value of the feature changes.

In Figure 3-8, we swap the output `MedInc` on the left with `Population` to see how the two features compare.

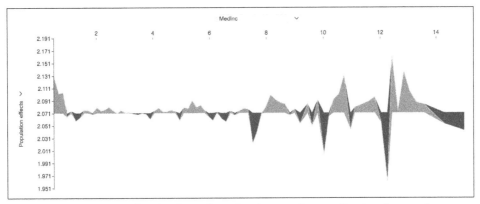

Figure 3-8. Comparing the Shapley value of `MedInc` to the `Population` feature shows that the influence on the model by the median income does not change in a meaningful way as the population changes.

For visualizing the global attributions of features, it may be more palatable to use SHAP's beeswarm plot (shown in Figure 3-9). These features are split into individual rows, with each row plotting all of the individual Shapley values along the x-axis, for all values of that feature. Each value of a feature is rendered as a point, so larger clusters of points (the beeswarm) show where many feature values had a similar Shapley value. SHAP also colors each point with a normalized heat mapping from the feature's lowest to highest values:

```
shap.plots.beeswarm(shap_values)
```

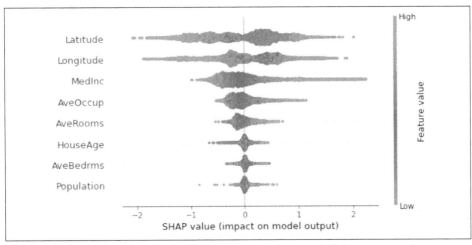

Figure 3-9. Beeswarm plot of Shapley values for all values of all features in a dataset. Note that the x-axis is the Shapley value while the heatmap color of points is related to the values in the dataset. (Print readers can see the color image at https://oreil.ly/ xai-fig-3-9.)

Finally, SHAP can also display the average Shapley value for each feature with a bar plot, as shown in Figure 3-10, using the command `shap.plots.bar(shap_values)`. This is often referred to as global feature attributions because it gives insight into the most influential features in the model, regardless of the specific input values.

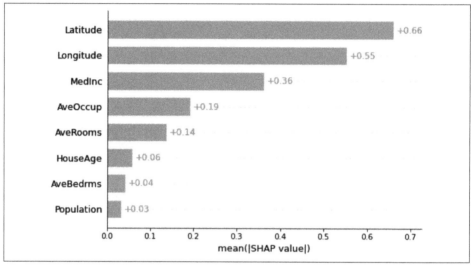

Figure 3-10. Bar plot of the average Shapley value for all features of the model.

Interpreting Feature Attributions from Shapley Values

Once you have Shapley values, what do they actually mean? Attributing the influence of features in the model with Shapley value gives three pieces of information:

- The numerical contribution to the prediction's score
- Whether the feature contributed in the model moving from the baseline prediction score toward the predicted score, or away from it
- The relative magnitude of the feature's contribution compared to other features in the dataset

What is meant by "toward" or "away"? Feature attribution values may be positive or negative, but that does not necessarily mean a positive attribution contributed to the model's prediction in a positive way. It may be that this feature was actually influencing the model toward a different prediction value but had less impact than other features. For a model with a prediction score that was –100 with a baseline prediction score of 0, then negative feature attributions would be contributing "toward" the final predicted score, and positive attributions away from it. Likewise, for a baseline prediction score that is greater than the predicted value, a negative attribution value would be contributing toward the final predicted value.

Managed Shapley Values

Many of the largest ML platforms offer a service for generating Shapley values to understand feature influence, and there are a number of open source libraries as well. Broadly, managed Shapley offerings fall into two groups: those that offer a hosted version of SHAP, and those that have built their own Shapley value library. Given our focus on the SHAP library so far, you may ask what the advantage is of going with a different implementation. While SHAP has become broadly popular, it is only one way of calculating Shapley values, and may not be the most accurate. For the purposes of demonstrating how to work with a managed Explainable AI service, we'll focus on using Google Cloud's Vertex AI Python SDK since that is what we are most familiar with.

Google Cloud Platform (GCP)—Explainable AI

Google Cloud's Explainable AI product supports calculating feature attributions based on Shapley values. While the implementation is proprietary, Google claims it provides faster sampled Shapley value calculations than other implementations and is more robust than many other tabular feature attribution techniques. The framework is model-agnostic and has native support for TensorFlow, PyTorch, XGBoost, and scikit-learn, and the ability to explain any model through the use of Vertex Custom Containers.

There are several ways to use Google Cloud's Explainable AI, as shown in Table 3-5.

Table 3-5. How to access GCP's Explainable AI

Access	Useful for
CLI (gCloud SDK)	Easy testing from the command line
REST API	Incorporating into an existing workflow
Vertex AI Python SDK	Generating cloud-based explanations from a notebook
Vertex AI Notebooks and Workbench	Computing explanations locally within the notebook's VM

If you already (or plan to) use other products in GCP's Vertex AI platform, an added advantage is that their Explainable AI product is built into several other products, such as AutoML, online and batch predictions, and Model Monitoring. Since all of these products rely on the same Explainable AI technology, this gives the flexibility of having portability in your explanations. For example, an AutoML model's global feature attribution values will be valid for understanding any feature attribution values calculated as part of an online prediction request when your model is served in production.

The Explainable AI framework is designed to offer flexibility with your model and your explanation technique. For most DNN models, it is easiest to use the Vertex AI SDK, which will try to infer the input and outputs of your model and generate a metadata configuration for you that we can augment to specify the technique we want (in this case, sampled Shapley) and the number of sample paths to compute. For the purposes of this example, we'll assume you already have a trained TensorFlow 2 model uploaded to Vertex AI (although Explainable AI works with TensorFlow and other frameworks):

```
from google.cloud import aiplatform
from google.cloud.aiplatform.explain.metadata.tf.v2 import
    saved_model_metadata_builder

explainable_ai_builder = saved_model_metadata_builder.SavedModelMetadataBuilder
    (path_to_my_model)
explainable_ai_metadata = explainable_ai_builder.get_metadata()

explanations_parameters = aiplatform.explain.ExplanationParameters({
    "sampled_shapley_attribution": {"path_count": 20}})

endpoint = model.deploy(machine_type="n1-standard-2",
            explanation_metadata=explainable_ai_metadata,
            explanation_parameters=explanations_parameters)
```

When a model is deployed to a prediction endpoint, we also (optionally) pass along the information needed to both tell Explainable AI how to understand our model's inputs and outputs (the metadata) and the parameters regarding what type of explainability we want.

To get an explanation, we then make a normal prediction call as shown in the following code. If we wanted to, we could also override some of our Explainable AI configuration for a particular prediction to change the number of paths, use a different baseline, or return the top K features by Shapley value:

```
instances = [{'dense_31_input': test_data.iloc[0].values.tolist()}]
explanation_spec_override = {"parameters":{"sampled_shapley_attribution":
        {"path_count": 5}}
endpoint.explain({"instances": instances, "explanation_spec_override":
        explanation_spec_override})
```

As part of the prediction response, Vertex will also return a payload with the feature attribution values (Shapley values in this case) and an approximation error, which represents how accurate the values were. We can then visualize these feature attributions with the included visualization widget using the following code snippet:

```
m = explainable_ai_sdk.load_model_from_vertex(my_project, 'us-central1',
        model_endpoint_id)
explanations = m.explain(instances)
explanations[0].visualize_attributions()
```

See "Sampled Shapley technique" on page 33 for a discussion of the trade-off between the number of sampled Shapley paths and the attribution error.

Microsoft Azure and AWS SageMaker

Of course, there are other cloud providers that provide model explainability, most notably Microsoft Azure and AWS SageMaker, both of which also use a version of SHAP. SageMaker's Clarity tool uses SHAP's KernelSHAP to generate feature attributions (as shown in this guide (*https://oreil.ly/45aWp*)), allowing the number of sampled paths, how to aggregate Shapley values, and baselines to be configured. Baselines can either be manually provided as a list or automatically sampled and calculated from a provided dataset.

Azure offers an Explainability service (*https://oreil.ly/T0m2X*) with support for `TreeExplainer`, `DeepExplainer`, `LinearExplainer`, and `KernelExplainer`. The service also has a `TabularExplainer` that is intended to be a high-performance improvement on SHAP, choosing the correct type of Explainer based on the model. `TabularExplainer` can also generate synthetic explanations based on extracting summary statistics from the training dataset. Likewise, `TabularExplainer` can sample explanations from the validation dataset. The explanation results can be visualized in Azure's ML Studio.

Explaining Tree-Based Models

Here's what you need to know about explanations for tree-based models:

- Decision trees are intrinsically explainable since each prediction can be described as a series of decision points for the model features, ultimately leading to the final prediction.
- For ensemble tree methods, like random forest, the explanation of the prediction is simply the average of the bias terms plus the average of the contributions of each feature within each tree in the forest.

Tree-based models can be anything from simple decision trees to gradient-boosted trees and random forests. Here are some general pros and cons to consider when thinking about explainability for these types of models.

Pros	Cons
• Explainability for decision trees is intuitive and easy to communicate to nontechnical audiences. • `treeinterpreter` is an easy-to-implement library that can be used to determine feature contributions for many of scikit-learn's tree-based models.	• Although inherently explainable, simple decision trees often do not perform as well as more complicated tree models, like random forest or gradient-boosted trees. • At this time, the `treeinterpeter` library does not support multilabel classification.

Decision trees are a popular tool for regression and classification problems and provide the epitome of interpretability, provided they don't go too deep. A decision tree consists of a series of nodes, each providing a split, or decision point, for various features that ultimately leads to the model output. The features and decision boundary points are determined by the training data in a way to minimize the mixing of class labels in the final leaves of the tree. This mixing is typically measured using entropy in the form of information gain, the Gini index, or the weighted mean square error in the case of a regression task.

 The Gini index is a number between 0 and 1, which represents the purity of the classification split. It's computed by subtracting the sum of the square probabilities of each class from one. A Gini index of 0 represents absolute purity of the classification; that is, each class is perfectly separated. A Gini index of 1 indicates a random distribution among the classes; that is, the classes are evenly split across subsets. Ideally, you want to split the examples in your dataset according to a feature that yields a low Gini index. Thus, when training a decision tree, the features and cutoff values to use at each split are chosen so that the Gini index of each split is minimized.

The process starts at the root node of the tree and each subsequent nonleaf node splits the data so that when you reach the leaf node, you have a predicted outcome. In this way, it's possible to follow the precise decision splits through the tree and explain how the features ultimately contributed to a certain prediction. Furthermore, because of this structure, decision trees easily allow for counterfactual analysis in that a user is able to ask (and answer!) what-if questions regarding how the model makes its decisions.

Looking again at the California Housing dataset and training a simple decision tree with a maximum depth of three nodes, we can visualize the final model, as shown in Figure 3-11. The full code can be found in the GitHub repository for this book. Notice that a feature might be used for more than one split, as in the two nodes that use the `MedInc` feature, or a feature might not be used at all, like the `Population`, `HouseAge`, or `AveBedrms` features:

```
dt_reg = DecisionTreeRegressor(max_depth=3)
dt_reg.fit(X_train, y_train)

dot_data = export_graphviz(dt_reg, out_file="ca_housing.dot",
                           feature_names=cal_features,
                           filled=True, rounded=True,
                           special_characters=True,
                           leaves_parallel=False)
graph = pydotplus.graphviz.graph_from_dot_file("CA_housing.dot")
Image(graph.create_png())
```

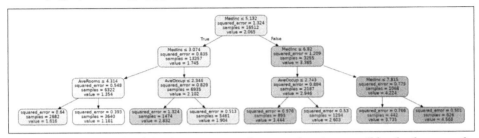

Figure 3-11. Each node of the decision tree indicates a decision cutoff for the features of the given instance.

With a maximum depth of only three nodes, the final model isn't difficult to visualize. From Figure 3-11, we see that the root node for this decision tree has MedInc ≤ 5.132 and each subsequent node is determined by a similar feature cutoff. If the condition of a node is met, the decision path moves to the left; otherwise, the decision path goes to the right. Figure 3-12 traces the decision path for a given instance in the test set. For this particular instance, following through each step of the decision tree, since MedInc ≤ 5.132, MedInc ≥ 3.074, and AveOccup ≥ 2.344, the predicted median house value is $190,400.

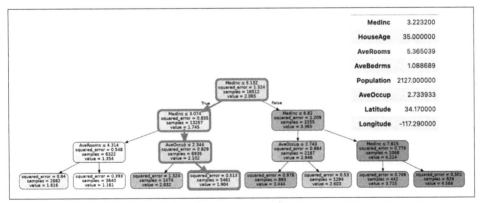

Figure 3-12. The decision path for a given instance can be traced through the decision tree according to the feature values for the instance and the learned decision cutoff of the tree.

The value of the root node is the mean of the labels taken from the training data. This is the initial bias of the model. To explain the prediction for this or any given instance, we start at the root node and add or subtract the feature contributions for each node in the decision path. Looking again at Figure 3-12 and the example instance there, we see that the prediction is given by 1.904 = 2.065 (the bias) – 0.32 (because MedInc ≤ 5.132) + 0.357 (because MedInc ≥ 3.074) – 0.198 (because AveOccup ≥ 2.344).

Each decision split is determined by a feature, sometimes a feature may be used more than once (as MedInc is), and each split either adds or subtracts from the current value until the final prediction outcome is returned. This gives the contributions of each decision split as in the example in Figure 3-12. By adding the contributions for each feature, we can see exactly how much each feature contributed to the prediction.

From Decision Trees to Tree Ensembles

Of course, the story becomes a bit more complicated once we move from simple decision trees to ensemble techniques like random forest and gradient-boosted trees. Ensemble methods are meta-algorithms that combine several machine learning models as a technique to decrease the bias and/or variance to improve model performance. By building several models, with different inductive biases, and aggregating their outputs, we hope to get a model with better performance.

Random forests use a bagging ensemble technique where many decision trees are trained in parallel and then their predictions are aggregated to create the final model prediction. Gradient-boosted trees and adaptive boosting algorithms build individual decision trees sequentially. The idea behind gradient boosting is to iteratively build an ensemble of models where each successive model focuses on learning the examples the previous model got wrong, ultimately taking a weighted average of those predictions to produce the final model.

Tree-Based Models and Extrapolation

Tree-based models like random forest and boosted trees are widely popular among ML practitioners and have become the go-to model, particularly for structured data. They can be used in regression, classification, or ranking problems, and they're easy to implement with packages available in scikit-learn and TensorFlow. However, as with any technique, this family of models does have its drawbacks that you should be aware of. Namely, they don't do well when predicting values that lie outside the range of the training data.

This is an artifact of how these models split up the input space of a given problem. Whether it's a random forest of decision trees, or an ensemble of decision trees with gradient-boosting framework, these models are trained to find partitions in the

---

feature sets of inputs sometimes many levels deep to bucket each instance into its corresponding label value. More formally, a decision tree with L leaves divides the features space into L regions and determines a set of rules from the training data so that it can output a value to leaves based on averages. These models are inherently noncontinuous functions and thus they can struggle to extrapolate to unseen or uncommon labels.

For example, since the California Housing dataset only has examples with the median values of homes between \$15,000 and \$500,000, our model will likely not do well when presented for predicting an instance that has the label \$1,000,000. Naturally, this is less of a problem for classification tasks as the label is either 0 or 1, but for regression tasks it is something to keep in mind.

Ensemble tree models are a favorite among machine learning practitioners and data scientists in industry because they are easy to train and yield very powerful models. In fact, for structured data, boosted tree algorithms are often considered the go-to model and you'll often see it show up on the leaderboard for many Kaggle competitions. However, due to their ensembled nature, these models often trade explainability for performance. In fact, even a single tree of depth 10 can already have thousands of nodes, meaning that using it as an explanatory model is almost impossible.

The main idea behind explainability of decision trees is that any prediction outcome can be traced from the root node, through the various node decision points, and ultimately to the leaf that determines the prediction. To explain why a certain prediction was made, you can trace through the decision path starting at the root node, either adding or subtracting the contribution at each node depending on the feature value and the learned decision cutoff. For random forests, since the prediction is the average of the predictions of all the trees in the forest, the explanation of the prediction is simply the average of the bias terms plus the average of the contributions of each feature within each tree.

The `treeinterpeter` package (*https://oreil.ly/sxXlm*) has a nice Python implementation and can be used on scikit-learn's `DecisionTreeRegressor`, `DecisionTree Classifier`, `RandomForestRegressor`, `RandomForestClassifier`, `ExtraTreeRegres sor`, `ExtraTreeClassifier`, `ExtraTreesRegressor`, and `ExtraTreesClassifier`.

For a given element of the test set, calling *predict* with the tree interpreter returns the trained models:

```
from treeinterpreter import treeinterpreter as ti
prediction, bias, contributions = ti.predict(rf_reg,
                                     X_test.iloc[[0]].values)
```

Recall, the `bias` is the average of the bias for each of the trees in the model. The `contributions` is a vector of size equal to the number of features in the dataset; in this case, 2.07. We can parse these values to get the following:

```
Bias term (training set mean): [2.06854048]
Feature contributions:
MedInc -0.96
Population 0.61
AveBedrms 0.12
AveRooms -0.11
AveOccup -0.06
Longitude -0.05
Latitude 0.02
HouseAge -0.02
```

This is a post hoc, local interpretation of the trained random forest for the given instance.

 So far we have discussed how to use the `treeinterpeter` library for regression and single label classification tasks. But what about multilabel classification tasks? Unlike normal classification tasks where the label consists of mutually exclusive labels over a collection of two or more potential classes, multilabel classification tasks have a label that consists of more than one nonmutually exclusive class label. For example, an image may contain both a dog and a cat in it, or a toxic comment might be both insulting and threatening, or a movie might be both action and adventure, or a patient might be at risk for heart disease as well as stroke. At the time of writing, the `treeinterpeter` library does not support multilabel classification.

SHAP's TreeExplainer

TreeSHAP is an algorithm that can also be used to compute Shapley values for tree-based models. The `TreeExplainer` library is built on the same principles for computing Shapley values as described in the previous section and optimized for tree-based models like XGBoost, LightGBM, CatBoost, PySpark, and most other tree-based scikit-learn models.

To use the `TreeExplainer`, we'll first train a simple XGBoost model using the same California Housing dataset as before. The full code for this example can be found in the treeinterpreter notebook in the GitHub repository (*https://oreil.ly/sdr6a*) accompanying this book:

```
import xgboost as xgb
xgb_reg = xgb.XGBClassifier(max_depth=3,
                            n_estimators=300,
                            learning_rate=0.05)
xgb_reg.fit(X_train, y_train)
```

Just as before, we'll create an `Explainer` class, passing it to our trained XGBoost model, only this time instead of using `Explainer`, we'll call `TreeExplainer`:

```
explainer = shap.TreeExplainer(xgb_reg)
```

Using this `explainer` object, we can then get explanations for an individual prediction, just as we did before. The following code block indicates how to create a "force" plot using the SHAP library; the resulting plot is shown in Figure 3-13:

```
shap_values = explainer.shap_values(X_train)
shap.force_plot(explainer.expected_value[1],
                shap_values[1][0,:],
                X_train.iloc[0,:])
```

Figure 3-13. SHAP's `TreeExplainer` is optimized for tree-based models. This graph shows the result of an explanation from an individual prediction from an XGBoost model.

Partial Dependence Plots and Related Plots

Partial dependence plots (PDPs), individual conditional expectation (ICE) plots, and accumulated local effects (ALE) plots are a closely related family of explainability tools that allow for visualizing the causal interaction between features and model predictions. These methods are related in that ICE and ALE plots are variations of PDPs and meant to address some of the shortcomings that PDPs may exhibit. We'll outline how each of these techniques works and highlight some of the pitfalls you should be aware of when using these techniques, particularly how ICE and ALE aim to be improvements over PDPs.

As you'll see in the sections to follow, this family of techniques is applied to a model after it has been fully trained and used to visualize the interaction between one or two features of the entire training dataset of the model and the output label. Using the taxonomy outlined in Chapter 2, these techniques are considered post hoc, model-agnostic explainability methods. As we'll see, partial dependence plots are global, whereas individual conditional expectations and accumulated local effects plots are local. In fact, since these methods aim to provide some insight into the causal relationship between feature and the predicted label, they are often thought of as interpretability methods. We'll start by discussing partial dependence plots since they are a bit more easily understood and a simpler entry point to these methods.

Partial Dependence Plots (PDPs)

Here's what you need to know about partial dependence plots:

- PDPs are a useful technique to visualize the marginal effect a specific feature has on a model's predictions.

Pros	Cons
• PDPs are easy to implement and have simple-to-understand interpretation. • When a feature is not correlated to other features, it is possible to infer a causal relationship between that feature and the model predictions.	• There is an underlying assumption of independence of features. • PDPs naively substitute feature values to measure feature dependence. When two features are correlated, the fake data points that are created are not a good representative of the true data distribution. • Sparsity of feature values in the distribution for a given feature (i.e., areas where a feature value lacks good representation) cause the partial dependence plot to be less reliable. • A PDP is really only useful for visualizing at most two features at a time.

PDPs are a useful tool to show how individual input features of a model contribute to the model's predicted outcome variable. This is done by measuring the marginal effect that a specific feature has on the label and plotting the result. By examining the resulting plot, one can easily visualize the causal relationship between the input feature and the label.

When we say we measure the marginal effect, this just means that we measure how the expected value of the model output changes with respect to the feature value. That is, given a trained model f, for any feature, we compute the corresponding partial dependence function as a function over the input feature values by taking the expected value, or average value, over the entire dataset. For example, suppose there are k features in a dataset consisting of n examples. Then we can write each example x_i as $\left(x_i^1, x_i^2, \cdots, x_i^k\right)$. For a regression model, the partial dependence function of the first feature x^1 is given by:

$$f_{pdp}^1(x) = \frac{1}{n} \sum_{i=1}^{n} f\left(x, x_i^2, \cdots, x_i^k\right)$$

where the values of x_i^2 through x_i^k are all the remaining feature values taken from all the n examples in the dataset. Similarly, the partial dependence function for the second feature x^2 is:

$$f_{pdp}^2(x) = \frac{1}{n} \sum_{i=1}^{n} f\left(x_i^1, x, x_i^3 \cdots, x_i^k\right)$$

and for the third feature x^3 is:

$$f^3_{pdp}(x) = \frac{1}{n} \sum_{i=1}^{n} f\left(x_i^1, x_i^2, x, x_i^4, \cdots, x_i^k\right)$$

and so on.

In this way, for any feature we can create and plot the function f^v_{pdp} for any feature v. This plot describes precisely how the predicted output variable changes on average with respect to the given feature. If there is a monotonic relationship between the feature and model predictions, it is immediately apparent.

Of course, in practice you'll use a library to implement this technique, and scikit-learn has a nice implementation called `PartialDependenceDisplay` in the class of inspection tools. As an example, let's look again at the California Housing dataset (*https://oreil.ly/zMb25*). This is a regression problem where the task is to develop a model that predicts the median house price `MedianHouseVal` using as input eight features of the census block. We'll build a model in scikit-learn using a neural network; see the following code block (the full code for this example is available in the notebook for partial dependence plots (*https://oreil.ly/9lnFi*) in the GitHub repository for this book):

```
mlp_reg = MLPRegressor(hidden_layer_sizes=[30, 20, 10],
                       max_iter=500)

# Create pipeline
transformer = ColumnTransformer([
    ('numerical', MinMaxScaler(feature_range=(-1,1)), cal_features),
])

mlp_pipeline = Pipeline(steps=[
    ('transform', transformer),
    ('model', mlp_reg)
])
```

Once the model is trained, to create the partial dependence plots, we'll use the `from_estimator` method of `PartialDependenceDisplay` specifying the model pipeline, the dataset, and which feature we want to visualize:

```
PartialDependenceDisplay.from_estimator(
    mlp_pipeline, X_train, features=['MedInc']
)
```

For the feature MedInc, the median income for the families within the census block, the partial dependence plot tells a very clear story. As shown in Figure 3-14, there appears to be a positive correlation between MedInc and the target value, the median house value: as median income increases, the median home value increases as well. Also note the similar trend we see represented for MedInc in Figure 3-3 as well. This makes sense with what we'd expect our model to learn.

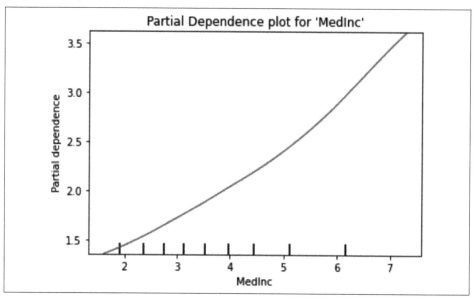

Figure 3-14. The partial dependence plot for the feature MedInc shows that as the median family income increases, so does the median home value. The tick marks on the x-axis represent the deciles of the MedInc features values.

In fact, for most features in this dataset, the relationship appears fairly straightforward. However, the feature representing the median house age HouseAge is more interesting. Figure 3-15 shows the partial dependence plot for the HouseAge feature. For houses less than 40 years old, the relationship is nearly constant, with a slight downward trend. However, for very old homes the median house value starts to increase dramatically. Furthermore, these examples only account for about 10% of the training data.

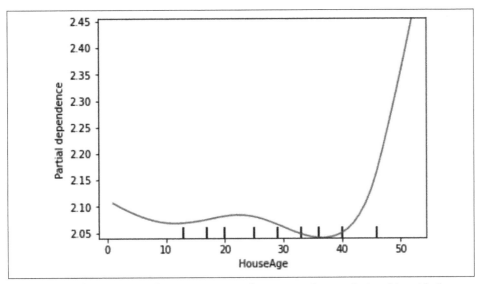

Figure 3-15. The HouseAge feature appears to have a quadratic relationship with the model predictions.

Working with classification models

For classification models, the partial dependence function is defined in exactly the same way. In the case of binary classification, the model predicts a probability that a given example belongs to the positive class. So, the partial dependence function returns the marginal effect a feature has on the predicted probabilities.

What about multiclass classification? So far, we've described how to apply partial dependence plots for regression tasks and binary classification tasks; but what if our model is multiclass? In this case, you can plot the partial dependence for a feature against each of the possible output labels. Take, for example, the Wine Quality dataset (*https://oreil.ly/mQMND*) from the UCI ML Repository. This dataset can be viewed as a classification task to predict the quality of the wine on a scale from 0 to 10 using physicochemical properties like acidity, citric acid, chlorides, and pH as features.

When building a multiclass model like this, we'll use the OnevsRestClassifier in scikit-learn as shown in the following code block (the full code for this example is contained in this book's GitHub repository (*https://oreil.ly/9lnFi*)):

```
from sklearn.multiclass import OneVsRestClassifier
multi_clf = OneVsRestClassifier(
    MLPClassifier(
        hidden_layer_sizes=[256, 128, 64, 32],
        max_iter=500)
    ).fit(X, y)
```

To visualize the partial dependence plots, we must create a plot for each target class. In this dataset, the target values are 3, 4, 5, 6, 7, and 8; the corresponding partial dependence plots are shown in Figure 3-16.

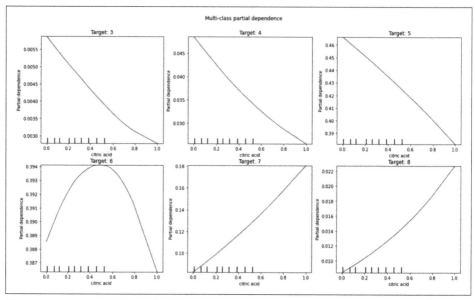

Figure 3-16. For multiclass classification, create a partial dependence plot for each target class.

We have to take extra care in interpreting the causal relationship between different target labels. For the wine quality dataset, we see that the "citric acid" feature is negatively correlated with the labels 3, 4, and 5, positively correlated with target labels 7 and 8 and somewhere in between for target label 6.

But what does this mean? One interpretation is that there is some tipping point for citric acid amounts when assessing the quality of red wines. However, as with all explainability techniques, this information should be viewed in relation to the other features. More likely, the concentration of citric acid interacts with other physicochemical properties of the wine that together influence the target quality label.

Assumption of independence

Partial dependence plots are a simple and intuitive way to explain how model features influence model predictions. When a feature is not correlated to other features, the partial dependence plot provides a direct causal connection by showing how model values change on average as the feature value changes. However, as with all explainability methods, the visualizations provided by partial dependence must be taken in context, especially because it's highly likely that some input features are at least somewhat correlated.

Look at the partial dependence plots for AveRooms and AveBedrms from the California Housing dataset (*https://oreil.ly/sxq3w*) side by side in Figure 3-17. In this dataset, AveRooms represents the average number of rooms per census block and AveBedrms indicates the average number of bedrooms per census block. Not surprisingly, their partial dependence plots are nearly identical.

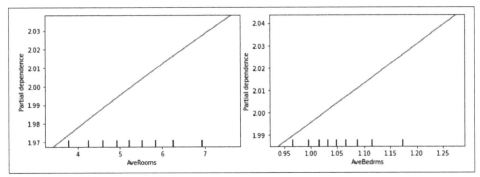

Figure 3-17. The partial dependence plots for AveRooms and AveBedrms are both positively correlated with expected median house value. However, these features are highly correlated.

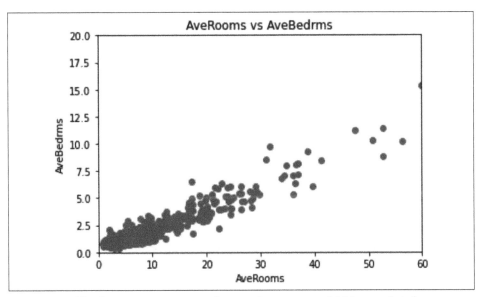

Figure 3-18. The features AveRooms and AveBedrms are very highly correlated.

However, these two features are positively correlated, as shown in Figure 3-18, with a Pearson correlation coefficient of 0.847. So, when it comes to explaining our model and interpreting how these features influence the model's predictions, it's unclear how much the AveRooms feature alone is affecting median house values or if AveBedrms is really a confounding variable between AveRooms and the target variable. The lack of independence distorts the causal interpretation of the partial dependence plot when attempting to explain our model predictions. One way to address this problem is to use a conditional distribution instead of the marginal distribution. We'll see how this is done in "Accumulated Local Effects (ALE)" on page 81.

Dealing with Highly Correlated Features in ML Models

In general, it is best practice to exclude highly correlated features when building classic machine learning models. For linear models, this is a must since multicolinearity (*https://oreil.ly/YstUb*) can yield solutions that vary wildly and are possibly numerically unstable. When there are multiple highly correlated features, the weight vector from the regression normal equation has high variance. This means that the model weights differ greatly depending on the training data causing numerically unstable solutions that don't generalize well. In addition, extraneous features typically only add noise to models during training and can lead to longer convergence times.

More generally, while correlated features might not harm your model, they certainly won't improve it either. So, while deep neural networks may not actually suffer too much with highly correlated features, it's still a good idea to remove extraneous features to assist in model training convergence. Ultimately, a simpler model is best when considering correlated features, both for training and especially when taking explainability into account. This is particularly true for partial dependence plots that assume features are uncorrelated.

Understanding feature distributions

Another concern for partial dependence plots is sparsity of feature values in the distributions for a given feature. In areas where a feature value lacks good representation, the partial dependence plot is less reliable. Take, for example, the MedInc feature again. As shown in Figure 3-19, the majority of feature values (about 97%) for the median income are less than $80,000 per year. However, when computing the partial dependence, we explore values in the entire range of the feature for median incomes as high as double that at $160,000.

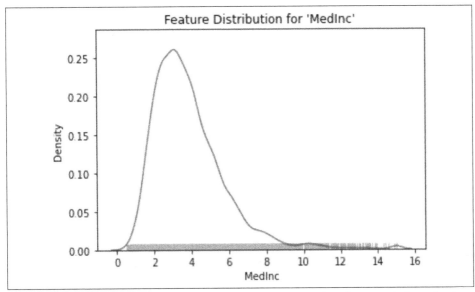

Figure 3-19. The majority of feature values, about 95%, are less than 7.5. When plotting partial dependence plots, it's helpful to plot the feature distributions as well.

These extreme values for the median income don't accurately represent the distribution of our training dataset. This can cause our model to make unreliable or unrealistic predictions that lead to unreliable or unrealistic partial dependence plots for those values. Remember, when computing the partial dependence function for a given feature value, say $m = 0.8$, the MedInc feature value is set to 0.8 for each training example and the model's average prediction is computed. In a way, it doesn't make sense to assign an outlier to apply such an outlier value to an arbitrary training example in the dataset. Our model may return an unrealistic prediction for such an unrealistic example.

One way this problem can be ameliorated is to plot the feature distribution on the same axes as the partial dependence plot, as shown in Figure 3-20. This can be done using the rugplot function in seaborn (*https://oreil.ly/3iHGB*), a well-known Python data visualization library:

```
PartialDependenceDisplay.from_estimator(
    mlp_pipeline, X_train, features=['MedInc'])
sns.rugplot(data=X_train, x='MedInc')
```

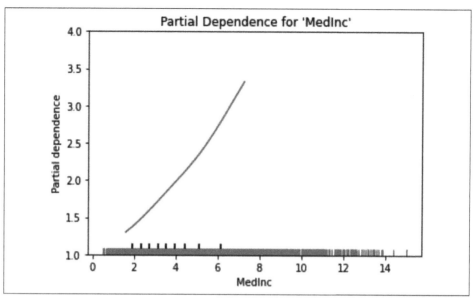

Figure 3-20. It is important to understand the feature value distribution when interpreting the partial dependence plot.

Looking at Figure 3-20, you're likely more inclined to trust the portions of the partial dependence plot where the feature distribution is denser as opposed to those areas where there are fewer feature values, e.g., above $80,000 per year.

Partial dependence plots provide a nice intuitive visualization that helps to explain how a feature is related to the model's target predictions. However, a partial dependence plot is really only useful for one feature at a time. It's not uncommon for some ML models to have tens or hundreds of input features, and each partial dependence feature plot must be examined individually. This quickly becomes intractable.

It is possible to plot two features at once, as in Figure 3-21, but visualizing three or more features in a meaningful way is not possible. To plot two features together, we simply specify a feature as an ordered pair, as in the following code block:

```
PartialDependenceDisplay.from_estimator(
    mlp_pipeline, X_train, features=[('HouseAge', 'MedInc')])
```

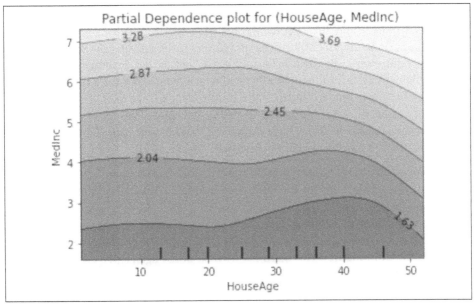

Figure 3-21. The partial dependence plot for two features in the California Housing dataset, HouseAge and MedInc. As HouseAge and MedInc increase together, the median house value also increases gradually. Decreasing MedInc and keeping HouseAge constant decreases median house value; however, the median house value is more stable with changes in HouseAge alone.

Individual Conditional Expectation Plots (ICEs)

Here's what you need to know about individual conditional expectation plots:

- ICE plots extend partial dependence plots by visualizing the dependence on a feature for each instance in the dataset.

Pros	Cons
• ICE plots address some of the shortcomings of partial dependence plots. • They illustrate the dependence of features for each example, giving a more holistic view in lieu of an aggregate. • They allow the user to see heterogeneity in a relationship between feature and model prediction, which is lost when averaging.	• ICE plots have many of the same issues as partial dependence plots, namely an assumption of feature independence. • Graphs quickly become overcrowded and noisy; it's only feasible to plot (at most) one feature at a time.

ICE plots can be thought of as an extension of partial dependence plots. While partial dependence plots graph the overall average of a specific feature value across the entire dataset, individual conditional expectations instead visualize the dependence on a feature for each individual instance. In this way, partial dependence plots are a *global* explainability technique while ICE plots are considered a *local* explainability technique. In short, for any feature, the partial dependence plot is an average of the model prediction values obtained from the ICE plot. One line in the ICE plot represents the predictions for a single instance in our dataset mapped as a function of varying feature value for the feature in question.

Partial dependence plots give aggregated information, but ICE plots allow you to visualize feature contributions on the individual example level. This can be really helpful, because aggregations can lose vital information. Take, for example, the HouseAge feature in the California Housing dataset (*https://oreil.ly/38qFE*), which represents the median age of the houses in the census block. Looking at the partial dependence plot, note the left plot in Figure 3-22: when the median house age is greater than 40 years, there is a strong positive correlation with the predicted target. This may be somewhat justifiable since older, historic homes could increase in value. However, that isn't always the case and it's important to not deduce a causal relationship that might not exist. Certainly, there are older housing blocks that do not have high median value.

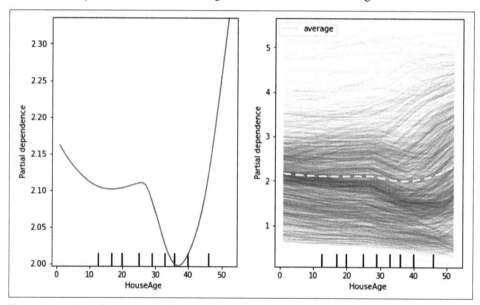

Figure 3-22. For the HouseAge feature, there are a few examples where an increase in the median age of houses after 40 years indicates a decrease in the median house value for that block. Note the range of the difference in the range of the y-axis in the two plots.

Using a partial dependence plot could hide the heterogeneous relationship between the houses' age and the median house value. However, looking at the ICE lines, we can see the overall trend and also note that there are some exceptions. We can see this in the individual conditional expectation plot on the right in Figure 3-22. Although the majority of lines do curve up (in fact, in the overwhelming majority), once HouseAge is greater than 40, there are a few examples where the median house value is decreasing.

Accumulated Local Effects (ALE)

Here's what you need to know about accumulated local effects plots:

- ALE plots improve upon partial dependence plots by taking into account the conditional dependence of correlated features and by computing the marginal effect by taking differences instead of averages.

Pros	Cons
• There are nice open source libraries that can be used to implement ALE plots. • ALE plots can still yield useful results when features are correlated.	• The implementation of ALE plots is much less intuitive than PDPs or ICE plots and they can be difficult to explain to nontechnical audiences. • Although ALE plots can handle correlated features, you should still be careful when interpreting results in this setting because strongly correlated features will vary together.

Similar to partial dependence plots, ALE plots visualize the relationship between the features of a model and the model's predictions. However, ALE plots improve upon partial dependence plots in two important ways:

- They take into account the conditional dependence of correlated features.

- They measure the marginal effect of a feature value by computing differences instead of averages.

These improvements allow ACE plots to represent a feature's influence more accurately without the confounding effects of correlated features. Take, for example, the first point. One of the biggest faults of partial dependence plots is that they handle correlated features in a very naive way. Recall that the algorithm for producing a partial dependence plot for a feature simply varies the value of that feature over a range of values in the feature space and measures the average model prediction value. When two features are correlated, this approach becomes problematic because the fake data points that are created when sampling the feature space are not a true representative of the data distribution.

Suppose you have a dataset that indicates the presence of heart disease in a patient from various patient features including sex, age, smoking history, height, and weight, among others. There is a positive correlation between a person's height and weight, so the partial dependence plot for either of these features would be very misleading. When computing the partial dependence plot for height, an entire range of height values are naively substituted into the dataset and their predictions are averaged to get a single value. However, for a sample feature value height of 5 ft., when you naively replace the height of all training examples to be 5 ft. then there could be some examples with height of 5 ft. and weight of 300 lb. Generally speaking, this would be considered an outlier for the dataset and not an accurate representation of the training dataset. As a result, the model that was trained on the training distribution, without examples like this, will have a very skewed prediction on this outlier and have a negative effect on the resulting PDP.

One way to address this issue of correlated features is to take into account the conditional distribution of one feature with respect to another so that these unlikely examples, like the patient that is 5 ft. tall and weighs 300 lb., are weighted less when computing the average of model predictions. This allows you to de-emphasize those examples that wouldn't normally occur in the dataset that would ultimately throw off the model predictions and ultimately the resulting partial dependence plot.

However, this approach still suffers from combining the effects of correlated features. Accumulated local effects plots go a step further, as described in the second point at the beginning of this section. That is, ALE plots mitigate this issue by taking the differences of model predictions in place of averages. By measuring the differences instead of the averages or conditional averages, the ACE plot is better able to gauge the effect of the given feature value on the model prediction.

So, for our height feature, to measure the local effect at a height of 5 ft., we'll compute the local effect by taking in the model's predictions for each example, first setting the height to be 4.9 ft. and then taking the height to be 5.1 ft. and computing the difference. In this way, the ALE technique separates out the effect of the height being 5 ft. without being influenced by the weight, or other correlated features. These local effects are then accumulated and plotted to produce the ALE plot for height.

To create ALE plots for our dataset and model, we'll use an open source Python library called Alibi (*https://oreil.ly/NvZm1*). This library has implementations of various local and global explainability methods and its interface is similar to that of scikit-learn, in that there are distinct initialize, fit, and explain steps. We'll look again at the California Housing dataset (*https://oreil.ly/DNVcC*).

To get some intuition about how ALE plots work, we'll start by looking at a linear regression model. By definition, linear models are intrinsically explainable, so it will be a nice toy model to verify the behavior we see in the plots. There are eight features in the dataset including the latitude, longitude, the average number of rooms, and average number of bedrooms per house in the block, as well as others. If we were to train a linear model on this dataset, it would have the form

$\widehat{y}(x) = w_0 + w_1 x_1 + \cdots + w_8 x_8$, and since the model is linear, there are no interactions between the various features. In fact, the effect of any feature would simply be the learned coefficient of that input feature value. So, if x_1 represents MedInc, the median income of a housing block in tens of thousands of US dollars, then the sign and magnitude of the coefficient w_1 indicates the positive or negative effect that the median income has on the predicted median house value for a given block.

We'll train a simple linear regression and examine that model's predictions with respect to the MedInc variable. Not surprisingly, there is a strong linear relationship: as median income increases, so does the median value of homes. For each example in the training dataset, Figure 3-23 plots the median income of each example on the x-axis and the model's prediction for that example on the y-axis. This is done using the following code block (see the ALE notebook (*https://oreil.ly/dez47*) in the GitHub repository for this book for the full code):

```
lr_reg = LinearRegression()
lr_reg.fit(X_train, y_train)

feature_names = data.feature_names
index = feature_names.index('MedInc')

fig, ax = plt.subplots()
ax.scatter(X_train[:, index], lr_reg.predict(X_train))
```

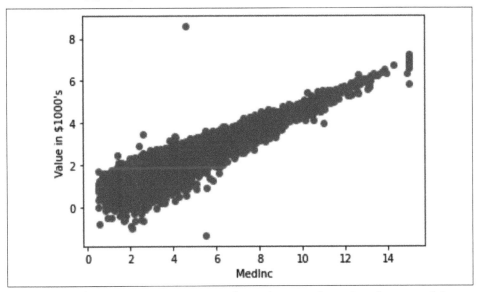

Figure 3-23. There is a strong positive correlation between the MedInc feature and the model predictions. As the median home income increases, so does the median value of homes.

We can print the learned coefficients from the linear model and find that the weight for the MedInc feature is about 0.439. This is approximately the slope of the line fit to the points in Figure 3-23. So, for each unit increase in the median income, the model's prediction for the median home value increases by a factor of 0.439. Of course, this doesn't take into account any effects with other, possibly correlated, features in the dataset. Using this simple linear regression as a model, we can see a bit more how ALE works "under the hood."

To start, we initialize the ALE object by passing it a predictor function from our trained linear regression model, a list of the feature names of the dataset, and the target variable name. We can then call the explain method, which returns an Explanation object that we can inspect and use for displaying the ALE plots. Since ALE plots are a global explainability technique, the explain method takes as an argument a batch of data on which to compute the ALE values. We'll use the entire training dataset X_train:

```
lr_ale = ALE(lr_reg.predict,
            feature_names=feature_names,
            target_names=['MedianHouseVal'])
lr_exp = lr_ale.explain(X_train)
```

Using the lr_exp Explanation object, we can visualize the effect of the MedInc feature by plotting the ALE values with plot_ale(lr_exp, features=['MedInc']), as shown in Figure 3-24. The feature deciles are also plotted on the x-axis.

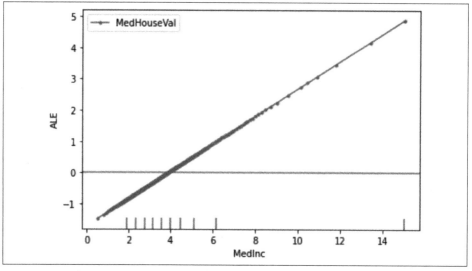

Figure 3-24. The ALE plot for MedInc shows the effect of median income on the linear regression's predicted value for median house value across the training dataset. When MedInc is less than 4, the effect is negative; i.e., lower median income causes the predicted value of down with respect to the average prediction.

The plot in Figure 3-24 is a line of slope approximately 0.43, which we would expect because our model is a linear regression and the learned weight coefficient for MedInc is 0.43. In fact, lr_exp contains a numpy array of ALE values for each feature in the dataset, so we can use plot_ale to plot any feature we request with the features argument. Calling the plot_ale function without arguments will plot the effects of every feature. Doing so, you'll see that the slopes of the ALE plots are precisely the coefficients of the linear regression model.

Remember how the algorithm for ALE works: first the feature MedInc is partitioned into a set of intervals covering the range of those feature values. For each interval, the feature value for MedInc for the data points within the interval are replaced with the upper and lower interval endpoints, and the difference in the model predictions are averaged across the examples. Since we have a linear model, all of the features (other than MedInc) nicely cancel each out in the difference and the only term remaining is the learned weight value taken across the interval.

Take, for example, the case when MedInc=12 in Figure 3-24. The y-axis represents the local effect of the median income; in this case, the ALE value is about 3.47, corresponding to an increase of about $3,500 for the predicted median house value solely due to the MedInc feature. The interpretation is that for neighborhoods where the median household income is about $120,000 per year, the model predicts an uplift of about $3,500 due to this median income feature when compared against the average model prediction.

We can explore this a bit deeper in the data by taking the examples in X_train that have MedInc values close to 12 and measuring the total expected uplift for median house value for neighborhoods in this range. In this example, the feature values are partitioned so that this corresponds to all training examples with MedInc between 11.78 and 13.39. We compute the average of the model predictions on this subset and compare against the average prediction on the entire dataset; this is the zeroth order effect of the linear model. See the notebook (*https://oreil.ly/dez47*) in the GitHub repository for the full code for this example:

```
subset = X_train[(X_train[:, index] > 11.78)
                & (X_train[:, index] < 13.39)]
lr_reg.predict(subset).mean() - lr_reg.predict(X_train).mean()
```

We get that the difference is about 3.7. This is the total expected uplift for housing blocks with median income close to $120,000.

Of course, for nonlinear models the story is a bit more complicated in that the model will learn more complicated relationships between different features and, as a result, the ALE plots are no longer linear. For example, when training a random forest model, the corresponding ALE plot for MedInc is nonlinear and nonmonotonic, as shown in Figure 3-25.

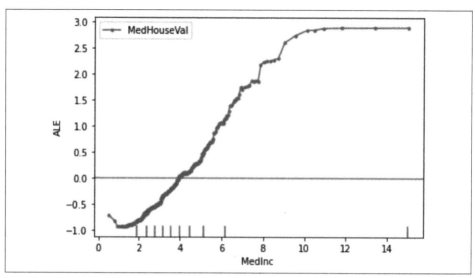

Figure 3-25. Since a random forest model is not linear, the ALE plots should not be expected to be linear either.

We can interpret the plot in Figure 3-25 in the same way as before. Namely, the ALE value at a point is the relative feature effect with respect to the mean feature effect of the random forest model. For example, in the plot, the ALE value for MedInc=8 is about 2.0. This means that for neighborhoods where the median household income is about $80,000 per year, the model predicts an uplift of about $2,000 for the median house value due to the median income feature with respect to the average model prediction.

Visualizing the ALE plots for each of the features together, as in Figure 3-26, we see that the features that have the largest influence on median house value are MedInc (the median income for households within a neighborhood, measured in hundreds of thousands of US dollars), AveOccup (average number of household members), and the Latitude and Longitude.

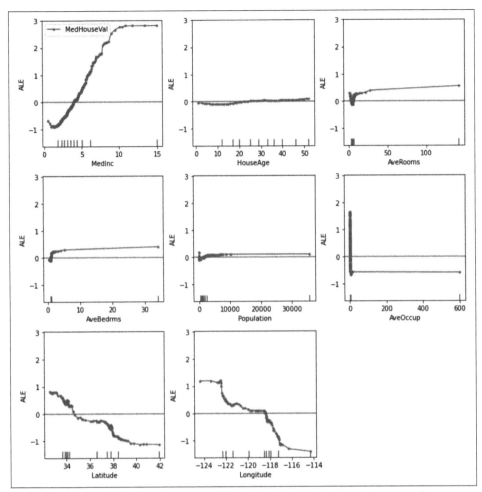

Figure 3-26. For the random forest model, the features that have the largest influence on median house value are the median income, the average number of household members, and the location.

Comparing the Effect of Features Across Different Models

We've seen how the behavior of ALE plots differs for linear versus nonlinear models. Namely, for linear models the ALE plots are linear, whereas for nonlinear models like a random forest, the ALE plots are not necessarily linear or even monotonic. But the differences don't stop there. For example, if we compare the effect of the AveRooms feature, we see that the models treat this feature quite differently.

From Figure 3-27, we can see that the random forest model puts a large emphasis on the AveRooms feature while the linear regression model doesn't. It's also interesting to note that the feature effects for the linear regression model are strongly negatively correlated while for the random forest there is a slight positive correlation. Also, not only is the feature effect for the random forest nonmonotonic, the effect becomes slightly negative for low values of AveRooms.

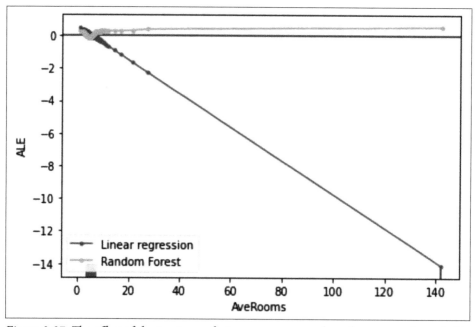

Figure 3-27. The effect of the AveRooms feature, average number of rooms per household, differs for the linear regression and the random forest model.

Summary

In this chapter, we saw a collection of explainability techniques that can be used for models trained on tabular datasets. We started with a discussion of feature importances for machine learning models and how they can be measured using permutation feature importance. As the name suggests, this is a perturbation-based explainability technique where the importance of a feature is determined by measuring the change in the model score after permuting the values of a given feature in the dataset. We then dove into Shapley values, starting first with SHapley Additive exPlanations (SHAP), an optimized way to compute Shapley values, and the importance of baselines. The main idea behind baselines is that if one can find a neutral value for a feature, that value will not influence the prediction and therefore not contribute to the Shapley value. The baseline then acts as a kind of placeholder in our model input so we can calculate the Shapley value across different coalitions.

Next, we looked at explainability methods for tree-based models, like decision trees and random forest. Although decision trees lend themselves well to interpretation and are intrinsically explainable for random forest and other more complex tree-based models, we saw how the `treeinterpreter` library could be used to shed light on explaining model predictions. Lastly, we looked at a family of closely related techniques including partial dependence plots (PDPs), individual conditional expectation (ICE) plots, and accumulated local effects (ALE) plots. Each of these techniques visualizes how certain model features contribute to the model predictions. ALE plots address many of the problems associated with PDPs and ICE plots. Namely, they are unbiased and still work well when features are correlated.

In the next chapter, we'll shift our focus to explainability techniques for image use cases. Some techniques we've covered in this chapter, like SHAP, are useful for images with slight modification, but we'll focus on a collection of other techniques designed with computer vision in mind.

## CHAPTER 4

Explainability for Image Data

Introduced in the 1980s, convolutional neural networks (CNNs), like DNNs, remained unused until the advent of modern ML, at which point they quickly became the backbone of contemporary solutions for computer vision problems. Since then, deep learning models based on CNNs have enabled unprecedented breakthroughs in many computer vision tasks ranging from image classification and semantic segmentation to image captioning and visual question answering, at times achieving near human-level performance. Nowadays, you can find sophisticated computer vision models being used to design smart cities, monitor livestock or crop development, build self-driving cars, or identify eye disease or lung cancer.

As the number of these intelligent systems relying on image models continues to grow, the role of explainability in analyzing and understanding these systems has become more important than ever. Unfortunately, when these highly complex systems fail, they can do so without any warning or explanation and sometimes with unfortunate consequences. Explainability AI (XAI) techniques are essential to build trust not only in the users of these systems but especially for the practitioners putting these models into production.

In this chapter, we'll focus on explainability methods you can use to build more reliable and transparent computer vision ML solutions. Computer vision tasks differ from other ML tasks in that the base features (i.e., pixels) are rarely influential individually. Instead, what is important is how these pixel-level features combine to create higher-level features like edges, textures, or patterns that we recognize. This requires special care when discussing and interacting with explainability methods for computer vision tasks. We'll see how many of these tools have been adapted to address those concerns. Just as CNNs were developed with images in mind, many of the explainability techniques we cover in this chapter were also developed for images or even CNNs.

Broadly speaking, most explainability methods for image models can be classified as either backpropagation methods, perturbation methods, methods that utilize the internal state, or some combination of these approaches. The techniques that we'll discuss in this chapter are representative of those groups. LIME's algorithm uses perturbed input examples to approximate an interpretable model. Like the name suggests, Integrated Gradients and XRAI depend on backpropagation, while Guided Backpropagation, Grad-CAM, and their relatives utilize the model's internal state.

Integrated Gradients (IG)

Here's what you need to know about Integrated Gradients:

- IG was one of the first successful approaches to model explainability.
- IG is a local attribution method, meaning it provides an explanation for a model's prediction for a single example image.
- It produces an easy-to-interpret saliency mask that highlights the pixels or regions in the image that contribute most to the model's prediction.

Pros	Cons
• IG was one of the first successful and most commonly used approaches to model explainability. • IG can be applied to any differentiable model for any data type: images, text, tabular, etc. • Implementation is easy and intuitive; even novice practitioners can apply it. In addition, there are easy-to-use implementations in many XAI libraries. • IG is better for low-contrast images or images taken in nonnatural environments such as X-rays.	• IG requires differentiability of the model and access to the gradients, so it does not apply well to tree-based models. • The results can be sensitive to hyperparameters or choice of baseline.

Suppose you were asked to classify the image in Figure 4-1. What would your answer be? How would you explain how you made that decision? If you answered "bird," what exactly made you think that? Was it the beak, the wings, the tail? If you answered "cockatoo," was it because of the crest and the white plumage? Maybe you said it was a "sulfur-crested cockatoo" because of the yellow in the crest.

Figure 4-1. What features tell us this is a sulfur-crested cockatoo? Is it the beak and wings? The white plumage? The yellow crest? Or all of the above?

Regardless of your answer, you made a decision based on certain features of the image, more specifically, because of the arrangement and values of certain pixels and pixel regions in the image. Perhaps the beak and wings indicate to you that this is a picture of a bird, while the crest and coloring tell you it is a cockatoo. The method of Integrated Gradients provides a means to highlight those pixels which are more or less relevant for a model's (in this case, your own brain's) prediction.

Using gradients to determine attribution of model features makes intuitive sense. Remember that the gradient of a function tells us how the function values change when the inputs are changed slightly. For just one dimension, if the derivative is positive (or negative), that shows the function is increasing (or decreasing) with respect to the input. Since the gradient is a vector of derivatives, the gradient tells us for each input feature if the model function prediction will increase or decrease when you take a tiny step in some direction of the feature space.[1] The more the model prediction depends on a feature, the higher the attribution value for that feature.

> For linear models, this relationship between gradients and attribution is even more explicit since the sign of a coefficient indicates exactly positive or negative relationships between the model output and the feature value. See also the discussion and examples in "Gradient x Input" on page 151.

---

[1] This is analogous to many loss-based functions for training DNNs that measure the gradient and performance change of the model in the loss space.

However, relying on gradient information alone can be problematic. Gradients only give local information about the model function behavior, but this linear interpretation is limiting. Once the model is confident in its prediction, small changes in the inputs won't make much difference. For example, when given an image of a cockatoo, if your model is robust and has a prediction score of 0.88, modifying a few pixels slightly (even pixels that pertain to the cockatoo itself) likely won't change the prediction score for that class. For example, once the model fully learns how the value of a specific pixel affects the model's predicted class, the gradient of the model prediction for that pixel will become smaller and smaller, and eventually go to zero. The gradient for the model's prediction with respect to that pixel has saturated.

 This notion of saturation of the gradient of the model prediction function with respect to a pixel value shouldn't be confused with the more general concept of neuron gradient saturation that may arise in training neural networks, though the two address a similar concept. In neural networks, activation functions like `sigmoid` or `tanh` map the set of real numbers into a range between 0 and 1 (or between −1 and 1 in the case of `tanh`). A neuron is said to be saturated when extremely large weights cause the neuron to produce values that are very close to the range boundary and thus have very small gradients.

In the context of measuring feature attribution via gradients of the model function, the idea of saturation with respect to a pixel is similar but now with respect to the model's prediction. Once the model has "learned" the predicted label, the gradient of the model prediction with respect to that pixel information will become very small. See, for example, Figure 4-3 where the model's prediction for the target class eventually becomes very flat.

To address this issue, the Integrated Gradients technique examines the model gradients along a path in feature space, summing up the gradient contributions along the path. At a high level, Integrated Gradients determine the salient inputs by gradually varying the network input from a baseline to the original input and aggregating the gradients along the path. We'll discuss how to choose a baseline in the next section. For now, all you need to know is that the ideal baseline should contain no pertinent information to the model's prediction, so that as we move along the path from the baseline to the image, we introduce information (i.e., features) to the model. As the model gets more information, the prediction score changes in a meaningful way. By accumulating gradients along the path, we can use the model gradient to see which input features contribute most to the model prediction. We'll start by discussing how to choose an appropriate baseline and then describe how to accumulate the gradients effectively to avoid this issue of saturated gradients.

Choosing a Baseline

To be able to objectively determine which pixels are important to our predicted label, we'll use a baseline image as comparison. As you saw in Chapter 2, baselines show up across different explainability techniques, and our baseline image serves a similar purpose to the baseline for Shapley values. Similarly for images, a good baseline is one that contains neutral or uninformative pixel feature information, and there are different baselines that you can use. When working with image models, the most commonly used baseline images are black image, white image, or noise, as shown in Figure 4-2. However, it can also be beneficial to use a baseline image that represents the status quo in the images. For example, a computer vision model for classifying forms may use a baseline of the form template, or a model for quality control in a factory may include a baseline photo of the empty assembly line.

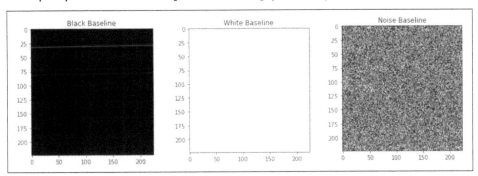

Figure 4-2. Commonly used baseline images for image models are a black image, a white image, and an image of Gaussian noise.

Other Baselines for Images

The easiest baseline and resulting feature path to understand for images is one that varies the brightness of the image. For brightness scaling, you can naively apply uniform scaling for all the values of all channels in the pixel from 0 to 100%, but this does not uniformly vary the perceived brightness in natural images.

Other common methods to create path in feature space include:

- Luminosity: using a color space for the image that has a separate channel for brightness and only changing the value of that channel
- Saturation: varying the intensity of colors in the image from desaturated (gray) to fully saturated (original colors)
- Blur: starting with a blurred version of the original image and then progressively applying less blur until arriving at the original, sharp image

While some gradient techniques are better suited for natural, real-world images, in principle any gradient-based method should work on an image that has a continuous scale for the values of its channels, even synthetic images such as LiDAR (light detection and ranging) depth maps or X-rays.

We'll start with using a simple baseline that consists of a completely black image (i.e., no pixel information) and consider the straight line path from the baseline to the input image, and then examine the model's prediction score for its predicted class, as shown in Figure 4-3. A linear interpolation between two points x, y is given by $\alpha y + (1 - \alpha)x$ where the values of α range from 0 to 1.

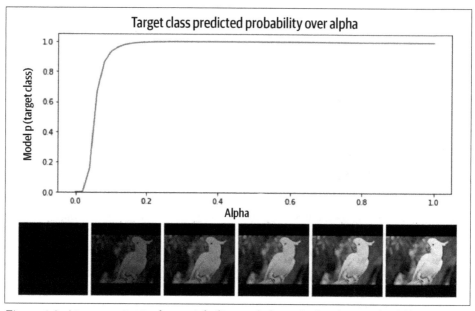

Figure 4-3. At some point in the straight line path from the baseline to the full input image, around when $\alpha = 0.1$, the model becomes very confident in the prediction "sulfur-crested cockatoo."

We can achieve this straight line path in Python with the `interpolate_images` function described here (see the Integrated Gradients notebook (*https://oreil.ly/9dnn8*) in the GitHub repository for the full code example):

```
def interpolate_images(baseline,
                       image,
                       alphas):
    alphas_x = alphas[:, tf.newaxis, tf.newaxis, tf.newaxis]
    baseline_x = tf.expand_dims(baseline, axis=0)
    input_x = tf.expand_dims(image, axis=0)
```

```
images = alphas_x * input_x + (1 - alphas_x) * baseline_x
return images
```

The `interpolate_images` function produces a series of images as the values of the α's vary, starting from the baseline image when $\alpha = 0$ and ending at the full input image when $\alpha = 1$, as shown in Figure 4-4.

Figure 4-4. As the value of α varies from 0 to 1, we obtain a series of images creating a straight line path in image space from the baseline to the input image.

As α increases and more information is introduced to our baseline image, the signal sent to the model and our confidence in what is actually contained in the image increases. When $\alpha = 0$, at the baseline, there is, of course, no way for the model (or anyone, really) to be able to make an accurate prediction. There is no information in the image! However, as we increase α and move along the straight line path, the content of the image becomes clearer and the model can make a reasonable prediction.

If we think of this mathematically, the confidence of the model's prediction is quantified in the value of the final softmax output layer. By calling `prediction` with our trained model on the interpolated images, we can directly examine the model's confidence in the label "sulfur-crested cockatoo":

```
LABEL = 'sulfur-crested cockatoo'
pred = model(interpolated_images)

idx_cockatoo = np.where(imagenet_labels==LABEL)[0][0]
pred_proba = tf.nn.softmax(pred, axis=-1)[:, idx_cockatoo]
```

Not surprisingly, at some point before the $\alpha = 1$ the model has an aha moment and the model prediction determined to be "cockatoo," as demonstrated in Figure 4-3 when $\alpha \approx .15$.

We can also see here the importance of our choice of baseline. How would our model's predictions have changed if we started with a white baseline? Or a baseline from random noise? If we create the same plot as in Figure 4-3 but using the white baseline and noise baselines, we get different results. In particular, for the white baseline, the model's confidence in the predicted class jumps somewhere around $\alpha \approx 0.25$, while for the Gaussian noise baseline, the aha moment doesn't happen until $\alpha \approx 0.9$, as seen in Figure 4-5. The full code to create these examples is in the repository for the book.

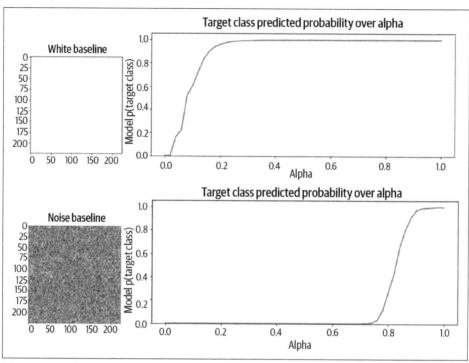

Figure 4-5. When using a white baseline (top) or a baseline based on Gaussian noise (bottom), the model takes longer to achieve the same confidence in the true label.

Accumulating Gradients

The last step for applying Integrated Gradients is then determining a way to use these gradients to decide which pixels or regions of pixels were the ones that most effectively contributed to that aha moment that we saw in Figure 4-3 when α was approximately 0.15 and the model's confidence was over 0.98. We want to know how the network went from predicting nothing to eventually knowing the correct label. This is where the *gradient* part of the Integrated Gradients technique comes into play. The gradient of a scalar valued function measures the direction of steepest ascent with respect to the function inputs. In this context, the function we are considering is the model's final output for the target class, and the inputs are the pixel values.

We can use TensorFlow's tf.GradientTape (*https://oreil.ly/uXw83*) for automatic differentiation to compute the gradient of our model function. We simply need to tell TensorFlow to "watch" the input image tensors during the model computation. Note that here we are using TensorFlow, but any library for performing automatic differentiation for other ML frameworks will work equally well:

```
def compute_gradients(images, target_class_idx):
    with tf.GradientTape() as tape:
```

```
            tape.watch(images)
            logits = model(images)
            probs = tf.nn.softmax(logits, axis=-1)[:, target_class_idx]
        return tape.gradient(probs, images)
```

Note that since the model returns a (1,1001)-shaped tensor with logits for each predicted class, we'll slice on `target_class_idx`, the index of the target class, so that we get only the predicted probability for the target class. Now, given a collection of images, the function `compute_gradients` will return the gradients of the model function.

Unfortunately, using the gradients directly is problematic because they can *saturate*; that is, the probabilities for the target class plateau well before the value for α reaches 1. If we look at the average value of the magnitudes of the pixel gradients, we see that the model learns the most when the value of alpha is lower, right around that aha moment at $\alpha \approx 0.1$. After that, when α is greater than 0.2, the gradients go to zero, so nothing new is being learned, as seen in Figure 4-6.

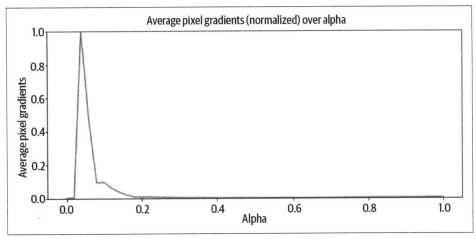

Figure 4-6. The model learns the most when the value of alpha is lower. After that, once $\alpha > 0.2$, the pixel gradients go to zero.

We want to know which pixels contributed most to the model's predicting the correct output class. By integrating over a path, Integrated Gradients avoids the problem of local gradients being saturated. The idea is that we accumulate the pixels' local gradients as we move along the straight line path from the baseline image to the input image. This way we accumulate a pixel's local gradients adding or subtracting its importance score to the model's overall output class probability. Formally, the importance value of the i-th pixel feature value of an image x for the model f is defined as:

$$\text{IG}_i(f,x,x') = \int_{\alpha=0}^{\alpha=1} (x_i - x_i') \frac{\partial f(x' + \alpha(x - x'))}{\partial x_i} d\alpha$$

Here x' denotes the baseline image. It may not look like it right away, but this is precisely the line integral of the gradient with respect to the i-th feature on the straight line path from the baseline image to the input image. To compute this in code, we'd need to use a numeric approximation with Riemann sums (see "Approximating Integrals with Riemann Sums" later in this chapter) summing over m steps. This number of steps parameter m is important, and there is a trade-off to consider when choosing the right value. If it's too small, then the approximation will be inaccurate. If the number of steps is too large, the approximation will be near perfect but the computation time will be long. You will likely want to experiment with the number of steps.

When choosing the number of steps to use for the integral approximation, the original paper (*https://oreil.ly/Z8dT9*)[2] suggests to experiment in the range between 20 and 300 steps. However, this may vary depending on your dataset and use case. For example, a good place to start for natural images like those found in ImageNet is $m = 50$. In practice, for some applications, it may be necessary to have an integral approximation within 5% error (or less!) of the actual integral. In these cases, a few thousand steps may be needed, though visual convergence can generally be achieved with far fewer steps. In practice, we have found that 10 to 30 steps is a good range to start with.

Once you have computed the approximations, you can check the quality of the approximation by comparing the attribution score obtained from using Integrated Gradients with the difference of the input image's attribution score and the baseline image's attribution score. The following code block shows how to do just that:

```
# The baseline's prediction and attribution score
baseline_prediction = model(tf.expand_dims(baseline, 0))
baseline_score = tf.nn.softmax(tf.squeeze(baseline_prediction))[target_class_idx]

# Your model's prediction and attribution score
input_prediction = model(tf.expand_dims(input, 0))
input_score = tf.nn.softmax(tf.squeeze(input_prediction))[target_class_idx]

# Compare with the attribution score from Integrated Gradients
ig_score = tf.math.reduce_sum(attributions)
delta = ig_score - (input_score - baseline_score)
```

If the absolute value of delta is greater than 0.05, then you should increase the number of steps in the approximation. For the full code, see the code for the check_convergence function in the Integrated Gradients notebook (*https://oreil.ly/9dnn8*) accompanying this book.

---

[2] Mukun Sundararajan et al., "Axiomatic Attribution for Deep Networks," Proceedings of the 34th International Conference on Machine Learning, PMLR 70 (2017).

Many of the large cloud providers offer managed implementations of various XAI techniques. For custom-trained models and for models trained via AutoML, Google Cloud offers explanations via sampled Shapley, Integrated Gradients, and XRAI (see "XRAI" on page 108). When requesting explanations for an instance, Google Cloud's implementation of Integrated Gradients calculates the approximation error for you as well and returns this error along with the explanations.

A high approximation error (for example, in excess of 0.05) indicates the quality of the explanation might not be reliable and you might need to adjust the XAI configurations. In particular, when you are working with custom-trained models, you can configure specific parameters to improve your explanations and decrease the approximation error by changing the following inputs:

- Increasing the number of integral steps
- Changing the input baseline(s)
- Adding more input baselines

Approximating Integrals with Riemann Sums

Riemann sums are a foundational tool in integral calculus and can be used to find an approximation of the value of a definite integral. When implementing Integrated Gradients, you use Riemann sums to approximate the actual value of the integral. This approximation is made by summing up many, many rectangles whose height is defined by the value of the curve, as in Figure 4-7. There are various implementations when computing Riemann sums; you can use a left endpoint to determine the height of the rectangle, the right endpoint, the midpoint, and you can even use more complicated polygons like trapezoids to get more accurate approximations.

For each technique, though, one important parameter is the number of partitions or rectangles you sum up to make the approximation. Formally, for well-behaved functions, as the number of partitions goes to infinity, the error between the Riemann sum approximation and the true area under the curve goes to zero. This presents a trade-off: with more rectangles the approximation is more accurate, but the computation cost also increases.

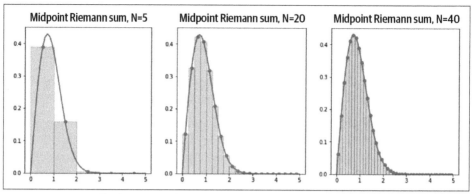

Figure 4-7. Formally, for reasonably well-behaved functions, as the number of rectangles goes to infinity, the error between the Riemann sum approximation and the true area under the curve goes to zero. This presents a trade-off when using Riemann sums to approximate continuous integrals.

Using the hyperparameter m for the number of steps, we can approximate the integral for computing Integrated Gradients in the following way:

$$\text{IG}_i^{\text{approx}}(f,x,x') = (x_i - x_i') \sum_{k=1}^{m} \frac{1}{m} \frac{\partial f(x)}{\partial x_i} \bigg|_{x = \text{interpolated images}}$$

In the notebook (*https://oreil.ly/9dnn8*) discussing Integrated Gradients in the GitHub repository for this book, you can see how each component of this sum is computed directly in Python and TensorFlow in the `integrated_gradients` function. First, the α's are created and the gradients are collected along the straight line path in batches. Here the argument `num` determines the number of steps to use in the integral approximation:

```
# Generate alphas.
alphas = tf.linspace(start=0.0, stop=1.0, num=m_steps+1)

# Collect gradients.
gradient_batches = []

# Iterate alphas range and batch speed, efficiency, and scaling
for alpha in tf.range(0, len(alphas), batch_size):
  from_ = alpha
  to = tf.minimum(from_ + batch_size, len(alphas))
  alpha_batch = alphas[from_:to]

  gradient_batch = one_batch(baseline, image, alpha_batch, target_class_idx)
  gradient_batches.append(gradient_batch)
```

Then those batch-wise gradients are combined into a single tensor and the integral approximation is computed, as shown in the following code. The number of gradients is controlled by the number of steps m_steps:

```
# Concatenate path gradients.
total_gradients = tf.concat(gradient_batches, axis=0)

# Compute Integral approximation of all gradients.
avg_gradients = integral_approximation(gradients=total_gradients)
```

Finally, we scale the approximation and return the integrated gradient results:

```
# Scale Integrated Gradients with respect to input.
integrated_gradients = (image - baseline) * avg_gradients
```

You can visualize these attributions and overlay them on the original image. The following code sums the absolute values of the Integrated Gradients across the color channels to produce an attribution mask:

```
attributions = integrated_gradients(baseline=black_baseline,
                                     image=input_image,
                                     target_class_idx=target_class_idx,
                                     m_steps=m_steps)
attribution_mask = tf.reduce_sum(tf.math.abs(attributions), axis=-1)
```

You can then overlay the attribution mask with the original image, as shown in Figure 4-8. See the notebook (*https://oreil.ly/9dnn8*) in the GitHub repository to see the full code for this example.

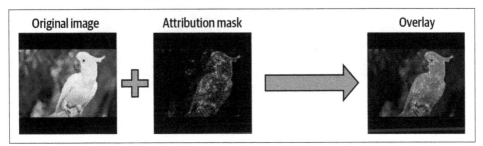

Figure 4-8. After computing feature attributions from the Integrated Gradients technique, overlaying the attribution mask over the original shows which parts of the image most contributed to the model's class prediction.

Baselines Matter

It's interesting to compare the result of applying Integrated Gradients on our cockatoo example when using a black baseline versus a white baseline. Remember the intuition when choosing a baseline is that the baseline should have "no information" and, typically, you can think that an all-white or all-black baseline as having no information. But in the example of a cockatoo, this isn't the case. The cockatoo is predominantly white, so a white baseline actually contains a lot of information of the features of a cockatoo. Not surprisingly, when we compare the result of applying Integrated Gradients with these two baselines, they look quite different, as shown in Figure 4-9 (see the notebook (*https://oreil.ly/9dnn8*) in the GitHub repository for the full code for this example).

There are also alternatives to using constant color baselines, such as using a maximum distance baseline, a blurred baseline (discussed later in the "Blur Integrated Gradients" section), a uniform baseline, or a Gaussian baseline (shown in Figure 4-2). Yet another option would be to average over multiple baselines.

Any baseline has its own pros and cons and, ultimately, choosing the right baseline remains a challenge. As a practitioner, it's important to be aware of the bias that is present when using a specific baseline and how certain baselines might affect your results. Therefore, we encourage you to experiment with multiple baselines to see which works best for your dataset and use case.

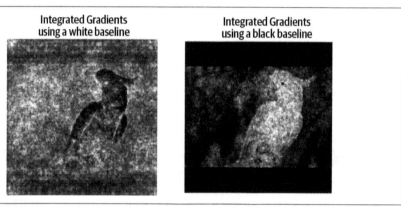

Figure 4-9. The results of applying Integrated Gradients with a white baseline versus a black baseline are quite different for a predominantly white image, like a sulfur-crested cockatoo.

The code and discussion in this section show what's really happening "under the hood" when implementing Integrated Gradients for model explainability. There are also more high-level libraries that can be leveraged and have easy-to-use implementations. In particular, the saliency library (*https://oreil.ly/kr02S*) developed by the People + AI Research (PAIR) group at Google contains easy-to-use implementations of Integrated Gradients, its many variations, and other explainability techniques. See the notebook (*https://oreil.ly/9dnn8*) in the book's GitHub repository to see how the saliency library can be used to find attribution masks via Integrated Gradients.

Improvements on Integrated Gradients

The method of Integrated Gradients is one of the most widely used and well-known gradient-based attribution techniques for explaining deep networks. However, for some input examples, this method can produce spurious or noisy pixel attributions that aren't related to the model's predicted class. This is partly due to the accumulation of noise from regions of correlated, high-magnitude gradients for irrelevant pixels that occur along the straight line path that is used when computing Integrated Gradients. This is also closely related to the choice of baseline that is used when computing Integrated Gradients for an image.

Various techniques have been introduced to address the problems that may arise when using Integrated Gradients. We'll discuss two variations on the classic Integrated Gradients approach: Blur Integrated Gradients and Guided Integrated Gradients.

Blur Integrated Gradients (Blur-IG)

In the section "Choosing a Baseline," you saw that when implementing Integrated Gradients, the choice of baseline is very important and can have significant effects on the resulting explanations. Blur Integrated Gradients (Blur-IG) specifically addresses the issues that arise with choosing a specific baseline. In short, Blur-IG removes the need to provide a baseline as a parameter and instead advocates to use the blurred input image as the baseline when implementing Integrated Gradients.

This is done by applying a Gaussian blur filter parameterized by its variance α. We then compute the Integrated Gradients along the straight line path from this blurred image to the true, unblurred image. As σ increases, the image becomes more and more blurred, as shown in Figure 4-10. The maximum scale σ_{max} should be chosen so that the maximally blurred image is information-less, meaning the image is so blurred it wouldn't be possible to classify what is in the image.

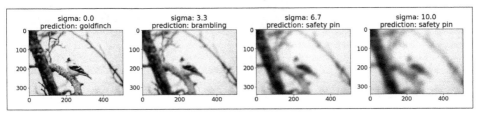

Figure 4-10. With no blur, the model predicts "goldfinch" with 97.5% confidence, but with $\sigma = 6.7$, the model's top prediction becomes "safety pin."

The idea is that for different scale values of σ, different features are preserved or destroyed depending on the scale of the feature itself. The smaller the variation of the feature, the smaller the value of σ at which it is destroyed, as seen in the detail in the wing patterns of the goldfinch in Figure 4-10. When σ is less than 3, the black-and-white pattern on the wings is still recognizable. However, for larger values of σ, the wings and head are just a blur.

We can compare the saliency maps produced from using regular Integrated Gradients versus Blur Integrated Gradients (shown in Figure 4-11). Using the `saliency` library, this can be done in only a few lines of code:

```
# Construct the saliency object.
integrated_gradients = saliency.IntegratedGradients()
blur_ig = saliency.BlurIG()

# Baseline is a black image.
baseline = np.zeros(im.shape)

# Compute the IG mask and the Blur IG mask.
integrated_gradients_mask_3d = integrated_gradients.GetMask(
    im, call_model_function, call_model_args, x_steps=25, x_baseline=baseline,
    batch_size=20)
blur_ig_mask_3d = blur_ig.GetMask(
    im, call_model_function, call_model_args, batch_size=20)
```

In this code block, the `call_model_function` is a generic function that tells how to pass inputs to a given model and receive the outputs necessary to compute the saliency masks. It can be used with any ML framework. See the notebook on Integrated Gradients (*https://oreil.ly/9dnn8*) for the full code for this example. For this example of an image of an American goldfinch, Blur-IG produces much more convincing attributions than the vanilla Integrated Gradients.

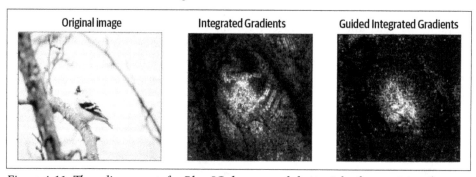

Figure 4-11. The saliency map for Blur-IG does a much better job of recognizing the parts of the image that make up the goldfinch.

Guided Integrated Gradients (Guided IG)

Guided Integrated Gradients (Guided IG) attempts to improve upon Integrated Gradients by modifying the straight line path that is used in the implementation. Instead of using a straight line path from the baseline to the input image, Guided IG uses an adapted path to create saliency maps that are better aligned with the model's prediction. Instead of moving pixel intensities in a fixed straight line direction from the baseline to the input, we make a choice at every step. More precisely, Guided IG moves in the direction where features (i.e., pixels) have the smallest absolute value of partial derivatives. As the intensity of the pixels becomes equal to those of the input image, they are ignored.

The idea is that the typical straight line path that is used by previous integrated gradient techniques we've discussed so far could potentially travel through points in the feature space where the gradient norm is large and not pointing in the direction of the integration path. As a result, the naive straight line path leads to noise and gradient accumulation in saturated regions that causes spurious pixels or regions to be attributed at too high of an importance when computing saliency maps. Guided IG avoids this problem by instead navigating along an adapted path in feature space, taking into account the geometry of the model surface in feature space. Figure 4-12 compares the result of applying vanilla Integrated Gradients with that of Guided Integrated Gradients. See the Integrated Gradients notebook (*https://oreil.ly/9dnn8*) in this book's GitHub repository for the full code for this example.

For the example image in Figure 4-12, the saliency map for the Guided IG example seems to focus on the goldfinch in the image more than the saliency map for Integrated Gradients, but both methods don't seem to do a particularly great job of producing convincing explanations. This may indicate that our model needs more training, or more data. Or maybe that both Integrated Gradients and Guided IG just aren't well suited for this task or this dataset and another method would work better. There is no one-size-fits-all XAI technique. This is why it's important to have a well-stocked toolkit of techniques that you can use when analyzing your model predictions.

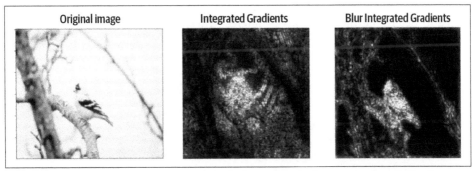

Figure 4-12. The saliency map for the Guided IG example focuses on the goldfinch in the image more than the saliency map for Integrated Gradients, but both methods don't seem to do a particularly great job of producing convincing explanations.

XRAI

Here's what you need to know about XRAI:

- XRAI is a region-based attribution method that builds upon Integrated Gradients.

- XRAI determines regions of importance by segmenting the input image into like regions based on a similarity metric and then determines attribution scores for those like regions.

- XRAI is a local explainability method that can be applied to any DNN-based model as long as there is a way to cluster the input features into segments through some similarity metric.

Pros	Cons
• XRAI improves upon other gradient-based techniques like vanilla Integrated Gradients.	• XRAI is only useful for image models.
• XRAI can be faster than perturbation-based methods like LIME that require multiple queries to the model.	• There is less granularity than a technique like Integrated Gradients that provides pixel-level attribution.
• It performs best on natural images, like a picture of an animal or an object, similar to those found in the benchmark ImageNet and CIFAR datasets.	• XRAI is not recommended for low-contrast images or images taken in nonnatural environments such as X-rays.

The saliency maps obtained from applying Integrated Gradients provide an easy-to-understand tool to visually see which pixels contribute most to a model's prediction for a given image. XRAI builds upon the method of Integrated Gradients by joining pixels into regions. So instead of highlighting individual pixels that were most important, the saliency maps obtained by XRAI highlight pixel regions of interest in the image.

A key component and the first step of the XRAI algorithm is the segmentation of the image to determine those regions of interest. Image segmentation is a popular use case in computer vision that aims to partition an image into multiple regions that are conceptually similar, as illustrated in Figure 4-13.

Figure 4-13. Image segmentation is a process of assigning a class to each pixel in an image. Here are some examples from the Common Objects in Context (COCO) dataset (https://cocodataset.org).

Image segmentation is a well-studied problem in computer vision, and deep learning architectures like U-Net, Fast R-CNNs, and Mask R-CNNs have been developed to specifically address this challenge and can produce state-of-the-art results. One of the key steps of the XRAI algorithm uses an algorithm called Felzenszwalb's algorithm to segment an input image into similar regions, much in the same way as a nearest neighbors clustering algorithm. The Felzenszwalb algorithm doesn't rely on deep learning.[3] Instead, it is a graph-based approach based on Kruskal's minimum spanning tree algorithm and provides an incredibly efficient means to image segmentation. The key advantage of Felzenszwalb's algorithm is that it captures the important nonlocal regions of an image that are globally relevant and, at the same time, is computationally efficient with time complexity $\mathcal{O}(n \log n)$ where n is the number of pixels.

The idea is to represent an image as a connected graph $G = (V,E)$ of vertices V and edges E where each pixel is a vertex in the graph and the edges connect neighboring pixels. The segmentation algorithm then iteratively tests the importance of each region and refines the graph partitions, coalescing smaller regions into larger segments until an optimal segmentation is found, resulting in a segmentation shown in Figure 4-14.

Figure 4-14. The Felzenszwalb segmentation algorithm realizes an image as a weighted undirected graph and then partitions the graph so that the variation across two different components is greater than the variation across either component individually.

---

3 Pedro F. Felzenszwalb and Daniel P. Huttenlocher, "Efficient Graph-Based Image Segmentation," *International Journal of Computer Vision* 59.2 (2004): 167–81.

The sensitivity to the *within* group and *between* group differences is handled by a threshold function. The strictness of this threshold is determined by the parameter k. You can think of this k as setting the scale of observation for the segmentation algorithm. Figure 4-15 shows the resulting image segmentations for various values of k. These images were created using the `segmentation` package of the `scikit-image` library. The code for this example is available in this book's GitHub repository. As you can see there, a larger value of k causes a preference for larger components, while a smaller value of k allows for smaller regions. It's important to note that k does not guarantee a minimum component size. Smaller components would still be allowed, they just require a stronger difference between neighboring components.

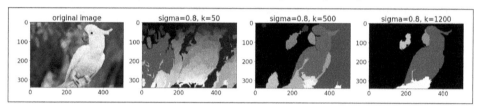

Figure 4-15. The parameter k controls the threshold function for Felzenszwalb segmentation algorithm. A larger value of k causes a preference for larger components while a smaller value of k allows for smaller regions.

How XRAI Works

XRAI combines the output from applying Integrated Gradients to an input image with the image segmentation provided by Felzenszwalb's algorithm described in the previous section. Intuitively, Integrated Gradients provides pixel-level attributions, so by aggregating these local feature attributions over the globally relevant segments produced from the image segmentation, XRAI is able to rank each segment and order the segments that contribute most to the given class prediction.

If one segment, for example the segment consisting of the body and crest of the cockatoo in Figure 4-14, contains a lot of pixels that are considered salient via Integrated Gradients, then that segment would also be ranked as highly salient via XRAI as well. However, a much smaller region, such as the segment representing the eye of the cockatoo, even if the pixels have high saliency measures according to the output from applying Integrated Gradients, XRAI would not rank that region as highly. This helps protect against individual pixels or small pixel segments that have spuriously high saliency from applying Integrated Gradients alone.

One thing to keep in mind, however, is the sensitivity of the segmentation result and how a certain choice of hyperparameters might bias the result. To address this, the image is segmented multiple times using different values (50, 100, 150, 250, 500, 1200) for the scale parameter k. In addition, segments smaller than 20 pixels are ignored entirely. Since for a single parameter the union of segments gives the entire image, the union of all segments obtained from all the parameters yields an area equal to about six times the total image area and with multiple segments overlapping. Each of the regions from this oversegmentation is used when aggregating the lower-level attributions.

So, bringing it all together, when implementing XRAI, first the method of Integrated Gradients is applied using both a black and white baseline to determine pixel-level attributions, as shown in Figure 4-16. Concurrently, Felzenszwalb's graph-based segmentation algorithm is applied multiple times using a range of scale parameter values for k = 50, 100, 150, 250, 500, 1200. This produces an oversegmentation of the original image. XRAI then aggregates the pixel-level attributions by summing the values from the integrated gradient output within each of the resulting segments and ranks each segment from most to least salient. The result is a heatmap that highlights the areas of the original image that contribute most strongly to the model's class prediction. Overlaying this heatmap over the original image, we can see which regions most strongly contribute to the prediction of "sulfur-crested cockatoo."

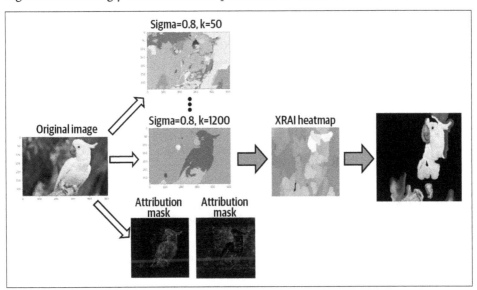

Figure 4-16. XRAI combines the results from the method of Integrated Gradients with the oversegmentation regions obtained from multiple applications of Felzenszwalb's segmentation algorithm. The pixel-level attributions are then aggregated over the oversegmented regions and ranked to determine which regions are most salient for the model.

Implementing XRAI

XRAI is a post hoc explainability method and can be applied to any DNN-based model. Let's look at an example of how to implement XRAI using the `saliency` library developed by the People + AI Research (PAIR) (*https://oreil.ly/QKjQl*) group at Google. In the following code block, we load a VGG-16 model pretrained on the ImageNet dataset and modify the outputs so that we can capture the model prediction m.output as well as one of the convolution block layers block5_conv3. The full code for this example can be found in the XRAI for Image Explainability notebook (*https://oreil.ly/gLqcn*) in this book's GitHub repository:

```
m = tf.keras.applications.vgg16.VGG16(weights='imagenet', include_top=True)
conv_layer = m.get_layer('block5_conv3')
model = tf.keras.models.Model([m.inputs], [conv_layer.output, m.output])
```

To get the XRAI attributions, we construct a saliency object for XRAI and call the method GetMask passing in a few key arguments:

```
xrai_object = saliency.XRAI()
xrai_attributions = xrai_object.GetMask(image,
                                        call_model_function,
                                        call_model_args,
                                        batch_size=20)
```

The image argument is fairly self-explanatory: it's the image on which we want to obtain the XRAI attributions passed in as a numpy array. Let's discuss the other arguments: the call_model_function and call_model_args. The call_model_function is how we pass inputs to our model and receive the outputs necessary to compute a saliency mask. It calls the model so it expects input images. Any arguments needed when calling and running the model are handled by call_model_args. The last argument, expected_keys, tells the function the list of keys expected in the output. We'll use the call_model_function defined in the following code, and we'll either get back gradients with respect to the inputs or the gradients with respect to the intermediate convolution layer:

```
class_idx_str = 'class_idx_str'
def call_model_function(images, call_model_args=None, expected_keys=None):
    target_class_idx = call_model_args[class_idx_str]
    images = tf.convert_to_tensor(images)
    with tf.GradientTape() as tape:
        if expected_keys==[saliency.base.INPUT_OUTPUT_GRADIENTS]:
            tape.watch(images)
            _, output_layer = model(images)
            output_layer = output_layer[:,target_class_idx]
            gradients = np.array(tape.gradient(output_layer, images))
            return {saliency.base.INPUT_OUTPUT_GRADIENTS: gradients}
        else:
            conv_layer, output_layer = model(images)
            gradients = np.array(tape.gradient(output_layer, conv_layer))
            return {saliency.base.CONVOLUTION_LAYER_VALUES: conv_layer,
                    saliency.base.CONVOLUTION_OUTPUT_GRADIENTS: gradients}
```

You may recall that when implementing Integrated Gradients, one hyperparameter you could adjust is the number of steps used to compute the line integral. Since XRAI relies on the output from Integrated Gradients, you may be wondering where and how you adjust that hyperparameter for XRAI. In the `saliency` library, those kinds of hyperparameters are controlled with a subclass called `XRAIParameters`. The default number of steps is set to 100. To change the number of steps to 200, you simply create an `XRAIParameters` object and pass it to the `GetMask` function as well:

```
xrai_params = saliency.XRAIParameters()
xrai_params.steps = 200

xrai_attributions_fast = xrai_object.GetMask(im,
                                        call_model_function,
                                        call_model_args,
                                        extra_parameters=xrai_params,
                                        batch_size=20)
```

Finally, we can plot the `xrai_attributions` object returned from calling `GetMask` to obtain a heatmap of attributions for the image, as shown in Figure 4-17.

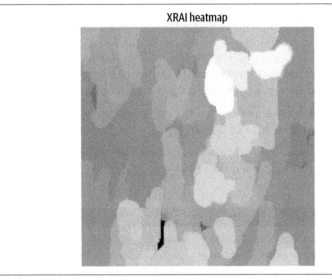

Figure 4-17. XRAI produces a heatmap of attributions for a given input image. For this image of a sulfur-crested cockatoo, the more relevant regions correspond to the body of the bird, its beak, and its distinct crest.

In order to see which regions of the original image were most salient, the following code focuses only on the most salient 30% and creates a mask filter overlaid on the original image. This results in Figure 4-18:

```
mask = xrai_attributions > np.percentile(xrai_attributions, 60)
im_mask = np.array(im_orig)
im_mask[~mask] = 0
ShowImage(im_mask, title='Top 30%', ax=P.subplot(ROWS, COLS, 3))
```

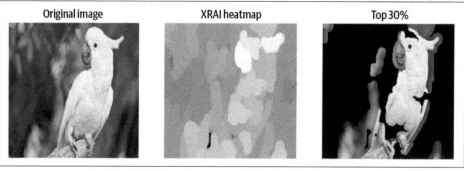

| Original image | XRAI heatmap | Top 30% |

Figure 4-18. Filtering the XRAI attributions, we can overlay the heatmap on the original image to highlight only the most salient regions.

Grad-CAM

Here's what you need to know about Grad-CAM:

- Grad-CAM is short for Gradient-weighted Class Activation Mapping. Grad-CAM was one of the first explainability techniques; it generalizes CAM that could only be used for certain model architectures.

- Grad-CAM works by examining the gradient information flowing through the last (or any) convolution layer of the network.

- It produces a localization heatmap highlighting the regions in an image most influential for predicting a given class label.

Pros	Cons
• Grad-CAM only requires a forward pass of the model, so it's computationally efficient and easy to implement by hand or with open source libraries. • Grad-CAM is applicable to a wide variety of CNN models and tasks, for example, CNNs with fully connected layers (used in classification tasks), CNNs with multimodal inputs (used in visual question answering), or CNNs for text outputs (used in image captioning). • Grad-CAM can be combined with other pixel-space visualizations to create high-resolution class discriminative visualizations (see "Guided Backpropagation and Guided Grad-CAM" on page 129).	• Grad-CAM produces low-resolution heatmaps that can have incorrect or misleading results by attributing regions in the image that were not influential for the model. Take caution when interpreting the results from Grad-CAM. • Grad-CAM doesn't perform as well as other XAI methods for multiclass classification models with a large number of class labels. • Grad-CAM fails to properly localize objects in an image if the image contains multiple occurrences of the same class; e.g., an image classifier for recognizing cat that is given an image with two cats will produce an unreliable-heat map.

Grad-CAM is one of the original explainability techniques developed for image models and can be applied to any CNN-based network. Grad-CAM is a post hoc explanation technique and doesn't require any architecture changes or retraining. Instead, Grad-CAM accesses the internal convolutions layers of the model to determine regions that are most influential for the model's predictions. Because Grad-CAM only relies on forward passes through the model, with no backpropagation, it is also computationally efficient.

How Grad-CAM Works

To understand how Grad-CAM works, let's first start with what Class Activation Map (CAM) is and how it works, since Grad-CAM is essentially a generalization of CAM. Typically, when building an image model, your model architecture is likely to consist of a stack of convolutional and pooling layers. For example, think about the classic VGG-16 model architecture shown in Figure 4-19. There are five convolution plus pooling blocks that act as feature extractors, followed by three fully connected layers (FC) before the final softmax prediction layer. CAM is a localization map of the image that is computed as a weighted activation map. This is done by taking a weighted sum of the activation maps of the final convolution layer in the model.

More precisely, and to illustrate with an example, suppose we take the final convolution layer (just before the last pooling layer) of the VGG-16 model in Figure 4-19 trained on the ImageNet dataset. The dimension of this final convolution layer is 7×7×512. So, there are 512 feature maps mapping to 1,000 class labels; that is, the labels corresponding to ImageNet.

Figure 4-19. VGG-16 consists of blocks of convolution and pooling layers. CAM is a weighted activation map applied to the final convolution layer.

Each feature map is indexed by i and j representing the width and height of the convolution layer (in this case $i = j = 7$). Notationally, A_{ij}^k denotes the activation at location (i,j) of the feature map A^k. Those feature maps are then pooled using global average pooling and CAM computes a final score Y^c for each class c by taking a weighted sum of the pooled feature maps, where the weights are given by the weights connecting the k-th feature map with the c-th class:

$$Y^c = \sum_k w_k^c \sum_{i,j} A_{ij}^k$$

If you then take the gradient of Y^c, that is, the score for class c, with respect to the feature maps, you can separate out the weight term w_k^c, so that (after a bit of math[4]) you get:

$$w_k^c = \sum_{i,j} \frac{\partial Y^c}{\partial A_{ij}^k}$$

This weight value is almost exactly the same as the neuron importance weight that is used in Grad-CAM! For Grad-CAM, you also pull out the activations A^k from the final convolution layer and compute the gradient of the class score Y^c with respect to these A^k. In some sense, these gradients capture the information flowing through the last convolution layer; you want to use this to assign importance values to each neuron for a particular class c. This importance weight is computed (similarly to CAM) as:

$$\alpha_k^c = \frac{1}{Z} \sum_{i,j} \frac{\partial Y^c}{\partial A_{ij}^k}$$

The last step of Grad-CAM is to then take a weighted combination of the activation maps using these α_k^c as weights and apply a ReLU to that linear combination, as shown in Figure 4-20. So,

$$L_{\text{Grad-CAM}}^c = \text{ReLU}\left(\sum_k \alpha_k^c A^k\right)$$

You use a ReLU here because we only care about the pixels whose intensity should be increased in order to increase the class score Y^c. Remember ReLU maps negative values to zero, so by applying ReLU after the weighted sum we only capture the positive influence on the class score. Because the shape of A^k is the same shape as the final convolution layer; it produces a coarse heatmap that can then be overlaid on the original image to indicate which regions were most influential in the model predicting class c. Also, due to the averaging and pooling of these feature maps, Grad-CAM works best at representing regions of influence in the image rather than exact pixels. An overview of the Grad-CAM process is shown in Figure 4-20.

---

4 Ramprasaath R. Selvaraju et al., "Grad-CAM: Visual Explanations from Deep Networks via Gradient-Based Localization," Computer Vision Foundation, *https://oreil.ly/cU9sG*.

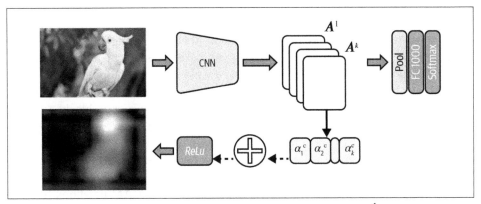

Figure 4-20. An overview of Grad-CAM. The final activation maps A^k are used to compute a weighted sum that is then passed through a ReLU layer.

The coarse heatmap created by Grad-CAM is problematic and can generate misleading results. Because the heatmap has the same dimensions as the final convolutional feature maps A^k, it is usually upsampled to fit the shape of the original image. For example, the last convolutional layer of VGG-16 is 7×7×512, so the heatmap determined from the weighted sum of the activation maps will have dimension 7×7, which then has to be upsampled to overlay on the original image that has shape 224×224. This upsampling has the strong potential for causing misleading results, particularly if your dataset consists of large images whose shape is much larger than the internal activation map or contains image patterns and artifacts that are not properly sampled by a convolution.

You may be wondering how exactly Grad-CAM improves upon CAM, especially if they are essentially using the same importance weights. The advantage of Grad-CAM is that the construction for CAM is very limiting. It requires feature maps to directly precede softmax layers. So, CAM only works for certain kinds of CNN model architectures, i.e., ones that have their final layers to be a convolution feature mapped to a global average pooling layer mapped to a softmax prediction layer. The problem is that this may not be architecture with best performance. By taking a gradient and rearranging terms, Grad-CAM is able to generalize CAM and works just as well for a wide range of architectures for other image-based tasks, like image captioning or visual question answering.

In the description of Grad-CAM, we only discussed taking the CAM from the final convolution layer. As you may have already guessed, the technique we described is quite general and can be used to explain activations for any layer of the deep neural network.

Implementing Grad-CAM

The Grad-CAM algorithm outlined in Figure 4-20 is fairly straightforward and can be implemented directly by hand, assuming you have access to the internal layers of your CNN model. However, there is an easy-to-use implementation available from the saliency library (*https://oreil.ly/unQm4*). Let's see how it works with an example. You start by creating a TensorFlow model. In the following code block, we load a pretrained VGG-16 model architecture that has been trained on the ImageNet dataset. We also select the penultimate convolution layer block5_3 that we'll use to obtain the activation maps. Note that when we build the actual model it returns both the convolution layer output and the VGG-16 outputs, so we can still make predictions. For the full code for this example, see the Grad-CAM notebook (*https://oreil.ly/h2zmh*) in the GitHub repository for this book:

```
vgg16 = tf.keras.applications.vgg16.VGG16(
    weights='imagenet', include_top=True)
conv_layer = m.get_layer('block5_conv3')
model = tf.keras.models.Model(
    [vgg16.inputs], [conv_layer.output, vgg16.output])
```

To apply Grad-CAM, you then construct a saliency object, calling the Grad-CAM method and then apply GetMask passing the example image, and the call_model_function. The following code block shows how this is done. The call_model_function interfaces with a model to return the convolution layer information and the gradients of the model. This returns a Grad-CAM mask that can be used to plot a heatmap indicating influential regions in the image:

```
# Construct the saliency object. This alone doesn't do anything.
grad_cam = saliency.GradCam()

# Compute the Grad-CAM mask.
grad_cam_mask_3d = grad_cam.GetMask(im, call_model_function,
call_model_args)
```

 Historically, Grad-CAM is an important technique. It was one of the first techniques to leverage the internal convolution layers of a CNN model to derive explanations for model prediction. However, you should take caution when implementing and interpreting the results from Grad-CAM. Because of the upsampling and smoothing step from the convolution layer, some regions of the heatmap may seem important when in fact they were not influential for the model at all. There have been improvements to address these concerns (see the next section, "Improving Grad-CAM," and the later section "Guided Grad-CAM"), but the results should be viewed critically and in comparison with other techniques.

Improving Grad-CAM

After publication of the original paper (*https://oreil.ly/g9dX9*) in 2017,[5] it was discovered that Grad-CAM could inaccurately attribute model attention to regions of the image that were not actually influential in the prediction. Grad-CAM applies a natural smoothing, or interpolation, to its original heatmaps in enlarging them to the size of the original dimensions of the input image. Figure 4-21 shows an example of what the Grad-CAM output looks like with and without smoothing.

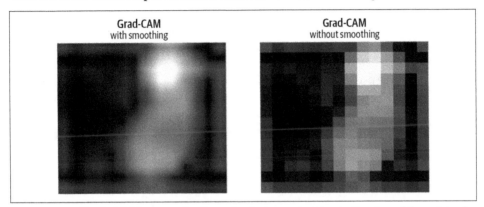

Figure 4-21. Grad-CAM upsamples from the feature map size to the size of the original image and applies a natural smoothing. This can cause misleading results and inaccurately attribute model attention to regions that weren't influential.

The smoothing results in a more visually pleasing image, with seamless changes in the colors of the heatmap, but can also be very misleading. Since the original region was focused on a much smaller image size, we can't say that the pixels that were lost would have had the same influence on the model as those remaining around it.[6] In response, researchers developed Grad-CAM++ and HiResCAM to address these issues. Figure 4-22 shows an example of how the outputs of Grad-CAM and Grad-CAM++ differ. These newer techniques helped to address these concerns and can produce more accurate attribution maps. However, even with the regional inaccuracy fixed, Grad-CAM remains a flawed technique due to how it upsamples from the original size of the feature maps to the size of the input image.

---

5 The Grad-CAM paper was revised and updated in 2019.

6 Defenders of Grad-CAM claim that this upscaling is acceptable because it mirrors the downsampling performed by the model's CNNs, but this argument does not have any strong theoretical grounding or evaluations to substantiate this claim.

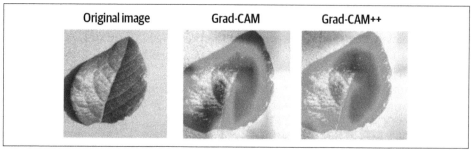

Figure 4-22. A heatmap from applying Grad-CAM and Grad-CAM++ for the classification of a healthy blueberry leaf. In the Grad-CAM image, the heatmap is most attentive in the center of the leaf but also highlights some influence from the background. For Grad-CAM++, the activated pixels are more evenly distributed throughout the leaf, although a highly influential region is still attributed to the background in the lower left. (Print readers can see the color image at https://oreil.ly/xai-fig-4-22.)

LIME

Here's what you need to know about LIME:

- LIME stands for *local interpretable model-agnostic explanations*. It is a post hoc, perturbation-based explainability technique.
- LIME can be used for regression or classification models, though in practice LIME is used primarily for classification models.
- LIME works by changing regions of an image, turning them on or off and rerunning inferences to see which regions are most influential to the model's prediction.
- LIME uses an inherently interpretable model to measure influence or importance of input features.

Pros	Cons
• LIME is a very popular technique for producing pixel-level attributions.	• Explanations are brittle and may not be accurate. Because LIME is a local interpretation of a complex model, explanations can be particularly bad for highly nonlinear models.
• It is easy to implement and has a well-maintained Python implementation (see GitHub repository (*https://oreil.ly/tcbtd*)).	• LIME is prone to misidentifying background regions as influential.
• It has an intuitive and easy-to-explain algorithm and implementation.	• Explanations can be very slow to generate, depending on the complexity of your model, since it queries the model multiple times on perturbations of the input.
• There are a wide variety of visualization options.	

Due to its age, LIME is one of the more popular explainability techniques. It can also be used for tabular and text data, and the algorithm is similar for each of these data modalities albeit with some modifications. We discuss the details of implementing LIME with images here because it gives a nice visual intuition of how LIME works in general (see Chapter 5 for a discussion of how LIME works with text).

How LIME Works

LIME is a post hoc, model-agnostic, perturbation-based explainability technique. That means it can be applied to any machine learning model (e.g., neural networks, SVM, random forest, etc.) and is applied after the model has been trained. In essence, LIME treats the trained model like an API, taking an example instance and producing a prediction value. To explain why the model makes a certain prediction for a given input instance, the LIME algorithm works by passing lots and lots of slightly perturbed examples of the original input to the model and then measures how the model predictions change with these small input changes. The perturbations occur at the feature level of the input instance; i.e., images, pixels, and pixel regions are modified to create a new perturbed input. In this way, those pixels or pixel regions that most influence the model's prediction are highlighted as being more or less influential to the model's predicted output for the given input instance.

To go into a little more detail, let's further explain two of the key components of implementing LIME: first, how to generate a perturbation of an image and second, what it means to measure how the model prediction changes on these perturbations.

For a given prediction, the input image is subdivided into interpretable components, or regions, of the image. LIME segments the image into regions called superpixels. A superpixel is a similarity-based grouping of the individual pixels of an image into similar components (see the discussion of Felzenszwalb's algorithm in the earlier section "XRAI"). For example, Figure 4-23 shows how the image of the sulfur-crested cockatoo can be segmented into superpixels. The superpixel regions represent the interpretable components of the image.

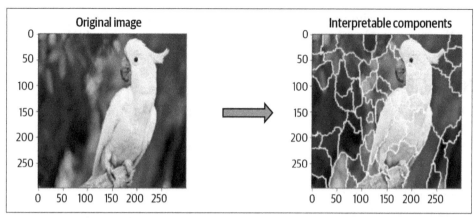

Figure 4-23. When implementing LIME, the original image is segmented into superpixel regions that represent the interpretable components of the image.

The superpixel regions in Figure 4-23 were created using the quickshift segmentation algorithm (*https://oreil.ly/jJVl4*) from the scikit-image library. This is the default segmentation algorithm used in the widely used, open source Python package LIME (*https://oreil.ly/ZM6ko*) (see the next section, "Implementing LIME"), although other segmentation functions could be used. Quickshift is based on an approximation of kernelized mean-shift and computes hierarchical segmentation at multiple scales simultaneously. Quickshift has two main parameters: the parameter sigma determines the scale of the local density approximation, and max_dist determines the level of the hierarchical segmentation. There is also a parameter ratio that controls the ratio between the distance in color space and the distance in image space when comparing the similarity of two pixels. The following code produces the segmentation in Figure 4-23. See the LIME notebook (*https://oreil.ly/RNL9g*) in the GitHub repository for this book for the full code example:

```
from skimage.segmentation import quickshift

segments = quickshift(im_orig, kernel_size=4,
                      max_dist=200, ratio=0.2)
```

LIME then perturbs these interpretable components by changing the values of the pixels in each superpixel region to be gray. This creates multiple new variations, or perturbations, of the input image. Each of these new perturbed instances is then given to the model to generate new prediction values for the class that was originally predicted. For example, in Figure 4-24 the original image is modified by graying out certain superpixel regions. Those perturbed examples are then passed to the trained model (in this case a deep neural network), and the model returns the probability that the image contains a sulfur-crested cockatoo. These new predictions create a dataset that is used to train LIME's linear model to determine how much each interpretable component contributes to the original prediction.

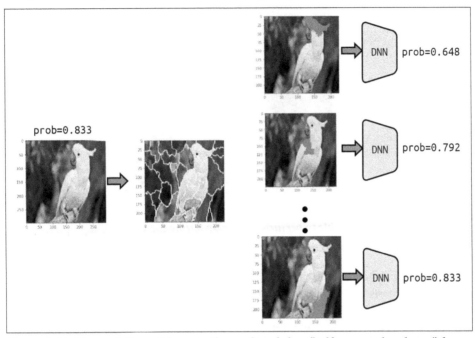

Figure 4-24. The model's confidence in the predicted class "sulfur-crested cockatoo" for the original image is 0.833. As certain superpixels are removed (by graying out the region), the model's top class prediction changes. For regions that are influential, the change is larger than for regions that are less important.

In the LIME implementation, superpixels are turned "on" or "off" by changing the pixel values of a segment to gray. This creates a collection of perturbed images that are passed to the model for prediction. It is also possible to instead change the superpixel regions to the mean of the individual pixel values in the superpixel region, as shown in Figure 4-25.

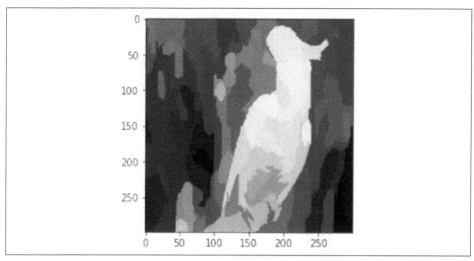

Figure 4-25. It is also possible to perturb images by setting the values of superpixel regions to be the average of the individual pixel regions in the image.

Let's now discuss how LIME quantitatively measures the contributions of the super-pixel feature inputs. This is done by training a smaller, interpretable model to provide explanations for the original model. This smaller model can be anything, but the important aspect is that it is inherently interpretable. In the original paper (*https:// oreil.ly/coFw3*),[7] the authors use the example of a linear model. Linear models are inherently interpretable because the weights of each feature directly indicate the importance of that feature for the model's prediction.

This interpretable, linear model is then trained on a dataset consisting of the perturbed examples and the original model's predictions, as shown in Figure 4-24. These perturbations are really just simple binary representations of the image indicating the "presence" or "absence" of each superpixel region. Since we care about the perturbations that are closest to the original image, those examples with the most superpixels present are weighted more than examples that have more superpixels absent. This proximity can be measured using any distance metric for images. The idea is that even though your trained model might be highly complex, for example a deep neural network or an SVM, the locally weighted, linear model can capture the local behavior at a given input instance. The more sensitive the complex model is to a given input feature, the more of an influence that feature will have on the linear, interpretable model as well.

---

7 Marco Tulio Ribeiro et al., "'Why Should I Trust You?' Explaining the Predictions of Any Classifier," Proceedings of the 22nd SIGKDD International Conference on Knowledge Discovery and Data Mining (August 2016).

Implementing LIME

There is a nice, easy-to-use Python package for applying LIME to tabular, image, and text classifiers that works for any classifier with at least two label classes. As an example, let's see how to implement LIME on the Inception v3 image classification model. The following code shows how to load the image in TensorFlow and make a prediction on an image. Note that when we load the incepton model, we specify `include_top=True` to get the final prediction layer of the model and we set `weights='imagenet'` to get the weights pretrained on the ImageNet dataset:

```
inception = tf.keras.applications.InceptionV3(
    include_top=True, weights='imagenet')
model = tf.keras.models.Model(inception.inputs, inception.output)
```

Now, given an image, we can create explanations for the Inception model's prediction by creating a `LimeImageExplainer` object and then calling the `explain_instance` method. The following code block shows how to do this:

```
explainer = lime_image.LimeImageExplainer()
explanation = explainer.explain_instance(image.astype('double'),
                                         inception.predict,
                                         top_labels=20,
                                         hide_color=0,
                                         num_features=5)
```

Most of the parameters in this code block are self-explanatory. The last two, however, are worth mentioning. Firstly, the parameter `hide_color` indicates that we'll turn off superpixel regions by replacing them with gray pixels. The parameter `num_features` indicates how many features to use in the explanation. Fewer features lead to more simple, understandable explanations. However, for more complex models it may be necessary to keep this value large (the default is `num_features=100000`).

To visualize the explanations for this example, we then call `get_image_and_mask` on the resulting explanation. This is shown in the following code block; see the LIME notebook (*https://oreil.ly/jQGJd*) in the book repository for the full code for this example:

```
temp, mask = explanation.get_image_and_mask(explanation.top_labels[0],
                                            positive_only=True,
                                            num_features=20,
                                            hide_rest=True)
plt.imshow(mark_boundaries(temp, mask))
plt.show()
```

The result is shown in Figure 4-26, which highlights the superpixel regions that most positively contributed to the prediction "sulfur-crested cockatoo."

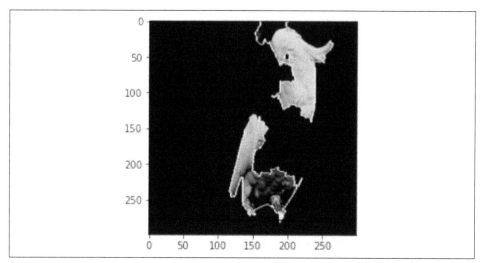

Figure 4-26. LIME uses a linear model trained on perturbations of the original input image to determine which superpixel regions were most influential for the complex model's prediction.

It is also possible to see which superpixel regions provide a negative contribution as well. To do this, set `positive_only` to `False`. This produces the output image as shown in Figure 4-27. The regions that positively contribute to the prediction are in green, while the regions that negatively influence the prediction are in red.

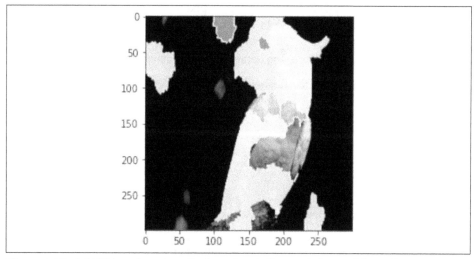

Figure 4-27. A LIME explanation. Regions that influenced the model are shown as a heatmap, with more influential regions having a deeper color, where green contributed positively to the classification, and red contributed negatively. (Print readers can see the color image at https://oreil.ly/xai-fig-4-27.)

This results in a segmented map of the image that is weighted according to how strongly that region influenced the model's prediction. Unlike Shapley values, there are no bounds or guarantees on the values of the region. For example, LIME could conceivably weight multiple regions as highly influential.

Unfortunately, LIME's elegance in generating weightings by turning regions of the image on and off is also its downfall. Since the perturbed images remove entire areas from the prediction, it effectively is shifting the model's attention to what remains visible in the image. In effect, LIME is asking the model not to do a "limited" prediction of the original image, but to look at an entirely new image. However, by not holistically perturbing the entire image, like Integrated Gradients, it is possible that learned concepts in the model are no longer activated. We are asking the model to tell us how it would predict the image by looking at how predictions change only with respect to one feature value and assuming that comparing across different features will result in something akin to how the model made its original prediction. This can sometimes lead to nonsensical explanations, as shown in Figure 4-28.

Figure 4-28. An example of how LIME's perturbation approach can lead to what seem to be nonsensical explanations. In the image of the goldfinch, there is a large portion of the background (nearly as much as the bird itself) contributing to the prediction. In the image of the cockatoo, we also see the background having a positive influence on the model, while parts of the bird have a negative influence as well. (Print readers can see the color image at https://oreil.ly/xai-fig-4-28.)

One way to address this problem is to adjust the parameters of the segmentation step: with more fine-grained segments, the less likely those superpixels will contribute to the image prediction. Ultimately, as with all implementations, it's important to be aware of this artifact both when implementing LIME as a technique and when interpreting the results.

As a further example of this, we used LIME on a nonnatural dataset, the PlantVillage dataset (*https://oreil.ly/1zVju*), which contains images of plant leaves with disease and tries to predict the type of disease. These images feature a combination of a very natural image (plant leaves) within a much more structured environment (interior lighting, monochrome background). The model used, Schuler (*https://oreil.ly/5hoWG*), was highly accurate, with an overall prediction accuracy of 99.8%. We also compared the LIME explanations to another, slightly less accurate model, Yosuke (*https://oreil.ly/8UzPG*).

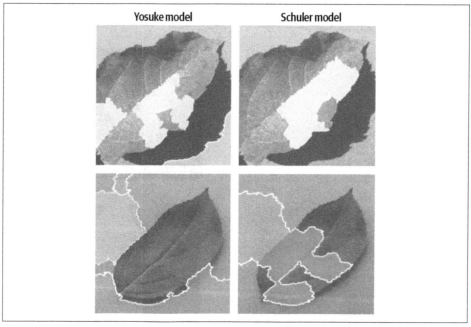

Figure 4-29. Examples of using LIME to explain the classifications between two different models. (Print readers can see the color image at https://oreil.ly/xai-fig-4-29.)

As you can see in the examples in Figure 4-29, LIME has determined that the backgrounds of the images are some of the most influential areas in the prediction. Given that the background is the same for all images in the dataset, this seems highly unlikely to be what is the cause for predictions!

Guided Backpropagation and Guided Grad-CAM

Here's what you need to know about Guided Backprop (often abbreviated this way) and Guided Grad-CAM:

- Guided Backprop builds on DeConvNets, which examines the interior layers of a convolution network.

- Guided Backprop corresponds to the gradient explanation, setting negative gradient entries to zero while backpropagating through a ReLU unit.

- Guided Grad-CAM combines the output of Grad-CAM and Guided Backprop through element-wise product to produce sharper visualizations in the saliency maps.

Pros	Cons
• Guided Backprop creates a sharper and more fine-grained visualization of saliency attribution maps. • Guided Grad-CAM saliency maps localize relevant regions but also highlight fine-grained pixel detail.	• Some evidence suggests that Guided Backprop and its variants fail basic "sanity" checks and show minimal sensitivity to model parameter randomization tests and data randomization tests.[a]

[a] Julius Adebayo et al., "Sanity Checks for Saliency Maps," arXiv, 2020, *https://arxiv.org/pdf/1810.03292.pdf*.

As we've seen throughout this chapter, the gradients of a neural network are a useful tool for measuring how information propagates through a model to eventually create a prediction. The idea is that by measuring the gradients through backpropagation, you can highlight those pixels or pixel regions that contributed most to the model's decision. Despite this intuitive approach, in practice the results of saliency maps that rely solely on gradient information can be very noisy and difficult to interpret. Guided Backprop also relies on model gradients to produce a saliency map but modifies the backpropagation step slightly in how it handles the ReLU nonlinearities.

Guided Backprop and DeConvNets

The technique of Guided Backprop is closely related to an earlier explainability method called DeConvNets. We'll start by describing how DeConvNets work first, then see how Guided Backprop improves upon that approach. As the name suggests, DeConvNets are built upon deconvolution layers, also known as transposed convolutions. You can think of a deconvolution as an inverse of a convolution layer, its job is to "undo" the operation of a convolution layer. Figure 4-30 shows the typical architecture of a DeConvNet.

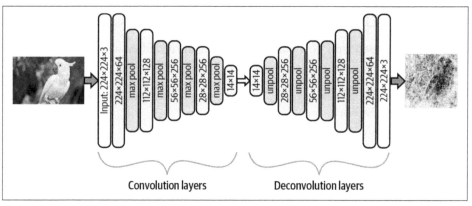

Figure 4-30. A typical deconvolution network with a VGG-16 backbone. The DeConv-Net architecture starts with the usual convolution and max pooling layers, followed by deconvolution and unpooling layers.

As you can see from the figure, the DeConvNet architecture starts with a usual convolution network. Each convolutional layer passes a kernel over the input channels and calculates an output based on the weights of the filter. The size of the output of a convolution layer is determined by the kernel size, the padding, and the stride. For example, if you have an input tensor with shape (5,5) and a convolution layer with kernel size 3×3, stride set to 2, and zero padding, the output will be a tensor of shape (2,2), as shown on the left in Figure 4-31. The nine values in the base (5,5) tensor are aggregated as a linear combination to produce the single value in the resulting (2,2) tensor. If the input has multiple channels, the convolution is applied to each channel.

The second part of the DeConvNet is the deconvolution (or transposed convolution) layers. DeConvNets are similar to convolutional networks but work in reverse (reversing filters, reversing pooling, etc.) so that they reconstruct the spatial resolution of the original input tensor. There are two components to the DeConvNet: the deconvolution and the unpooling layers. We'll discuss how the deconvolution layers work first. The deconvolution also uses a convolution filter but enforces additional padding both outside and within the input values to reconstruct the tensor with larger shape. For the convolution step we just described, the deconvolution maps the (2,2) tensor back to a tensor of shape (5,5), as shown in the image on the right in Figure 4-31. The deconvolution filter has size 3×3. In order to upsample the (2,2) tensor to a tensor of shape (5,5), we add additional padding on the outside and between input values (in red in Figure 4-31).

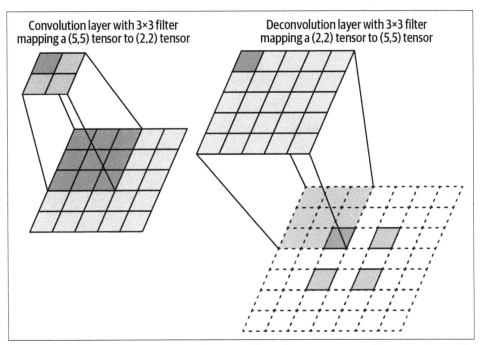

Figure 4-31. A deconvolution layer, shown on the right, reconstructs the original spatial resolution of the input to a convolution layer, shown on the left.

The next component of the DeConvNet to discuss are the unpooling layers. The max pooling layers of a convolution network pass a filter over the input and record only the maximum of all values in the filter as the output. By nature, max aggregation loses a lot of information. To perform unpooling, we need to remember the position where the maximum value occurred in the original max pooling filter. These locations are called switch variables. When performing unpooling, we place the max value from max pooling back in its original position and leave the rest of the values in the filter as zero, as shown in Figure 4-32.

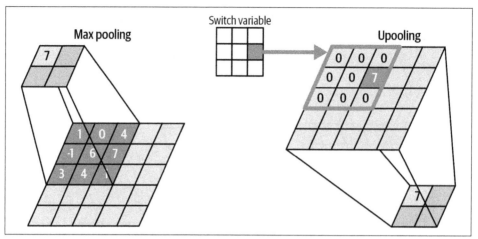

Figure 4-32. When reversing a max pooling layer using "unpooling," the switch variable keeps track of where the max value was located.

The idea of using DeConvNets as an explainability method is to visualize the internal activation layers of a trained CNN by "undoing" the convolution blocks of a CNN using deconvolution layers block by block. Ultimately, the DeConvNet maps the filter of an activation layer back to the original image space, allowing you to find patterns in the images that caused that given filter activation to be high.

 Applying a convolution and max pooling causes some information of the original input tensor to be lost. This is because the convolution filter is aggregating values and the max pooling returns only one value from the entire filter, dropping the rest. The deconvolution reverses the convolutions step but it is an imperfect reconstruction of the original tensor.

The method of Guided Backpropagation is similar to DeConvNets. The difference is in how Guided Backprop handles backpropagation of the gradient through the ReLU activation functions. A DeConvNet only backpropagates positive signals; that is, it sets all negative signals from the backward pass to zero. The idea is that we are only interested in what image features an activation layer detects, not the rest, so we only focus on positive values. This is done by multiplying the backward pass by a binary mask so that only positive values are preserved. In Guided Backprop, you also restrict just the positive values of the input to a layer. So, a binary mask is applied both for the backward pass *and* the forward pass. This means there are more zero values in the final output, but it leads to sharper saliency maps and more fine-grained visualizations.

Here the name "Guided" indicates that this method uses information from the forward pass in addition to the backward pass to create a saliency map. The forward pass information helps to guide the deconvolution. This is similar in spirit to how Guided Integrated Gradients differs from vanilla Integrated Gradients in that it uses information about the baseline and the input to guide the path when computing a line integral.

Guided Grad-CAM

Guided Grad-CAM combines the best of both Grad-CAM and Guided Backprop. As we saw in the section on Grad-CAM, one of the problems with Grad-CAM was that the coarse heatmap produced from the activation layers must be upsampled so that it can be compared against the original input image. This upsampling and the subsequent smoothing leads to a lower-resolution heatmap. The original authors of Grad-CAM proposed Guided Grad-CAM as a way to combine the high-resolution output from Guided Backprop with the class-specific gradient information obtained from Grad-CAM alone. This doesn't alleviate all of the concerns with Grad-CAM since it still relies on the output of the Grad-CAM technique, which has some fundamental concerns (see "Grad-CAM" on page 114 for more in-depth discussion on this), but it is an improvement. Guided Grad-CAM combines Grad-CAM and Guided Backprop by taking an element-wise product of both outputs, as shown in Figure 4-33.

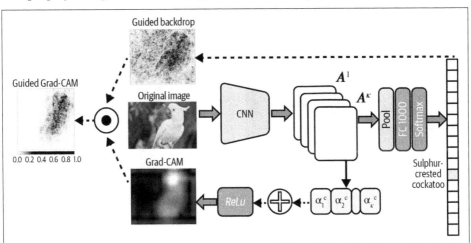

Figure 4-33. Guided Grad-CAM combines the output of Grad-CAM and Guided Back-propagation by taking the element-wise product. This produces a visualization.

Both Guided Backprop and Guided Grad-CAM have easy-to-use implementations available in the Captum library (*https://captum.ai*). Let's look at an example to see how these techniques are implemented in code. Captum is built on PyTorch, so let's start by loading an Inception v3 model that has been pretrained on the ImageNet dataset. This is done in the following code block (see the Guided Backprop notebook (*https://oreil.ly/0NuAh*) in this book's GitHub repository for the full code for these examples):

```
import torch
model = torch.hub.load('pytorch/vision:v0.10.0',
                       'inception_v3',
                       pretrained=True)
model.eval()
```

In this code block, `model.eval()` tells PyTorch that we're using the model for inference (i.e., evaluation), not for training. To create attributions using Guided Backprop, only a couple lines of code are required. First, we create our `GuidedBackProp` attribution object by passing the Inception model we previously created, then we call the `attribute` method passing the input example (as a batch of one) and the target class ID that we want to create explanations for. Here we set `target=top5_catid[0]` to use the top predicted class for the given input image, as shown in the following code block:

```
gbp = GuidedBackprop(model)
# Computes Guided Backprop attribution scores for class 89 (cockatoo)
gbp_attribution = gbp.attribute(input_batch, target=top5_catid[0])
```

This returns an attribution mask that we can then visualize using Captum's visualization library. The result is shown in Figure 4-34.

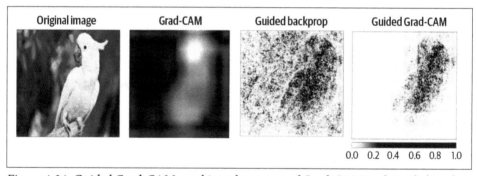

Figure 4-34. Guided Grad-CAM combines the output of Grad-CAM and Guided Backprop by taking an element-wise product of the output of the two methods.

You can implement Grad-CAM using the Captum library in a very similar way. Remember, Grad-CAM works by creating a coarse heatmap from the internal activation layers of the CNN model. These internal activations can be taken from any of the convolution layers of the model. So, when implementing Grad-CAM you specify which convolution layer to use for creating the heatmap. Similarly, for Guided Grad-CAM you specify which layer of the model as well. This is shown in the following code block. When creating the `GuidedGradCam` object, we pass the model as well as the layer `model.Mixed_7c`; this is the last convolution layer of the Inception v3 model:

```
from captum.attr import GuidedGradCam

guided_gc = GuidedGradCam(model, model.Mixed_7c)
ggc_attribution = guided_gc.attribute(
input_batch, target=top5_catid[0])
```

Once we have the attributions, we can visualize the result using Captum's visualization library as before. See the Guided Backprop notebook (*https://oreil.ly/0NuAh*) in the GitHub repository for the full code for this example.

Summary

Computer vision models have critical applications in a wide range of contexts, from healthcare and security to manufacturing and agriculture. Explainability is essential for debugging a model's predictions and assuring a model isn't learning spurious correlations in the data. In this chapter, we looked into various explainability techniques that are used when working with image data.

Loosely speaking, explanation and attribution methods for computer vision models can be fit into a few broad categories: backpropagation methods, perturbation methods, methods that leverage the internal state of the model, and methods that combine different approaches. The explainability techniques we discussed in this chapter are representative examples of these categories, and each method has their own pros and cons.

Integrated Gradients and its many variations fall in the category of back-propagation techniques. XRAI combines Integrated Gradients with segmentation-based masking to determine regions of the image that are most important in the model's prediction. By oversegmenting the image and aggregating smaller regions of importance into larger regions based on attribution scores, this produces more human-relatable saliency maps instead of pixel-level attributions obtained via Integrated Gradients alone. Methods like Grad-CAM and Grad-CAM++ also rely on gradients, but they leverage the internal state of the model. More specifically, Grad-CAM uses the class-activation maps of the internal convolutional layers of the model to create a heatmap of influential regions for an input image.

LIME is a model-agnostic approach that treats the model as opaque and determines pixels that are relevant to the model's prediction by perturbing input pixel values. These methods use gradients of the model to create saliency maps (also called sensitivity maps or pixel attribution maps) to represent regions of an image that are particularly important for the model's final classification. Lastly, we discussed Guided Backpropagation and Guided Grad-CAM, which combine different approaches. Guided Grad-CAM combines Guided Backprop and Grad-CAM using an element-wise product, getting the best of both methods, and addresses some of the problems that arise when using Grad-CAM.

In the next chapter, we'll look into explainability techniques that are commonly used for text-based models and how some of the techniques that we've already seen can be adapted to work in the domain of natural language.

## CHAPTER 5

Explainability for Text Data

Language models play a central role in modern-day deep learning use cases and the field of natural language processing (NLP) has advanced rapidly, especially over the last few years. NLP is focused on understanding how human language works and is at the heart of applications such as machine translation, information retrieval, sentiment analysis, text summarization, and question answering. The models built for these applications rely on text data to understand how human language works, and many of the deep learning architectures commonly used today, like LSTMs (long short-term memory), attention, and transformer networks, were developed specifically to handle the nuances and difficulties that arise when working with text.

Perhaps the most significant of these advances is the transformer architecture, introduced in the paper "Attention Is All You Need."[1] Transformers rely on the attention mechanism and are particularly well-equipped for handling sequential text data. This is partly because of their computational efficiencies and because they are better able to maintain context since text is processed as a whole rather than sequentially. Soon after transformers hit the scene, BERT, which stands for Bidirectional Encoder Representations from Transformers, was introduced and it beat all the GLUE[2] (General Language Understanding Evaluation) benchmarks for NLU (natural language understanding) tasks ranging from sentiment classification, textual entailment, text similarity, and grammatical correctness. Since BERT, other record-breaking, transformer-based models have emerged, leading to better and better (and increasingly larger and larger) language models such as OpenAI's GPT2 and GPT3, Google's T5, DeepMind's Gopher, and more recently PaLM, a 540 billion parameter

---

[1] Ashish Vaswani et al., "Attention Is All You Need," *Advances in Neural Information Processing Systems* 30 (2017).

[2] For more information on GLUE, see *https://gluebenchmark.com*.

dense decoder transformer model that is capable of mathematical reasoning, code writing, and even explaining jokes.[3]

With these impressive developments, there is an increased desire to better explain how these models work. Explainable NLP has become a strong focus in the current research community aimed at better understanding how these large language models work and what they are learning. Of course, there is an important distinction to be made between standard, day-to-day text models used by the typical ML practitioner and these state-of-the-art (SOTA) models like T5, GPT3, or PaLM. Models like T5, GPT3, and PaLM are the AI equivalent of a Formula One racing car,[4] and indeed, many of these models are outside the realm of the typical practitioner. These models train for weeks on end and require compute resources that the average practitioner or business does not have access to.

However, their underlying technology has become commonplace and, with easy-to-use implementations available in the Hugging Face library, many of these advanced architectures aren't so out of reach. In fact, it's likely model architectures like BERT, XLNet, and GPT2 will find their way into your day-to-day toolkit, if they haven't already. Just as we have seen when training image models, there is immense value in leveraging a pretrained version of the large language models either directly or for fine-tuning on a more task-specific use case.

The focus of this chapter is to discuss commonly used explainability techniques and understand how they are applied when working with text data. The goal here is not to explain how complex architectures like T5 or transformers work in general; instead, we'll focus more on text models more closely aligned with the general ML practitioner. In this chapter, we'll introduce some new techniques but also revisit some of the techniques that we saw in previous chapters, such as LIME and Integrated Gradients. We'll show how these familiar methods can be adapted to work for text data due to the unique constraints of building language models. We'll also look into some of the tools that have been developed by the community to help explain text models.

Overview of Building Models with Text

In a way, natural language models are no different than models built on tabular or image data. As when building any machine learning model, features are extracted from the data and preprocessed for training. Oftentimes a deep neural network or some other advanced model architecture is used. The model's output prediction is compared against the true label and the weights are updated via a variant of gradient

---

3 See "Pathways Language Model (PaLM): Scaling to 540 Billion Parameters for Breakthrough Performance" (*https://oreil.ly/GnH5H*) on the Google AI blog.

4 See this recent tweet (*https://oreil.ly/2tQWH*) from Hugging Face cofounder and CEO Clement Delangue.

descent through backpropagation. When it comes to natural language models, however, the raw data is text, so special tricks and techniques are needed to handle the nuances of a textual dataset. In fact, because the techniques for working with text are so specialized, NLP is an active research area in its own right and there are a number of courses and specializations designed to specifically address how to work with natural language models.

In this section, we'll discuss at a high level the main ideas and key aspects to have in mind when building text models. This will also allow us to set up common terminology and introduce concepts that we'll need later. As we proceed through the chapter, we'll introduce other more advanced treatments, but it's important to keep these initial steps in mind because they can affect the explainability of the model downstream.

Tokenization

The first step to building a text-based model is to preprocess the text data into a format that can be used by the model. Machine learning models are numeric machines so, one way or another, text needs to be converted into a numeric quantity. Perhaps the most basic or naive way to convert a word into a vector is through one-hot encoding. One-hot encoding is a preprocessing step in which categorical variables are converted into a sparse vector consisting of a single one as a placeholder for a given categorical value, with all other indices set to zero (e.g., [0,0,1,0,0]). In the text setting, the words are the categorical variables. This poses a problem because our vocabulary could easily be on the order of tens or hundreds of thousands of words. This means that one-hot encoding maps a word like *cockatoo* to a vector of shape 100,000 with all zeros and a single one representing the word *cockatoo*. Figure 5-1 shows an example of one-hot encoding to a sentence of words.

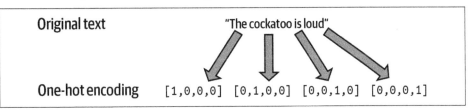

Figure 5-1. Transforming the sentence "The cockatoo is loud" into a sequence of one-hot encoded vectors. Here, the one-hot encoding is for a vocabulary of just those four words; in reality, the vocabulary could easily be on the order of tens or hundreds of thousands of words.

For some simple models and use cases, taking a vocabulary to be the 10,000 most frequently used words in a corpus and an "out-of-vocabulary" bucket for everything else works well enough. But more sophisticated models, in particular transformer models, require a more comprehensive vocabulary. There is a bit of a trade-off.

The larger the vocabulary, the more expressive the model can be in learning the relationship between a wide variety of words. However, a larger vocabulary also leads to more sparse one-hot encoded vectors.

So, what should our vocabulary be? There are more than 500,000 words in the English language. The goal is to find the most meaningful, and preferably the smallest, representation that will make sense for our model. Should we include punctuation? Should we include rarely used words like *crapulous* or *ostensibly*? Should we include words from Old English like *ye Olde Worlde*? Or more recently, how do we deal with emoticons and emojis, like "⁻_(ツ)_/⁻" and "🪦"? Should we split up word pairs like *Costa Rica* into two separate words *Costa* and *Rica*, or does it deserve its own token? How do we treat two words with a common root, like *chirp* and *chirping*? What about misspellings that are bound to arise, like *recieve* instead of *receive*? Or words that are spelled correctly but used in context incorrectly, like *affect* versus *effect* or *surreptitious* versus *serendipitous*. What if our model is multilingual? How do we incorporate the vocabulary of all the languages we want our model to accommodate? Should our vocabulary now include all languages and their idiosyncrasies? Surely there is a sweet spot.

This is where tokenization comes in. Given a character sequence (e.g., a sentence) and a defined document unit (e.g., a movie review), *tokenization* is the task of splitting up the character sequence into essential pieces, called *tokens*, and discarding irrelevant characters. Tokenization is at the forefront of any NLP pipeline when preprocessing text for machine learning. It is the translator from human-readable text into a numeric categorical representation that the machine learning model can use. If you've had experience working with natural language models, it's likely you are already familiar with tokenization. If not, or if you've forgotten the details, we'll quickly discuss the basics here. As we'll see in this chapter, the artifacts of tokenization often appear in the final explanations we may receive and even affect how some techniques are implemented. Let's begin by discussing what tokens are and how they're used in natural language processing.

Tokens are integer representations of a word or word piece and can be used to split a sentence into words or subwords. A subword is obtained by breaking down a word into smaller meaningful words. For example, the word *cockatoos* or *let's* is broken down into the subwords *cockatoo* and *s* or *let* and *'s*, respectively. You train a tokenizer just as you might train a large neural network. Of course, instead of learning parameter weights, you're passing over the entire dataset to determine which tokens to use and how to split words or sentences in your dataset. There are a number of popular tokenization algorithms, and determining an efficient and effective tokenization is an active area of current research.

To illustrate the general approach to tokenization, we'll discuss one of the most common algorithms: byte pair encoding (BPE), which builds a tokenizer vocabulary from an alphabet of bytes. Other commonly used tokenization algorithms are WordPiece, Unigram, and SentencePiece.

To train a BPE tokenizer, you start by tokenizing all characters in the entire training corpus. Then, passing over the dataset, you identify common pairs of tokens and merge the pairs into a single token. For example, after seeing *m*, *o*, *v*, *i*, and *e* enough times, the tokenizer will merge these five tokens into a single token *movie*. You iteratively repeat this process until the number of tokens in the vocabulary reaches the size you want. As with most things in machine learning, there is a trade-off when choosing the size of the vocabulary. If the vocabulary size is too small, then the vocabulary is too coarse, and different words may end up being tokenized as the same. However, increasing the vocabulary size too much increases the computational cost unnecessarily. A BPE tokenizer is nice because you don't have to pre-prescribe words in your vocabulary, and you don't need special tokens for unknown words. Word tokens are learned by passing through the data, and BPE ensures that the most common words are represented as a single token, while rare words are broken down into subwords.

Transfer learning is a technique that allows you to take advantage of the learned embeddings of a model that was trained on a large dataset. It provides an advantage over training from scratch. Just as transfer learning leverages pretrained weights of a model, pretrained tokenizers are a useful resource for the average practitioner. The quality of your model is heavily dependent on the quality of your tokenizer vocabulary, so it's to your benefit to take advantage of a tokenizer that was pretrained on a corpus likely much larger than yours. Luckily, Hugging Face has an entire library of pretrained tokenizers that can easily be loaded and incorporated into your ML workflows. For example, the BERT tokenizer is a class inside the Hugging Face transformer library and can be loaded with just a few lines of code:

```
from transformers import BertTokenizer
tokenizer = BertTokenizer.from_pretrained("bert-base-uncased")
```

BERT was trained using the WordPiece tokenization algorithm. With the tokenizer loaded, we can then easily tokenize a sample text using the `tokenize` method and convert the tokens to integer IDs, as shown in the following code block and illustrated in Figure 5-2. These IDs can then be used to create embeddings for training the model, which we'll discuss in the next section:

```
sample_text = "If you like the original, you'll love this movie."
tokens = tokenizer.tokenize(sample_text)
ids = tokenizer.convert_tokens_to_ids(tokens)
```

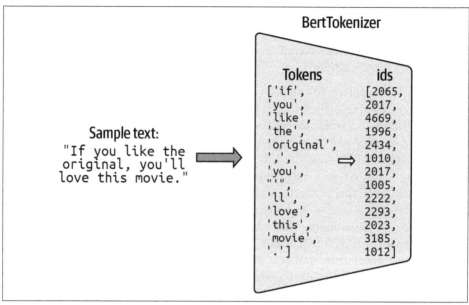

Figure 5-2. The BERT tokenizer is our translator from human-readable text into a numerical encoding that our machine learning model can use. Words and word pieces are first tokenized, then converted to integer IDs before being passed to the model.

Word Embeddings and Pretrained Embeddings

After tokenization, the words of our text dataset can be represented by an integer ID, and sentences can be represented as sequences of integers. This is only half the battle, however. The next step is to convert these tokens into a meaningful representation. Although the tokens are numeric, they don't have meaningful magnitude; the tokens are merely numeric placeholders. Converting each token into a vector creates a meaningful numeric representation of the word that can be processed by the model.

Essentially, the IDs are categorical features. Each ID represents a single token in our vocabulary. As with any categorical feature, these IDs must be encoded before being passed to the model. If the features don't have any relationship with one another, then one-hot encoding is a common approach. However, these categorical IDs represent words in our corpus (or, more specifically, tokens in our vocabulary), and there are close relations between some words. So, a naive one-hot encoding won't work. Another issue with one-hot encoding is the high cardinality of our vocabulary. Our tokenizer vocabulary could consist of tens or hundreds of thousands of tokens. One-hot encoding the token IDs would lead to very sparse tensors and really inhibit the learning process.

Instead, you typically use an embedding layer to encode token IDs. A *word token embedding* converts the categorical ID representing a given word token into a dense vector. This essentially turns the sequence of token IDs into a sequence of dense vectors. First, the sentence is broken down into word tokens, then tokens are converted into categorical IDs, and finally the IDs are mapped to an embedding space, as shown in Figure 5-3. The embeddings are a mathematical vector representation that captures different aspects of the data so that similar words are mapped to points that are close to each other. For example, in Figure 5-3, each word is mapped to a vector in 8-dimensional Euclidean space. The sequence of IDs is just a placeholder for each word token. This sequence of dense vectors in the embedding space is ultimately what is passed to the model during training.

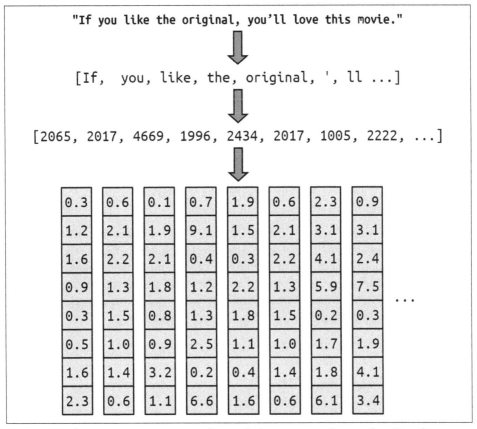

Figure 5-3. The movie review text is tokenized, then converted into token IDs, then passed through an embedding layer. The resulting sequence of dense vectors is then passed to the model for training.

To add an embedding layer in Keras, for example, you specify the embedding dimension for the output vector space, as shown in the following code. This makes the embedding layer a component of the network, and the weights for mapping from the categorial token IDs to the word embedding is then learned during the training process (see the notebook (*https://oreil.ly/lotg0*) in this book's GitHub repository for the full code):

```
model = tf.keras.models.Sequential()
model.add(
    tf.keras.layers.Embedding(input_dim=vocabulary_size,
                output_dim=embedding_dim,
                input_length=MAX_SEQUENCE_LENGTH)
)
```

As usual with deep learning, it's a good idea to leverage a pretrained embedding whenever possible. TensorFlow makes this easy with TensorFlow Hub (*https://oreil.ly/GniR0*), where there are many pretrained text embeddings that can be used. We can load Google's neural network language model (NNLM) architecture that has been pretrained on the English Google News 7B corpus with just a couple lines of code:

```
import tensorflow_hub as hub
embedding = "https://tfhub.dev/google/nnlm-en-dim50/2"
hub_layer = hub.KerasLayer(embedding, input_shape=[],
                    dtype=tf.string, trainable=True)
```

Given a string of text, this `hub_layer` outputs a 50-dimensional dense vector that can be used for training a text classification model. In fact, we use this embedding to train a sentiment analysis classifier on the IMDB movie review dataset. See this book's GitHub repository for the full code. We'll use the trained model to illustrate some of the explainability methods we discuss in this chapter.

Now that we've reviewed some of the basics of working with text data, let's now turn our attention to explainability methods. Since explainability methods rely on model features and feature importances, it's helpful to keep in mind these tokenization and embedding preprocessing steps when interpreting the results of an explainability technique. Also, we'll see how some techniques we've already discussed, like LIME and Integrated Gradients, are applied in the context of text data.

LIME

What you need to know about LIME:

- LIME stands for *local interpretable model-agnostic explanations.*
- When working with given text, LIME perturbs a given example text by randomly removing words.
- The cosine distance is used to compute proximity measure between the input instance and the sampled perturbations.
- LIME performs better with around 1,000 perturbations, especially for longer inputs. Beyond that, there isn't much improvement.

Pros	Cons
• LIME is model agnostic, so it can be applied to any machine learning model in any framework.	• The proximity measure uses a kernel smoothing that can be very sensitive to the kernel width. Slight modifications to the kernel width can lead to quite different explanations.
• This is an easy-to-implement Python package with easy-to-interpret visualizations.	• LIME provides an explanation based on a linear approximation of the local behavior of a model. It does not work as well for highly nonlinear models.
• LIME is available in the Language Interpretability Tool (LIT).	• LIME doesn't take into account the sequential nature of the text data, and repeated words in a sentence are treated as a single feature.
	• The publicly available Python package implementation `lime` is only for text classification.

We already saw how to use LIME for image data in Chapter 4. One useful aspect of this technique is that it can also be applied to text (or tabular) data. However, it's important to understand how the LIME algorithm changes when working with text as opposed to images. LIME is a post hoc, local perturbation technique, so it provides interpretability for a trained model's prediction on a specific example by measuring how the model's predictions change with small perturbations to the feature inputs. By measuring how the predictions change under these local perturbations, LIME reflects the contribution of each feature of a data sample. More (or less) important feature values will have more (or less) influence on changing the model's predictions.

For images or tabular data, this process is fairly straightforward. Afterall, an image is represented by RGB pixel values, so we can perturb the feature of an image by turning pixel values on or off. In fact, the input image is segmented into interpretable regions or superpixels, and these components are changed to be gray. Similarly in tabular data, for continuous feature values, we can sample values nearby to any given feature value. But the features for a text model are words. How does one perturb or add noise to a word? In fact, this could be achieved in a few ways.

How LIME Works with Text

As we discussed in "Overview of Building Models with Text" on page 138 the word pieces of a sentence are represented by a token, which is then mapped to some embedding space. This embedding space essentially represents each word as a k-dimensional vector that can then be perturbed just as a continuous feature value as before by sampling other vectors nearby in the embedding space.

However, this formulation is problematic. LIME uses an exponential smoothing kernel to define a neighborhood of a data instance. The smoothing kernel defines the size of a neighborhood by measuring the proximity of points in relation to the given data instance. The smaller the kernel width, the closer points need to be in order to be considered within the neighborhood, whereas a larger kernel width will include instances farther away in the neighborhood.

However, when working with text, just because a vector is "close" to another in the vector space, this doesn't mean that the perturbed vector also actually represents another word "close" to the input. In fact, most likely it does not! Also, it's known that LIME is very sensitive to the kernel width. It is a subtle but very important hyperparameter when implementing LIME, since modifying the kernel width to be larger or smaller can result in completely different explanations.

Instead, we must go a bit further "upstream" and modify the words directly in a way more akin to the kind of example perturbations that are made when implementing LIME on images. That is, individual words are turned "on" or "off" to create a new, nearby example for inference.

Let's take as an illustration this snippet from an example in the IMDB dataset of 50K movie reviews: "If you like the original, you'll like this movie." This is the beginning of a positive review from the dataset. When passing this example text to the `LimeTextExplainer`, it is modified by replacing words with empty spaces, creating a distribution of nearby examples to pass to the model for prediction (see Figure 5-4).

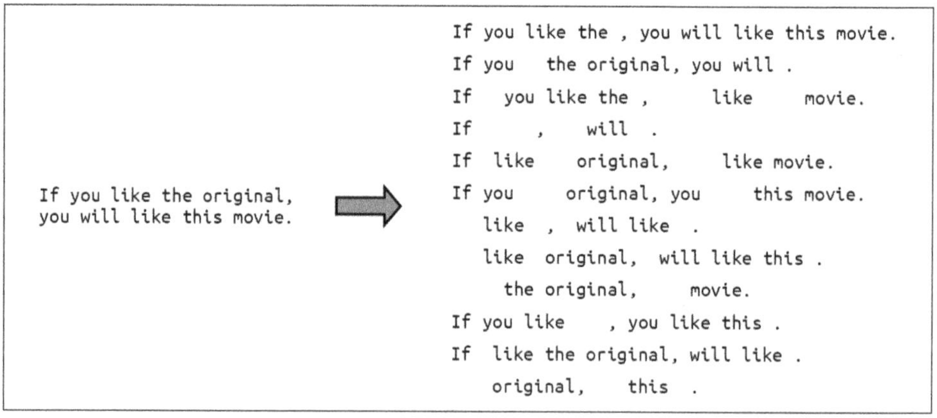

Figure 5-4. Given an input text for explanation, LIME creates new text to test the model predictions by randomly replacing words with spaces.

The next thing to consider when applying the LIME algorithm is how to measure the proximity of the perturbed inputs with the original example instance in question. This proximity is used to weight the generated samples to measure the influence of the features on the model's predictions. The public implementation of LIME uses as default an exponential smoothing kernel that takes the distance of two data instances and returns a proximity measure defined by:

$$\text{proximity}_\kappa\left(x_i, x_j\right) = \sqrt{e^{-d\left(x_i, x_j\right)^2 / \kappa^2}}$$

where κ is the kernel width and d represents a distance metric; e.g., $d(x_i,x_j)$ could be the Euclidean distance between the vectors x_i and x_j.

Choosing the Kernel Width in LIME

One of the most sensitive hyperparameters in applying LIME is the choice of the proximity measure. This is true when applying LIME with text or with images or tabular data as well. This proximity is used to weight the generated samples, so the more nonlinear your model function is, the smaller you want the kernel width to be.

The default for text classification takes the distance to be the cosine distance and sets the kernel width at 25. However, the Python package for LIME[5] allows for users to modify the distance function d and the kernel width κ. You'll probably want to experiment with different values, though, and compare LIME explanations across different hyperparameters.

In the field of text mining there are various ways to measure the distance between two sentences; for example, the Euclidean distance, the cosine distance, Jaccard similarity, or a measure related to the proportion of words missing from the original. The default distance in LIME is the cosine distance that computes the cosine of the angle between the two sentences expressed as vectors. The cosine distance of two sentences will range from 0 to 1; the larger the cosine similarity, the more words in common the two sentences have and the more similar they are. It is possible to change the distance metric when implementing LIME, and just as kernel width impacts the LIME explanations, so can the distance metric.

LIME then trains an interpretable model such as a logistic regression on these examples weighted by the proximity measure of the sampled instances. The weights of this linear model indicate the feature importance for each word. One nice thing about LIME is that it can be used as an interpretability technique for any model. The implementation treats the model as an opaque box.

Let's see how this works in practice for a text classification model trained on the IMDB dataset. Each example in this dataset is a movie review, not preprocessed in any way, and the corresponding label. The label is an integer value where 0 is a negative review, and 1 is a positive review. We'll train a TensorFlow model and use the `LimeTextExplainer` to explain a prediction by calling the `explain_instance` method as shown in the following code (see the notebook (*https://oreil.ly/lotg0*) in this book's GitHub repository for the full code):

---

5 See *https://github.com/marcotcr/lime* for more information on LIME.

```
from lime.lime_text import LimeTextExplainer
explainer = LimeTextExplainer(class_names=['negative', 'positive'])
sample_text = "If you like the original, you will love this movie."
exp = explainer.explain_instance(text_instance=sample_text,
                                 classifier_fn=predict_prob,
                                 num_features=10)
```

The argument num_features indicates how many features (i.e., words) we'll use for the explanation and the classifier_fn is LIME's entry point to our model function. The classifier function must take a list of strings and output a two-dimensional array with prediction probabilities for each class. Since our TensorFlow model was built as a binary classification, we'll wrap our model in a function so that it has the appropriate signature:

```
def predict_prob(texts):
    preds = imdb_model.predict(texts)
    return np.concatenate((preds, 1-preds), axis=1)
```

Since 0 indicates a negative review and 1 indicates a positive review, for a given prediction pred for an example instance we return a tuple (preds, 1-preds). The following code snippet calls predict_prob on the sample text "If you like the original, you will love this movie.", followed by the model's prediction:

```
predict_prob(["If you like the original, you will love this movie."])
> array([[0.04230487, 0.9576951 ]], dtype=float32)
```

Our model is 95% confident that this sample text is a positive review. We can then examine the output of the explainer as a list by calling exp.as_list(label=1) to see which words most contributed to the model's prediction with the target class 1:

```
[('you', 0.184102135),
 ('love', 0.177897292),
 ('will', 0.135323892),
 ('movie', -0.043178052),
 ('original', 0.0382655165),
 ('this', -0.0227692068),
 ('the', 0.01647684757),
 ('If', 0.0088829997),
 ('like', 0.0060883934)]
```

Here the numbers represent the attribution score for each of the features, in this case, words. The absolute value of each score informally represents their relative importance to the model prediction or performance. The positive or negative sign indicates their positive or negative influence on the target class.

For example, the word *love* has an attribution score of 0.178 and the model predicts the target class of 1, that is, a positive movie review. This means the word *love* has a relatively large positive influence on the model predicting this statement as a positive review. On the other hand, the word *movie* has an attribution score of –0.04, which indicates this word has a negative, though relatively small, influence on the model predicting this statement as a positive review.

When calling the method `as_list(...)`, we include the argument `label=1` to tell the explainer that we want attribution scores that contributed to the positive label. This is because our model predicted the positive class for this input. If instead we wanted to list attribution scores for the negative label class, we would have used `exp.as_list(label=0)`.

In the way LIME is implemented for text data, each word in a sentence is treated as an individual feature. LIME itself does not take into account the sequential nature of the words in a sentence. This means that repeated words have a single feature importance. For example, in the sentence "If you like the original, you will love this movie.", the word *you* appears twice in the sentence. However, their importance is measured in aggregate just once. Be aware as this can cause misleading results.

Here we see that *you* has the strongest positive influence on the model, followed by *love*. The attribution for *you* is perhaps a bit misleading, but the positive attribution for *love* makes sense. Overall, the top three features with positive influence are *you*, *will*, *love*, which, when viewed together, makes sense.

There are also visualizations that can be used to represent the feature attributions, and we can display these in the notebook as well. For example, the method `as_pyplot_figure(label=1)` visualizes the attributions for each feature of the local example as green and red bars on a bar plot. Green indicates a positive influence for the model prediction, and red indicates negative influence on the model prediction. The result for this example is shown in Figure 5-5.

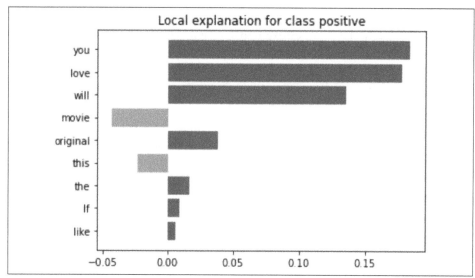

Figure 5-5. Local explanations can be visualized as a pyplot figure with green bars indicating positive influence for the model prediction (in this case the positive class) and red bars indicating negative influence for the model prediction.

We can also visualize these results within the notebook using `exp.show_in_note book()` to see the influence of each feature value, as in Figure 5-6, both as a bar chart and as a heatmap overlaid on the original text.

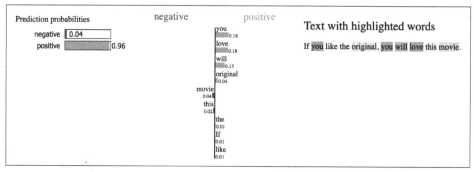

Figure 5-6. For this text example, the model predicts a positive sentiment. The LIME visualizations show that the words in the text that most contributed to this prediction are you, will, and love. (Print readers can see the color image at https://oreil.ly/xai-fig-5-6.)

Gradient x Input

Here's what you need to know about Gradient x Input:

- It's one of the simplest attribution methods, relying on gradients of the machine learning model. Gradient x Input can be referred to as "Grad cross Input," "Grad times input," or "Grad dot Input."
- Grad x Input is a saliency method and produces saliency scores proportional to the dot product of the gradient and the input.
- Saliency scores for word tokens can be positive or negative, indicating the influence that token had on the model prediction.
- Grad x Input was initially proposed as a technique to improve the sharpness of attribution maps generated by sensitivity analysis.
- Some studies suggest Grad x Input works better for BERT than it does for LSTM, based on its ability to find shortcuts in text classification tasks.[6]

Pros	Cons
• Easy and fast to implement for machine learning libraries like TensorFlow, PyTorch, and JAX; it can be applied to any differentiable model. • Gradient x Input has been shown to be the best performing explainability technique for transformers. • It is available in the Language Interpretability Tool.	• The gradients of a deep neural network can be, and typically are, noisy and sensitive to functions inputs. • Gradient x Input should be used in conjunction with other gradient-based techniques and especially sensitivity methods, like Grad L2-norm (also discussed in this section). • It requires differentiability of the ML model.

Gradients x Input (often referred to simply as Grad x Input) is a type of gradient-based attribution method. It's a favorite among practitioners because it's fast, easy to implement, and, particularly for transformers, known to perform well across various text classification datasets.[7]

More specifically, Grad x Input is a saliency method of explainability (later in this section, we discuss the difference between saliency and sensitivity methods). When working with text models, the salience scores for a certain word are proportional to the dot product of the word embeddings and the gradient of the model function with respect to that input. This gives a directional score for each input feature (i.e., word token). A positive score can be interpreted as that token having a positive influence on the prediction, while a negative score indicates that the prediction would be stronger if that token was not present.

---

6 Bastings et al., "Will You Find These Shortcuts? A Protocol for Evaluating the Faithfulness of Input Salience Methods for Text Classification," arXiv, 2021, *https://arxiv.org/abs/2111.07367*.

7 Pepa Atanasova et al., "A Diagnostic Study of Explainability Techniques for Text Classification," arXiv, 2020, *https://arxiv.org/pdf/2009.13295.pdf*.

Intuition from Linear Models

Suppose we have a simple linear model to estimate a baby's weight y in pounds based on two input variables: the mother's age x_1 and the duration of the pregnancy in days x_2. Using a linear regression model, we would learn a function:

$$y = w_0 + w_1 x_1 + w_2 x_2 + \epsilon$$

where the w_i's are the model weights and bias and ϵ is the residual error. If we learn through the data model parameters $w_1 = 0.1$ and $w_2 = 0.02$, then we have a clear explanation of the model's predictions using these model weights (to keep things simple, we'll take a zero bias $w_0 = 0$). The attribution for each input feature is simply the partial derivative of the target variable y with respect to the input feature x_i:

$$\text{feature attribution for mother's age} = \frac{\partial y}{\partial x_1} = w_1 = 0.1$$

$$\text{feature attribution for gestation days} = \frac{\partial y}{\partial x_2} = w_2 = 0.02$$

Since the feature attribution for the mother's age is substantially larger than that of gestation days, you might think it's obvious that the mother's age plays a more important role when predicting baby weight using our model.

But let's take an explicit example. Suppose we had a 30-year-old mother who had carried the baby for 40 weeks. In this case, our model would predict a baby weight of 8.6 pounds. Due to the linearity of the model, we can see that the final prediction for the baby weight is explained as the sum of the effect from the two input variables: 3 pounds from the mother's age and 5.6 pounds from the gestation period. That is to say, for this local explanation, we get the following feature attributions:

$$\text{feature attribution for mother's age} = x_1 \cdot \frac{\partial y}{\partial x_1} = (30)(0.1) = 3$$

$$\text{feature attribution for gestation days} = x_2 \cdot \frac{\partial y}{\partial x_2} = (280)(0.02) = 5.6$$

The feature attributions have flipped. Now the more important feature is the gestation period for the pregnancy. We have two possible explanations for the model's prediction and both are based on the gradient of the model function. One involves the gradient alone, and the other involves multiplication of the gradient at the input value.

Both methods described in the example are valid. They illustrate the differences between sensitivity and saliency methods. The first approach involving just the gradient is a sensitivity method. The second method, involving the gradient and the input value, is a saliency method and illustrates exactly the intuition behind the Grad x Input explainability technique we'll discuss in this section.

From Linear to Nonlinear and Text Models

Using the intuition from linear models, we can better appreciate how Grad x Input is defined. The attribution for a feature input is computed by taking the signed gradient of the model prediction function at a given input and multiplying component-wise with the (embedded) input itself.

To make this more precise with an example, suppose we have a text classification model to predict the sentiment of a given review from the IMDB dataset of movie reviews. Let's take the review "If you like the original, you'll love this movie." and suppose our model predicts (correctly) a positive sentiment for this input instance. After tokenizing and embedding the words in the review, we have a sequence of vector embeddings we'll represent by $x_{1:n}$ where $n = 10$ since there are 10 words in the review. If we let f represent the model function, the attribution for the i-th word in the review is given by:

$$\nabla_{x_i} f(x_{1:n}) \cdot x_i$$

The dot product of these two vectors will give a scalar value. This scalar can be positive or negative, depending on the influence the input word embedding x_i has on the model prediction function f.

Grad L2-norm

Grad L2-norm is closely related to Grad x Input. The idea is that we want a single scalar value to provide a relevance score for each feature (word) input. Taking the dot product between the gradient and the input produces such a scalar value. However, there are, of course, other ways to obtain a scalar value. Another commonly used approach is to take the L2-norm. Just as with Grad x Input, we compute the gradient of the neural network with respect to the inputs (note the subscript x in the gradient).

Just as we use auto differentiation for backpropagation during training to update the parameter weights, we can also compute the gradient with respect to the inputs. Thus the Gradient L2-norm indicates how much a change in a word's embedding affects the output of the model. The smaller the gradient, the less sensitive the model function is to small changes in the input. The larger the gradient, the steeper the model function and the more sensitive it is. Figure 5-7 illustrates this idea in one dimension.

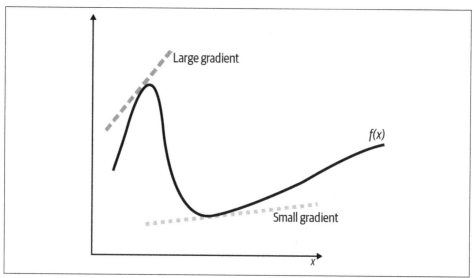

Figure 5-7. In this one-dimensional example, we see that the larger the gradient, the steeper the function. The smaller the gradient, the flatter the function, indicating the function is less sensitive at that input value.

Using the same notion as in the previous section, we can express the Gradient L2-norm as:

$$\nabla_{x_i} f(x_{1:n}) \cdot x_i$$

that is, the L2-norm of the gradient of the model function with respect to the inputs. Recall, the x_i here are the word embeddings. So, the Gradient L2-norm indicates how much a change in a word's embedding affects the output of the model. Note also, in comparison with the Grad x Input, the L2-norm is essentially the dot product of the gradient with itself and so lends itself to a similar interpretation. One caveat of Grad L2-norm is that because it is a norm measure, the saliency value is unsigned and always positive. However, it is still a common technique and often used when working with text.

Comparing sensitivity and saliency methods

There are two broad categories of explainable attribution methods: sensitivity methods and salience methods. A *sensitivity* method describes how the output of the network changes when one or more input features are perturbed. For differentiable models, this can be represented by the derivative or gradient of the prediction function with respect to the input features. This gives a first order Taylor expansion of a nonlinear function so, just as Taylor series are accurate within a small neighborhood of an input, a sensitivity measure for a nonlinear function is only accurate within a very small perturbation. Since Grad L2-norm depends only on the gradient of the model function, it is a sensitivity method.

A *saliency* method, on the other hand, describes the marginal effect of a feature on the model prediction. Grad x Input is a saliency method because the attribution is computed by taking the (signed) partial derivatives of the output with respect to the input and multiplying them feature-wise by the input itself. The saliency score that is produced describes the contributions of the different input variables to the final model output. Thus, saliency methods take into account the input as well as the model gradient when computing the feature attributions.

As the example involving baby weights illustrates, the two methods are equally valid but answer different questions and show that the two attribution methods cannot be directly compared.

Layer Integrated Gradients

Here's what you need to know about Layer Integrated Gradients:

- Layer Integrated Gradients (LIG) is a variation of Integrated Gradients, but it focuses on a single layer of the network instead of input features; LIG provides attributions with respect to layers inputs or outputs.
- Similar to Integrated Gradients, LIG is a gradient-based attribution method.
- The implementation is available using the Captum library.

See also the pros and cons of Integrated Gradients in Chapter 4.

Pros	Cons
• LIG is useful for text to isolate the embedding layer for computing Integrated Gradients. • It can be applied to any differentiable model for any data type, images, text, tabular, etc. • There is an easy and intuitive implementation that even novice practitioners can apply.	• LIG requires differentiability of the model and access to the gradients, so it does not apply well to tree-based models. • The results can be sensitive to hyperparameters or choice of baseline.

As stated above, LIG is a variation on the classic IG method. The need for variation is in how text models are built. As we discussed in the beginning of this chapter, when working with text data, the text must be preprocessed to be fed to a machine learning model. The first step of preprocessing is tokenization. These tokens are then converted to categorical IDs and passed to an embedding layer. These embeddings are numeric vector representations of each word token.

The issue that arises is the step from tokenization to categorical IDs. Integrated Gradients is a gradient-based attribution method, but this step is not differentiable. Of course, there is a natural solution. In order to explain text features via Integrated Gradients, we need to compute the gradients with respect to the embeddings, not the token indices. One solution is to use Layer Integrated Gradients.

A Variation on Integrated Gradients

In Chapter 4, we discussed how the method of Integrated Gradients works for image-based models. At a high level, the method of Integrated Gradients determines feature attributions for a model's prediction by measuring how the model gradient with respect to the feature inputs changes along an integral path in the input feature space. More precisely, this integral path is a straight line from a given baseline to the input example, and the gradients are cumulated (integrated) over the straight-line path. This produces feature attributions for the input features, which in the case of images, can be represented as a saliency map indicating which pixel most contributed to the model's prediction.

The main difference in LIG is that where IG assigns an importance score to the model's input features, Layer Integrated Gradients assigns an importance score to a given layer's inputs (or outputs); i.e., it allows us to apply Integrated Gradients on the interior of the model. Layer Integrated Gradients is a layer attribution where Integrated Gradients is a feature attribution method, as depicted in Figure 5-8.

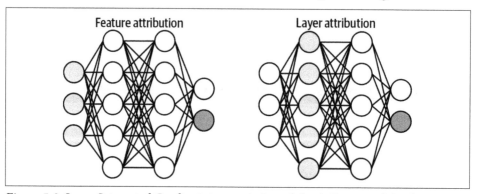

Figure 5-8. Layer Integrated Gradients is a variation of classic Integrated Gradients. They differ in where they measure attributions (the light shaded circles) of the model. For Integrated Gradients, attribution of the model output (the dark shaded circles) is assigned to the features, whereas for Layer Integrated Gradients, the attribution is assigned to internal layers of the model.

The other consideration when implementing Integrated Gradients is the choice of baseline. We saw in Chapter 4 that when using Integrated Gradients for images, the baseline plays an important role. The same is true for text. When working with text, a common baseline is just a sequence of the zero embedding vectors or, at the word level, a sequence of zero tokens. The zero embedding vector is a vector of all zeros with the same dimension of the embedding space. This is the baseline recommended in the original paper (*https://oreil.ly/MSkvi*) on Integrated Gradients.[8] During training, unimportant words tend to have small norms, and since the baseline is meant to represent an information-less feature, the all-zero input vector is a natural choice, even though it doesn't actually represent a valid input for the model in the same way an all-black image would for an image model.

The zero token represents any token or value you would use when padding a sequence. This makes the zero token a good candidate to use as a baseline. For example, when working with the BERT tokenizer, the pad token is simply a zero PAD. Therefore, the baseline sequence for the text "If you like the original, you'll love this movie." would be [CLS, PAD, PAD, PAD, PAD, PAD, PAD, PAD, PAD, PAD, PAD, SEP] or, when converted to integer tokens, [101, 0, 0, 0, 0, 0, 0, 0, 0, 0, 0, 102].

There is a nice implementation of Layer Integrated Gradients (among many other layer attribution methods) available in the PyTorch Captum library. One very useful library built on top of Captum is the Transformer Interpret tool designed to work specifically with the Hugging Face transformers package (*https://oreil.ly/JLT0J*).

For example, suppose we want to use a BERT sentiment classifier to classify movie reviews from the IMDB database. BERT is a transformer-based natural language model released in 2018 by Google AI Language. The Transformers Interpret tool has an easy-to-use interface to provide a saliency map built on top of Captum's Layer Integrated Gradients. As when building any text model, we start with tokenization. To do this, we'll use a pretrained tokenizer that was used for training the BERT model. We can also use a pretrained BERT model. The following code block shows how to load the pretrained BERT tokenizer and pretrained BERT model for sequence classification. The predict function shows how to call this model to make classification predictions given an input text sequence:

```
from transformers import BertTokenizer

# load tokenizer
tokenizer = BertTokenizer.from_pretrained('./model')
# load model
model = BertForSequenceClassification.from_pretrained('./model')
def predict(inputs):
    return model(inputs)[0]
```

8 Mukund Sundararajan et al., "Axiomatic Attribution for Deep Networks," International Conference on Machine Learning, PMLR, 2017.

To generate explanations of this model using Layer Integrated Gradients, we'll use the `LayerIntegratedGradients` class in Captum. This is done by specifying the layer where you want to compute the attributions, as shown in the following code block. Technically, we can use any layer in our model. Here, we'll use the BERT embeddings layer given by `model.bert.embeddings`:

```
from captum.attr import LayerIntegratedGradients
lig = LayerIntegratedGradients(custom_forward, model.bert.embeddings)
```

When instantiating the `LayerIntegratedGradients` class, we provide two arguments: a forward pass of the model and the layer for which we want to compute attributions. Here we set the forward pass of our model to be a custom function defined by:

```
def custom_forward(inputs):
    preds = model(inputs)[0]
    return torch.softmax(preds, dim = 1)[0][1].unsqueeze(-1)
```

This way, `custom_forward` takes as an argument the input IDs of a tokenized text (e.g., a movie review) and returns the model prediction as a probability of positive sentiment. We can then compute the attributions for the tokenized input text (see the Layer Integrated Gradients notebook (*https://oreil.ly/nYuLQ*) in this book's GitHub repository for the full code):

```
lig_attributions, delta = lig.attribute(inputs=input_ids,
                                        baselines=ref_input_ids,
                                        n_steps=700,
                                        internal_batch_size=3,
                                        return_convergence_delta=True)
```

Given the input text "If you like the original, you'll love this movie," our model classifies that statement as having positive sentiment with probability 0.998. We can also visualize the saliency map for the word importance for the model's prediction using the `Transformers Interpret` library. As shown in Figure 5-9, we see that the words that most contribute to the positive sentiment prediction were *love*, *this*, and *movie*.

Figure 5-9. The visualization provided by Transformers Interpret and Captum indicates the word importance for the model's prediction. We see that phrases like love this movie have positive influence, but also (confusingly) if and the. (Print readers can see the color image at https://oreil.ly/xai-fig-5-9.)

However, the visualization also indicates a positive influence from the words *if* and *the*, which is somewhat less convincing. Also, the model appears to give a negative importance to *you* and *like*. Although this could indicate that there are more improvements to be made on our sentiment classification model, it's also a good reminder that explainability results should be taken in context. In Chapter 7, we'll discuss some of the considerations you should keep in mind as a human interacting with explainability.

Conductance

Conductance is another notion of attribution that is often considered in conjunction with feature attribution and layer attributions. The idea of conductance was introduced to extend the idea of attribution to better understand the importance of hidden units. Conductance is meant to be a natural refinement of Integrated Gradients. Instead of measuring the importance of a feature, conductance measures the importance of a single hidden unit to a model's prediction (see Figure 5-10).

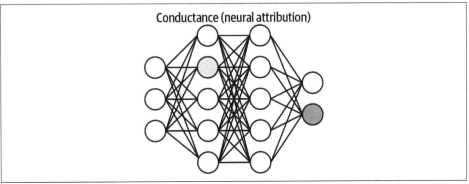

Figure 5-10. The conductance at a specific neuron (the light shaded circle) in a hidden layer is computed in a similar way to how Integrated Gradients compute attribution for a feature input.

Layer-Wise Relevance Propagation (LRP)

Here's what you need to know about Layer-Wise Relevance Propagation:

- LRP is a saliency method of explainability that measures the attributions of a given layer by backpropagating the contributions of all neurons in a layer to the neurons of the previous layer.
- At each layer, a special backward pass backpropagates the top-level relevance given by the model prediction to the inputs to that layer. The relevance is redistributed all the way back to the input layer.
- For models with only ReLU activations and max pooling nonlinearities, LRP is equivalent to the Gradient x Input method.

Pros	Cons
• The implementation is very modular. That is, each type of layer has its own propagation rules (there are different rules for redistribution for feed-forward layers and LSTMs), and different propagation rules can be applied for different layers in the network. • This can be applied to various data types (images, text, audio, video, etc.) and neural architectures (DNNs, CNNs, and LSTMs). • LRP has been shown to work better than gradient-based methods on text classification tasks.	• LRP requires implementing a custom backward pass, and the relevance is redistributed differently for feed-forward layers versus LSTMs. • Attribution values tend to concentrate on only a few features, which can inhibit performance for less common words. • Depending on your use case, you may want to combine different propagation rules for the best results. This can require some extra experimentation and hyperparameter tuning.

LRP is one of the most commonly used explainability techniques because it can be applied to various data types (not just text) and works well across various model architectures, such as DNNs, CNNs, and LSTMs. The purpose of LRP is to provide an explanation of any neural network's output in the domain of its input.

 LRP is similar in spirit to DeepLIFT (Deep Learning Important FeaTures). DeepLIFT was introduced in 2016; it is a method for decomposing the output prediction of a neural network by back-propagating the contributions of all neurons to every feature of the input. The activation of each neuron is compared to its "reference activation," and the attribution scores for each neuron are determined by the difference between the activation and the reference. This allows for positive and negative contributions for any neuron.

How LRP Works

As the name suggests, LRP is considered a propagation explainability technique. This means that the feature attributions are achieved by recursively propagating some measure of the model's relevance for a prediction back through the network and to the instance's input features. At each level of the network, the propagation procedure must satisfy a conversation property so that whatever has been received by a neuron from a higher layer has to be fully redistributed to the neurons of the previous layer. This way the total relevance from upper-level layers to lower-level layers remains constant (see Figure 5-11).

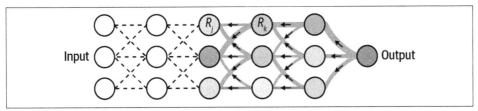

Figure 5-11. The top-level relevance is redistributed to the lower layers of the model so that whatever has been received by a neuron from a higher layer has to be fully redistributed to the neurons of the previous layer.

In Figure 5-11, let R_j and R_k denote the relevance of the neurons j and k located at layer l and $l+1$, respectively. The relevance score for neuron j is determined by propagating the relevance from every neuron in level k onto the neurons in level j according to the rule:

$$R_j^{(l)} = \sum_k \frac{z_{jk}}{\sum_j z_{jk}} R_k^{(l+1)}$$

The quantity z_{jk} is a general contribution measure that measures how much neuron j contributes to neuron k. When implementing LRP, you can determine how to compute this quantity. Defining z_{jk} can take some experimentation, though there are commonly used implementations and formulas that you can use as a starting point, as we'll soon see. The important thing to note is that when summing both sides of the equation with respect to j, a conservation property is satisfied; namely, the sum of the relevance for all neurons in a layer is constant.

Let's look at a familiar example from text classification. Suppose we had the input text from the IMDB dataset of movie reviews, "If you like the original, you'll love this movie." Each word is mapped to an embedding layer to create a sequence of n vectors $x_{1:n}$. This is then passed to the model to determine the top-level relevance $f(x_{1:n})$. The aim of LRP is to propagate this relevance score, the model's output, back through the individual neurons and layers of the model with the rule that at each layer the total relevance is maintained, as in Figure 5-12.

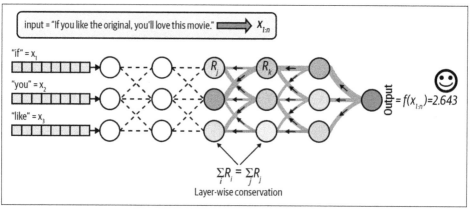

Figure 5-12. Each layer preserves the total relevance of the model's prediction on the input instance. This top-level relevance is propagated back through the network and ultimately to the model inputs to assign feature attributions to each feature (i.e., word) input.

The way that relevance of a neuron is distributed to its contributing neurons from the previous layer (i.e., defining the contribution measure z_{jk}) can be defined according to different schemes. It's even possible to have different propagation rules for different layers. For deep neural networks with ReLU activation functions, the recommended contribution measure is defined by $z_{jk} = x_j w_{jk}$, where x_j are the input values and w_{jk} are the parameter weights. In this setting, the basic rule for propagation then becomes:

$$R_j^{(l)} = \sum_k \frac{x_j w_{jk}}{\sum_j x_j w_{jk}} R_k^{(l+1)}$$

This is often referred to as the LRP-0 rule and is arguably the simplest rule you can use for Layer-Wise Relevance Propagation (the reason for the zero in the name will become evident in the next paragraph).

One way to improve upon LRP-0 is by incorporating a constant ϵ in the denominator. This is done for two main reasons. First, adding a small constant to the denominator helps in capturing the relevance when the contributions of an input neuron are small. With larger values of ϵ, only the most important explanation factors still make enough of a difference to be recognized. Second, from a computational perspective, the ϵ helps make the fraction more stable. The LRP-ϵ rule is given by:

$$R_j^{(l)} = \sum_k \frac{x_j w_{jk}}{\epsilon + \sum_j x_j w_{jk}} R_k^{(l+1)}$$

Thus, when $\epsilon = 0$, we have the original LRP-0 rule from before. The LRP-ϵ propagation rule can help in creating explanations that are less noisy and sparser in terms of input features.

One of the advantages of LRP is that the propagation rules can be implemented efficiently and modularly. Different LRP rules can be applied at different levels of the network. For example, at the upper layers it's better to use the basic LRP rule (with $\epsilon = 0$) to have a propagation rule close to the function and its gradient. While in the middle layers, it helps more to use LRP-ϵ for some positive ϵ value to help filter out spurious variations within the network and highlight only the most salient features. There are other propagation rules that are mentioned in the original paper,[9] if you are interested in exploring others, but LRP-0 and LRP-ϵ will get you pretty far.

The relationship between LRP and Grad x Input

It's interesting to note that when all the activation functions of a deep neural network are ReLU functions, the Layer-Wise Relevance Propagation method is equivalent to Grad x Input.[10]

ReLU stands for Rectified Linear Unit and is a piecewise linear function that outputs the input when the input is positive and returns zero otherwise (see the graph in Figure 5-13).

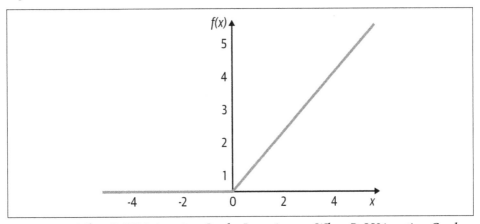

Figure 5-13. When ReLU is inactive, Grad x Input is zero. When ReLU is active, Grad x Input is equal to the output.

---

9 Alexander Binder et al., "Layer-Wise Relevance Propagation for Deep Neural Network Architectures," *Information Science and Applications (ICISA)*, Springer (Singapore, 2016): 913–22.

10 Avanti Shrikumar et al., "Not Just a Black Box: Learning Important Features Through Propagating Activation Differences," arXiv, 2017, *https://arxiv.org/abs/1605.01713*.

As shown in the graph, for negative values, the ReLU activation is equal to zero and the gradient is zero. So, when ReLU is inactive, the Grad x Input is zero and LRP assigns zero signal to that unit. On the other hand, when ReLU is positive and the unit is active, the gradient is equal to one and Grad x Input is equal to the output, and LRP assigns full signal to the unit.

Deriving Explanations from Attention

Since the transformer architecture was introduced in 2017, *attention* mechanisms have played an increasingly important role in natural language models and can achieve state-of-the-art results for almost all NLP tasks. Attention mechanisms were introduced to address the shortcoming that arose when training more traditional encoder-decoder sequence models, particularly when decoding long sequences.

As the name suggests, a traditional encoder-decoder model consists of two components, the encoder and the decoder. The encoder steps through each time step of the input sequence and encodes the input into a fixed-length context vector. The decoder then takes that context vector and decodes it into a meaningful output sequence, one time step at a time. Encoder-decoders are a useful architecture for sequence-to-sequence models, but they struggle when decoding long sequences. Attention addresses this issue by keeping track of the hidden state for each time step of the input sequence, rather than encoding the entire input sequence into a single context vector. With attention, the context vector *plus* all of the input sequence hidden states are passed to the decoder at each time step during the decode step. This way, attention allows the decoder model to focus on different parts of the input sequence at each stage of decoding. This helps to preserve the input sequence context, particularly when decoding long input sequences.

Attention now dominates the field of text processing and has even become popular in computer vision tasks as well. Given their wide range of applications and impressive results, there have also been attempts to crack open the attention mechanism of transformers to derive some form of explanation into the model's predictions.

The heart of the transformer is the self-attention block. Self-attention is similar to the attention mechanism we just described for encoder-decoder models, but it also applies attention to elements of the input sequence, allowing the encoder to look at other words in the input sequence as it encodes a word at a certain time step. So, attention is used by the decoder when decoding the context received by the encoder, while self-attention is used by the encoder to create the context the encoder produces.

Self-attention layers assign a pair-wise attention value to every two words (or tokens) in an input sequence. Since attention is ultimately a matrix of learned weights, it is possible to visualize a transformer model by examining the learned relevancy score for input features. A larger weight value indicates a stronger attribution for that feature. As an example, consider the task of machine translation. Given our sample input sentence "If you like the original, you'll love this movie.," our model returns the Spanish translation "Si te gusta la original, encantara esta pelicula." The alignment matrix between the input and target sentence, shown in Figure 5-14, illustrates which part of the input sequence is more or less important at each decoding step. Each row of the matrix indicates the learned weights associated with the annotations for that hidden state. The (i, j)-th element of the matrix indicates the weight of the annotation of the *j*-th input word for the *i*-th output word. Note that the alignment of words between English and Spanish is almost perfectly aligned word for word with strong weights along the diagonal of each matrix.

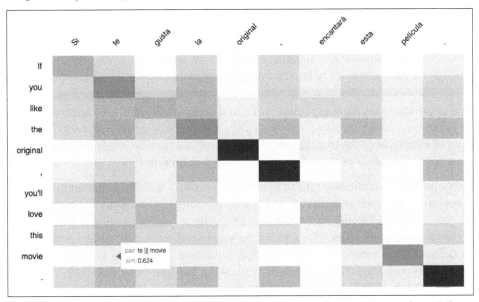

Figure 5-14. For machine translation, we can visualize how the model attends to different parts of the input and target sentence.

While we can visualize an alignment matrix for the single attention layer of an encoder-decoder model (as in Figure 5-14), this is much more difficult for a typical transformer. Transformers build on the idea of self-attention in an encoder-decoder, and a typical transformer will have multiple self-attention layers (and multiple attention heads) that are combined one after the other with nonlinearities in between, much like the fully connected layers of a deep neural network.

Be careful in trying to derive too much explanatory power from visualizing alignment matrices from attention. A self-attention head in a transformer model involves computation of queries, keys, and values, and when attention is applied over hidden states, there is inherently information about other time steps automatically mixed in. Any attempt to reduce self-attention to only values learned in the attention matrix doesn't capture the entire picture. In fact, some research shows that the attention weights that are learned through training can be uncorrelated with the results of gradient-based methods for determining feature importances.[11]

So, although there has been some work in visualizing attention weights to infer explainability or interpret which layers the model was focusing on for certain predictions, these visualizations should be taken with a grain of salt, and it's better to rely on saliency methods if you want quantitative importance scores.

One approach to deriving explanations for self-attention models is to borrow an idea of Layer-Wise Relevance Propagation (LRP) to compute scores for each attention head in each layer of the transformer. These scores can then be integrated throughout the attention graph to provide a final feature attribution score.[12]

To see how this technique works in practice, let's create a text classification model that relies on transformer architecture and is trained using the IMDB movie review dataset. We'll use the Hugging Face transformer library to load a pretrained BERT model for sequence classification. Then, using the pretrained tokenizer, we can evaluate the model on IMDB movie reviews to predict a positive or negative sentiment, shown in the following code (the full code is available in the LRP notebook (*https://oreil.ly/zFRqy*) from this book's GitHub repository):

```
model = BertForSequenceClassification.from_pretrained("bert-base-uncased-SST-2")
tokenizer = AutoTokenizer.from_pretrained("textattack/bert-base-uncased-SST-2")
# initialize the explanations generator
explanations = Generator(model)

classifications = ["NEGATIVE", "POSITIVE"]
```

Here, Generator is a class that is instantiated using the pretrained BERT model.[13] This class contains the methods we'll use to generate explanations using LRP. Let's

---

11 Sarthak Jain and Byron C. Wallace, "Attention Is Not Explanation," *Proceedings of NAACL-HLT 2019*, *https://aclanthology.org/N19-1357.pdf*.

12 Hila Chefer et al., "Transformer Interpretability Beyond Attention Visualization," Proceedings of the IEEE/CVF Conference on Computer Vision and Pattern Recognition, 2021.

13 See *https://github.com/hila-chefer/Transformer-Explainability* for more information.

take the sample review text "If you like the original, you'll love this movie." We can tokenize and pass to our explainer using layer-wise propagation:

```
sample_txt = ["If you like the original, you'll love this movie."]
encoding = tokenizer(sample_txt, return_tensors='pt')

# true class is positive - 1
true_class = 1

# generate an explanation for the input
expl = explanations.generate_LRP(input_ids=input_ids,
                                 attention_mask=attention_mask,
                                 start_layer=0)[0]
```

Using Captum's library for visualization, we can explore the explanations that were generated (see Figure 5-15).

Figure 5-15. For this input example, the model predicts positive sentiment (the true label), and the word importance score using LRP creates a saliency mask over the words that contributed most to that prediction. (Print readers can see the color image at https://oreil.ly/xai-5-15.)

Which Method to Use?

So far, you've seen a number of explainability techniques that can be used when working with text data. You're probably wondering which is the best method and which one you should use for your next (or current) ML project. Of course, there is no clear answer to that question. If anything, we've tried more to illustrate the *what* and *how* of each technique and not claim to suggest that any one method beats out all the rest. They each have their pros and cons and, moreover, the technique that is best for you and your use case will depend heavily on your data, your model, and how you plan to use the explanations (see Chapter 7 where we discuss in detail human interaction aspects of explainability).

With that in mind, our advice would be to try various techniques and see which explanations ring the truest for you given what you know about your data, your model, and your use case. Of course, implementing even one of the techniques we discuss in this chapter could be a lot of development time and effort. We'll end this chapter by discussing the Language Interpretability Tool (LIT) developed by Google's People + AI Research (PAIR) (*https://oreil.ly/Rvrrr*) team. LIT is an incredibly useful tool for any practitioner hoping to explain their NLP model and provides an easy-to-use interface that you can use to help you decide which explainability method to use.

Language Interpretability Tool

The Language Interpretability Tool (LIT)[14] is a visual, interactive model-understanding platform for NLP models developed by the PAIR group at Google. LIT is similar in spirit to the What-If Tool that allows ML practitioners the ability to analyze and debug their models and datasets without the need to write a lot of code. However, LIT is focused on the specific challenges that arise when working with NLP models and has an intuitive interface that allows you to explore and interact with your dataset and model predictions. The main workspace contains modules for exploration and analysis, including UMAP (uniform manifold approximation and projection) and t-SNE (t-distributed stochastic neighbor embedding) embeddings of your dataset, data tables, and editors to explore individual examples and a slicer editor that allows you to create and examine slices of interest in your dataset. The group-based workspaces can be set up to focus on performance, predictions, explanations, or counterfactuals; this is the workspace that we will primarily be focusing on.

Like LIT, the What-If Tool (WIT) was also developed by the PAIR group at Google. It is designed to provide an easy-to-use interface for exploring and understanding the predictions of classification and regression ML models. The plugin allows you to apply inference on a large subset of examples and visualize the result in a number of different ways.

You can explore how your model prediction would change if a feature value was different or examine how different features affect each model's prediction in relation to each other. You can examine global statistics of your dataset to uncover hidden biases or correlations among features. You can even explore slices of your dataset and evaluate model performance metrics on subgroups to check for model fairness.

The LIT platform has an extensive list of capabilities to assist practitioners in explaining their model's predictions, covering a wide range of NLP tasks from text classification to sequence generation. Many of the XAI techniques we discussed in this chapter are also available in LIT along with nice visualizations. For example, there are built-in modules for visualizing attention and saliency maps and features for aggregation metrics for your text samples. There is also support for counterfactual generation for model examples and side-by-side comparison for two different models to easily see how they differ or agree. There is a wide range of features, and we highly encourage you to go explore the functionality that is available. In terms of analyzing different explainability techniques, one of the nicest properties is that LIT allows you to easily

---

14 More information is available at *https://pair-code.github.io/lit*.

compare the results of different explainability methods without having to develop and experiment with each one yourself.

There are a number of demos available that illustrate some of the capabilities of LIT. For example, let's look at the demo for sentiment analysis. This demo uses the Stanford Sentiment Treebank consisting of movie reviews, similar to the IMDB dataset we've seen already in this chapter. Let's provide a test sentence: "If you like the original, you'll love this movie." Within the LIT UI, under the Predictions tab, we see that the model predicts a positive sentiment for this example with probability 0.979. There is a lot of functionality within the LIT platform that can be explored, but let's focus on the explanations for this input instance. LIT currently supports a collection of explainability methods, including Grad x Input, Integrated Gradients, LIME, and Grad L2-norm. Clicking on the Explanations tab, we can see a visualization of the saliency maps for each of these methods (see Figure 5-16), allowing for quick and easy comparison of the different techniques. This way you can easily see which techniques most resonate with what you know about your data, your model, and your use case. A large discrepancy between different techniques might be cause for concern or suggest further analysis, whereas a similar consensus among techniques sends a clearer signal on the current state of the model.

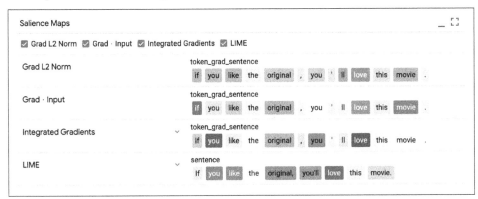

Figure 5-16. The Language Interpretability Tool allows for easy comparison of several commonly used explainability techniques, including many that we discussed in this chapter. The color intensity indicates salience with blue and purple, indicating positive attribution, and red indicating negative. (Print readers can see the color image at https://oreil.ly/xai-5-16.)

Summary

In this chapter, we focused on explainability methods for natural language models. We started with a brief overview of the nuances of working with text data and the role played by tokenizers and embedding layers. It's important to be aware of these preprocessing steps as their artifacts make their way downstream to explainability tasks later either directly or indirectly. We then turned to techniques, starting with LIME. LIME is a common explainability method and can be used for images, tabular data, and text; we saw in detail how LIME is implemented when working with text.

We then turned our attention to two related techniques: Grad x Input and Grad L2-norm. These two techniques have been shown to work well with transformer models, and they give a good comparison of sensitivity and saliency techniques in XAI. Next, we discussed Layer Integrated Gradients, which is really just an extension of the classic Integrated Gradients technique to provide layer attribution within a mode. This approach is particularly useful when working with text since examining a model on the input token ID level is problematic because integer IDs are not differentiable. Instead, it's necessary to evaluate the Integrated Gradients at the embedding layer of the model.

Lastly, we looked at Layer-Wise Relevance Propagation, which provides a way to distribute the relevance score of a model's prediction to the internal neurons of the network. By propagating the relevance through the network, we can ultimately determine which input features contain more relevance for a given prediction. We then explored the Language Interpretability Tool as a platform for exploring features of NLP models and, in particular, explainability methods. LIT has a suite of capabilities and an interactive platform that can be run in a Jupyter notebook. It's a great way to apply the explainability techniques we discussed in this chapter to your own NLP model.

In the next chapter, we'll look at some other advanced techniques and recent trends in explainability that you might also like to add to your explainability toolkit.

## CHAPTER 6

Advanced and Emerging Topics

with Sheeraz Ahmad

The focus of the book so far has been on well-established techniques, modalities, and use cases. However, Explainable AI (XAI) continues to be an active area of research, so that new techniques are continually being developed and existing techniques are improved and scrutinized further. Feature-based explanations such as Shapley values and Integrated Gradients introduced in the previous chapters can cover many use cases, especially as applied to text, tabular, and image data. However, there are several emerging techniques and topics that can be valuable in your explainability toolbox in specific situations.

In this chapter, we will discuss three broad, emerging topics. First, we will introduce alternative explanation techniques like attribution to inputs (as opposed to features) and making models explainable by design. Second, we will briefly cover how some of the previously introduced techniques can be more generally applied to data formats that are not text, tabular, or image, specifically focusing on time-series and multimodal data (text + image). Third, we will discuss how explainability techniques can be evaluated in a systematic way, as opposed to spot checks on a handful of data points.

Alternative Explainability Techniques

In this section, we will discuss two alternative explainability methods, namely, alternate input attribution, which is attribution to training data points or user-defined concepts, as well as explainability by design, which involves intervening in the modeling process to make it inherently more explainable.

Alternate Input Attribution

Although reasoning based on an example's features is a sensible way to approach explainability, predictions can also be attributed to other inputs such as other examples in the training data or examples in some supplementary data. Note that feature attributions are also indirectly affected by the training data since after all, training data is what the model uses to learn about a task, and feature attribution techniques require querying the trained model in various ways. However, this indirect effect (training data → model → feature attribution) is hard to trace, making it tricky for us to answer the question of which points in the training data a correct (or erroneous) prediction should be attributed to.

We will now discuss techniques that allow us to directly attribute credit (or blame) to individual data points in the training set, or to data in a supplementary set that can be curated by a domain expert. We'll discuss three broad types of alternate input attribution methods: example-based explanations, influence functions, and concept-based explanations. Example-based explanations provide insight into model behavior by surfacing elements of the training dataset that the model treats as similar (or different). Influence function-based explanations also utilize examples from the dataset but focus on those examples that significantly affect model behavior. Here, the influence of a training example is measured by how much the model parameters or predictions change if that example were to be removed from the training dataset. Lastly, concept-based explanations use the internal state of the model to compare how high-level, abstract concepts compare with input instances and model predictions. The advantage is that these concepts align better with human intuition than individual features might.

Example-based explanations

Here's what you need to know about example-based explanations:

- These provide insight into model behavior by surfacing approximate nearest neighbor-based explanations for model instances.
- They work equally well with different data modalities—image, text, and tabular.
- Example-based explanations are primarily considered model agnostic and provide explanations based on elements of the datasets, not model features.
- Counterfactual explanations are a form of example-based explanations.

Pros	Cons
• These explanations are useful for debugging models as well as closing the loop with stakeholders. • They are a very intuitive, human-understandable representation of model behavior. • Example-based explanations are helpful in building a mental model for understanding your ML model predictions and give additional insight into complex data distributions, surfacing hidden data issues or outliers. • It's quick to get started with generating example-based explanations using open source libraries like ScaNN (*https://oreil.ly/oJa95*).	• Example-based attribution does not offer guarantees in completeness—summing up the distances of each training data point from a given test point doesn't sum up to anything meaningful. • These explanations don't offer any insights into the causal relationship between the test point and the corresponding example-based explanations. • It can be difficult to scale up example-based explanations beyond ~1–10K examples locally; beyond that, you'd want to use a cloud service.

Example-based explanations are an intuitive way to communicate a model's reasoning. Akin to feature attribution where the objective is to assign partial responsibility of the prediction to individual features, the objective for example-based explanations is to do the same to individual points in the training data. For instance, the question of why the leftmost image in Figure 6-1 was classified as a husky, a breed of dog, can be answered in different ways. We can point to the contributing features, in this case pixels (using a technique like Integrated Gradients) or regions (using a technique like XRAI). Alternatively, we can point to other similar examples in the training data that were huskies, as potential explanations.

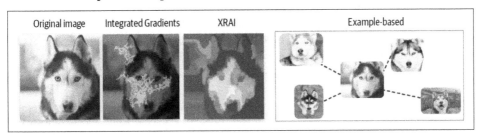

Figure 6-1. Possible explanations for a prediction of "husky" (leftmost image). From left to right: Integrated Gradients, XRAI, and example-based explanations.

Example-based explanations work by first transforming any given input into a meaningful representation using the learned internal state of the model, and then finding the nearest neighbors in the training data for a query point, based on a predefined notion of distance such as Euclidean or cosine distance. For deep learning models, such representations are often called embeddings and are expected to capture semantics of the data distribution for a well-trained model.

The term *embeddings* is used across various domains to mean similar things. In essence, it is a vector representation (i.e., an element of the latent space) of the data often learned by a model as a by-product of performing its intended task. For example, in case of text, we can think of it as capturing semantic properties of the word like polarity (positiveness), gender, level of formality, etc., each by one element of this embedding vector and from a range of 0 to 1. A model might have learned this vector as it tried to perform sentiment classification. Similarly for images, each embedding vector element might capture saturation, humanness, soft versus sharp contours, etc., which a model might have learned as it tried to perform pedestrian detection. Of course, these are made up of examples, and we can't be sure a specific aspect is clearly captured by an element of the embedding. In general, they seem to be useful and often appear to capture meaningful aspects of the data.

With the assumption that meaningful embeddings have been learned by the model, example-based explanations return results often aligning with user intuition. Such explanations can then be used for applications such as *misprediction analysis*—if the example-based explanations for a mispredicted test point have labels that agree with the predicted label and disagree with the true label, it might point to issues with data quality. Figure 6-2 illustrates one such case where the explanations for a misclassified bird are largely from the airplane class, and subsequent manual inspection reveals the uniqueness of this bird image and how it indeed looks similar to an airplane. This in turn points to a potential data sparsity for silhouetted birds.

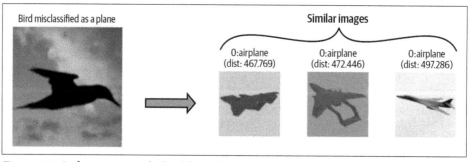

Figure 6-2. Left: an image of a bird from the STL10 dataset (https://oreil.ly/NTG3k) that was misclassified as a plane by a fine-tuned MobileNet model. Right: example-based explanations (using the penultimate layer output as embeddings and Euclidean distance) that in fact look similar to the query image but come from the airplane class.

We saw how example-based explanations can be useful in some specific applications, and to help you figure out whether they can be a good fit for your needs, let us look at their pros and cons.

One of the primary advantages of example-based explanations is that they provide very intuitive, human-understandable representation of model behavior. This makes this method particularly useful for debugging models as well as closing the loop with stakeholders. By surfacing related examples from the training dataset, example-based explanations are helpful in building a mental model for understanding your ML model predictions and give additional insight into complex data distributions that can be useful in surfacing hidden data issues or outliers. Example-based applications are uniquely useful for identifying issues with training data and pinpointing when more data might need to be collected. In addition, it's quick to get started[1] with generating example-based explanations thanks to the availability of open source libraries like ScaNN (*https://oreil.ly/jnrUs*).

On the other hand, unlike many feature attribution techniques, this simple example-based attribution does not offer guarantees in completeness—if we compute distances of each training data point from a given test point, they don't sum up to anything meaningful. This means that it does not point to or quantify a specific property of an input or image. Instead, a data scientist has to fill the gap and determine what the example-based attribution reveals, such as in Figure 6-2. In explanations that have a completeness property, one can quantify how much something contributes to a decision without much need to fill in the interpretability gap.

Another issue to keep in mind is scalability: it can be difficult to scale up example-based explanations beyond ~1,000–10,000 examples using OSS solutions and local processing power, and you will likely need to use a cloud service if your example set is larger than that. Furthermore, example-based explanations don't offer any insights into the causal relationship between the test point and the corresponding example-based explanations—how would the prediction of the test point change if one of the explanation points was removed from the dataset? Intuitively, if the dataset is rich enough, removing one of the explanation points for any test point would have negligible effect on the model prediction. This goes somewhat against the idea from feature attribution where high attribution generally implies high importance to the prediction. Relatedly, a nonsimilar example can still be useful since it can impart more discriminative power to the model.

One approach that has been proposed to address this issue and better consider the perspective of individual data points is influence function-based explanations. We discuss this technique in the next section.

---

1 Have a look at this ScaNN demo using the GloVe dataset (*https://oreil.ly/xAItz*).

Influence function-based explanations

Here's what you need to know about influence function-based explanations:

- Influence functions describe model behavior through the lens of the training data and influential examples. They are used to understand the relative importance of different points in your training data.

- An influential training example is an example such that removing it from the training data would cause considerable changes to the model parameters or predictions. Influence function-based explanations measure how model predictions would change if that example was removed.

- Computing the influence of specific training data points requires computing second-order derivatives. The influence can be positive or negative, which indicates whether a particular data point helped or hurt the prediction.

Pros	Cons
• This is a flexible technique that can be applied to debug models, detect dataset errors, and even create visually indistinguishable adversarial examples. • The explanations they offer align better with intuition— how important is a training data point to the model's prediction. • They work well for small or moderately sized models.	• They don't scale well to large models or large datasets. • Influence functions lack a systematic way to account for correlated data points. The influence of a given data point might appear low if there's another data point that is strongly correlated with it. • These explanations require the model to be twice differentiable.

Using influence functions[2] (IFs) to explain model predictions was proposed in a 2017 paper by Koh et al. and was inspired by a classical technique in the field of robust statistics from 1974.[3] In the context of explainability, IFs provide an alternate way to assign attribution to training data points by asking the question of how would the loss on a specific test point x_{test} change if a given training data point was removed from the training set. That is, we want to measure:

$$L\left(x_{test}; \theta_{X \setminus x}\right) - L\left(x_{test}; \theta_X\right)$$

where X is the full dataset, $X \setminus x$ represents the dataset with a single example x removed, and θ_X denotes the model parameters learned using X (similarly for $\theta_{X \setminus x}$).

---

2 Pang Wei Koh and Percy Liang, "Understanding Black-Box Predictions via Influence Functions," International Conference on Machine Learning, PMLR, 2017.

3 F. R. Hampel, "The Influence Curve and Its Role in Robust Estimation," *Journal of the American Statistical Association* 69, no. 346 (June 1974): 383–93.

While this may appear to be a sensible approach, a naive implementation would be prohibitively costly, requiring us to retrain the model with different subsets of training data. This practical hurdle should sound familiar—an exact implementation of Shapley values runs into a similar issue requiring rebuilding and retraining the model with different subsets of input features.

To address this scalability problem, approximations are needed. We start by considering how the model parameters would change if we upweighted a single training example $z = (x,y)$ by a tiny, tiny bit called ϵ. Of course, upweighting by a tiny, tiny amount is the same as removing that example completely. If we let $L(z_i,\theta)$ denote the loss function at the point z_i with the parameters θ then the new model parameters, with this example z upweighted by ϵ, would be:

$$\widehat{\theta}_{z,\epsilon} = \arg\ \min_{\theta} \frac{1}{n} \sum_{i=1}^{n} L(z_i,\theta) - \epsilon\, L(z,\theta)$$

The idea of influence functions is to approximate what the change in the loss for the parameters learned on the full dataset θ_X versus the loss for the parameters learned on the full dataset minus one test example $\theta_{X \setminus x}$. So, the influence on the loss of upweighting and element x at a test point x_{test} can be approximated (by chain rule, omitting the derivation) by:

$$\text{Influence}(x,x_{test}) = \left.\frac{dL\left(x_{test}, \widehat{\theta}_{x_{test},\epsilon}\right)}{d\epsilon}\right|_{\epsilon=0} \approx \frac{1}{n}\nabla_{\theta}L(x_{test}; \theta_X)^T H_{\theta_X}^{-1}\nabla_{\theta}L(x; \theta_X)$$

where ∇ and H are the first- and second-order derivatives, respectively.

The general idea is that θ_X is a stationary point of the loss function, and thus a solution for $\nabla_{\theta}L(X; \theta) = 0$. This equation can be approximated by a first-order Taylor series expansion giving rise to the Hessian term. Since matrix inversion is still computationally expensive, the authors of the original IF paper proposed further approximations to make the evaluation more efficient. In the subsequent years, somewhat related approaches like representer points[4] and TracIn[5] were published that generalize and expand on the ideas pioneered by IF.

The influence of specific training data points can be positive or negative that indicates whether a particular data point helped or hurt the prediction. Figure 6-3 shows the

---

4 Chih-Kuan Yeh et al., "Representer Point Selection for Explaining Deep Neural Networks," *Advances in Neural Information Processing Systems* 31 (2018).

5 Garima Pruthi et al., "Estimating Training Data Influence by Tracing Gradient Descent," *Advances in Neural Information Processing Systems* 33 (2020): 19920–30.

helpful data points for two different image classification models, a support-vector machine (SVM) and Inception network. Lower-level features such as contrast and texture seem to have higher influence for SVM, whereas higher-level features such as shape and patterns seem to have higher influence for Inception net. Even an image from a different class (dog) can help the classification for another class (fish) by effectively helping a model learn to differentiate them better.

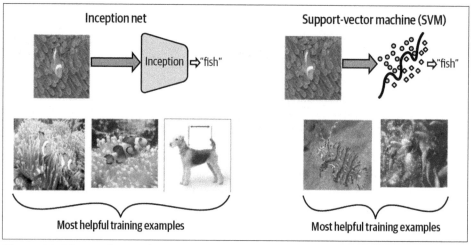

Figure 6-3. Using influence functions, we can determine which were the most helpful training images for each model. For the SVM model, fish close to the test image were mostly helpful, while dogs were harmful for the SVM model. However, for the Inception network, one of the most helpful training images was also a dog, presumably because it helped to determine what a fish doesn't look like as well.

Influence functions have their own set of pros and cons. The explanations they offer align better with intuition—how important is a training data point to the model's prediction. The approximations in the original paper also make it computationally feasible to generate influence functions for moderately sized models and datasets. However, the algorithm doesn't scale well for large models and datasets since it requires computing second-order derivatives and matrix-vector products in high dimensions. Influence functions also lack a systematic way to account for correlated data points, so that the influence of a given data point might appear low if there's another data point that is strongly correlated with it. Even with these caveats, influence functions are a useful tool to understand the relative importance of different points in your training data.

Concept-based explanations

Explanations can also be based on concepts[6]—abstractions that are at a higher level compared to individual features. Here's what you need to know about concept-based explanations, and in particular TCAV:

- One of the commonly used techniques is TCAV (Testing with Concept Activation Vectors). TCAV is a global explainability method.
- Concept activation vectors (CAVs) are a way for machines to represent examples (e.g., images) using the internal layers of a neural net's embedding space.
- TCAV uses CAVs and directional derivatives to quantify how much a user-defined concept is important for the model's prediction.
- The TCAV score is a proportion and always lies between 0 and 1. Values closer to 1 indicate that more of the images of the label class are positively influenced by a concept vector, whereas values closer to 0 indicate less of an influence.

Pros	Cons
• The TCAV score is a proportion, so it's easily interpretable. • Users can determine or explore any concept they define or care about (e.g., gender, textures, patterns); they are not limited to concepts considered during training. • TCAV works without any retraining or modifications to the ML model. • TCAV can interpret entire classes or sets of examples (not just individual data inputs) with a single quantitative measure.	• TCAV can be difficult or expensive to curate a collection of enough examples that illustrate a concept. • TCAV may not perform as well for shallow networks that don't have the capacity to separate internal states as well. • This has been used primarily for images, less so for text or tabular datasets.

For the sake of concreteness in this section, we will focus on concept-based explanations for images. Such explanations can align better with human intuition, which is not attuned to pixel-level perception, as shown in several papers where changes to the pixel values that were imperceptible to humans could be highly significant to a machine learning model. This article by Goodfellow et al. (*https://oreil.ly/pxKTK*)[7] provides an example. Figure 6-4 shows these concept-based explanations for an example image where predictions are attributed to conceptual categories as opposed to Integrated Gradients and XRAI that assign attributions to pixels and regions, respectively.

---

6 Been Kim et al., "Interpretability Beyond Feature Attribution: Quantitative Testing with Concept Activation Vectors (tcav)," International Conference on Machine Learning, PMLR, 2018.

7 Ian J. Goodfellow et al., "Explaining and Harnessing Adversarial Examples," arXiv, 2014.

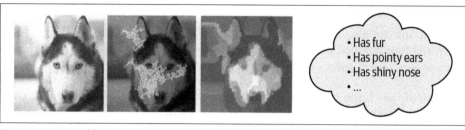

Figure 6-4. Possible explanations for a prediction of "husky" (leftmost image). From left to right: Integrated Gradients, XRAI, and concept-based explanations.

In order to generate concept-based explanations, we need to address two questions. First, how can concepts be provided to the model? And second, how can we measure how such abstractions are learned by the model? We'll discuss how these two questions are addressed with TCAV as an example. For the first question, to implement TCAV, you, the practitioner, provide a set of examples that represent a certain concept or find an independent dataset with that concept already labeled.

The TCAV technique is flexible enough that it can be applied to any user-defined concept (e.g., gender, patterns, textures, or job titles); you just need to curate a collection of examples that exhibit that concept if it doesn't already exist. We recommend roughly 50–200 images per concept and target class for the TCAV algorithm to really be able to pick up on the idea of the concept. That being said, depending on your use case and the complexity of the concept, you can likely get away with only 10–20 pictures, but 200 is generally pretty safe.

For example, in the case of images and animal classification, to measure your model's utilization of the concept of "stripes," as for recognizing zebras, you would provide a set of supplementary images representing the "stripe" concept, and a set of random images representing nonstripes (to facilitate discriminative learning). Or, if you're interested in assessing your model against various fairness metrics, you might collect a database of images representing gender or protected classes to determine how much your model has come to depend on those concepts.

Luckily, for basic concepts there is an easy alternative to creating your own database of images: the Broden (Broadly and Densely Labeled) dataset,[8] which contains images with labels of both low-level concepts such as colors and patterns as well as high-level concepts such as objects. The dataset contains over 1,000 visual concepts ranging across different abstraction levels including scenes, objects, materials, textures, colors, and patterns. This can then be augmented with user-defined concepts that might not be well represented in the existing 1,000 concepts. Figure 6-5 shows some example concepts from the Broden dataset.

Figure 6-5. The Broden dataset contains over 1,000 visual concepts in different abstraction levels including materials, textures, and colors. Here are some examples of the images that represent the concepts "striped," "zigzagged," and "dotted."

The second question we needed to address is how such abstractions can be learned so that they can be used during attribution. As a potential solution, consider an intermediate embedding layer for a deep learning model, or any other meaningful representation for the broader class of models. We will use the term embedding in the broader sense of a meaningful representation as opposed to the stricter sense of a layer's output. A linear classifier that separates the images representing the stripe concept from the ones in the nonstripe concept is a hyperplane describing the decision boundary between the two. The concept activation vector is defined as the normal to this hyperplane, and in general the images representing the stripe concept will have a larger (signed) projection on this vector compared to the ones representing the nonstripe concept. Figure 6-6 illustrates this process of concept learning.

---

8 David Bau et al., "Network Dissection: Quantifying Interpretability of Deep Visual Representations," Proceedings of the IEEE Conference on Computer Vision and Pattern Recognition, 2017.

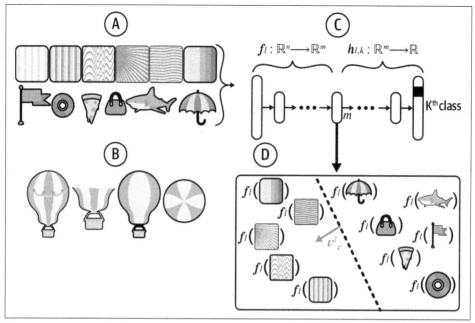

Figure 6-6. Process for learning concept vectors: (a) user-defined set of examples for a concept (e.g., "striped"), and random examples for nonconcept (e.g., "nonstriped"); (b) labeled training data for the specific class (e.g., "hot air balloons"), (c) and a trained network; (d) concept vectors are learned by training a linear classifier to distinguish between the embeddings produced by a concept's examples versus a nonconcept's examples at a given layer. The concept plane is the decision boundary, and the concept activation vector is the vector orthogonal to the decision boundary.

With these prerequisites in place, we can generate global, aggregated explanations that summarize what fraction of images were on the stripe side of the hyperplane. More formally, if we denote by f_l the l-th layer of a neural network and let $h_{l,k}$ logit for the model's predicted class k. That is, $h_{l,k}$ is the part of the neural network that maps the activations of the l-th layer to the k-th class prediction. The directional derivative of that function in the direction of a unit vector CAV v for a concept C is then given by:

$$D_{C,k,l}(x) = \nabla h_{l,k}(f_l(x)) \cdot v_C$$

where x is a specific image input. The dot product measures how aligned two vectors are. If the vectors are orthogonal, then the dot product is zero. The dot product is maximal when the vectors are parallel. So, $D_{C,k,l}$ measures how aligned the gradient and the concept vector are, in essence quantitatively measuring the sensitivity of the model predictions for any layer l and for any concept vector v_C. The TCAV score is then an aggregation of that sensitivity measure across all images. Letting X_k denote the class of all images with the label k, we want to count the fraction of k-class inputs whose l-layer activation vector was positively influenced by the concept C. Thus, the TCAV score is computed via:

$$\text{TCAV}_{C,k,l} = \frac{|x \in X_k : D_{C,k,l}(x) > 0)|}{|X_k|}$$

Since, by definition, the TCAV score is a fraction, the value will always lie between 0 and 1. When TCAV is closer to 1, more of the images of the k-label class are positively influenced by the concept vector associated with the concept C. When the TCAV score is closer to 0, that concept vector doesn't have as much of an influence.

Note that it's also possible to provide local (individual test point) concept-based explanations, but with the caveat that their quality will depend highly on the user-curated concepts, whereas global aggregation can smooth some of that variability that would occur with a smaller sample size.

There are two main issues with the formulation of concept-based explanations we just discussed. First, for less standard concepts, like those that are not found in the Broden dataset or other similarly curated dataset, the onus of providing meaningful concepts and sufficient examples is on you, the practitioner, and is an error-prone requirement. Second, it's unclear precisely how many concepts are required to suffi-ciently explain a prediction. In other words, while for some domains only 10 concepts might be needed to explain every prediction, for another it might be 1,000 concepts. To address this second issue, a follow-up work to TCAV[9] also proposes generating supplementary image[10] concepts as patches from the original training data, and learning enough concepts such that a model using only the concept scores (like the distance from the concept hyperplane) can achieve an accuracy as high as the full raw images. However, issues such as redundant concepts, effect of embedding choice, and so on still remain, and concept-based explanation continues to be an active area of research.

Explainability by Design

Another way to approach explainability is by incorporating transparency principles into the model from the get-go. One way this can be done is by choosing models that are inherently explainable, such as linear models or tree models. Using the terminol-ogy from Chapter 2, such models are often referred to as interpretable models.

---

9 Chih-Kuan Yeh et al., "On Completeness-Aware Concept-Based Explanations in Deep Neural Networks," *Advances in Neural Information Processing Systems* 33 (2020): 20554-565.

10 The idea generalizes to other modalities and has been applied to text with reasonable success.

Consider the loan approval models in Figure 6-7, and let's look at an applicant with an income of $80K, a credit score of 750, and a height of 5 ft. 10 in. Note that, here we're purposefully including height as an irrelevant feature and expect that the models will learn to not rely on it. For both the models, the decision is to approve the loans, and there is a clear explanation for how the different features do or do not contribute to the decision: high income and high credit score make the loan approval more likely, whereas height does not affect the decision at all. We can make these observations without the need of a post hoc explanation technique like Shapley values. Of course, more sophisticated models can potentially offer better performance. What follows are alternatives for making models more explainable by design beyond adhering to simple model architectures.

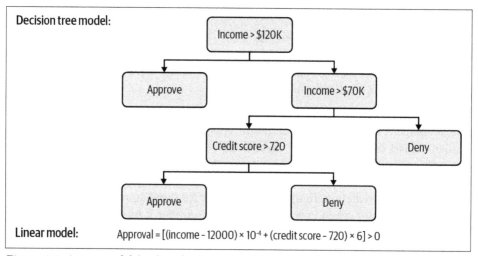

Figure 6-7. A tree model (top) and a linear model (bottom) for predicting loan approval decisions. Both provide inherently transparent decisions, and how the decision will change with respect to the features "income" and "credit score."

Other ways explainability can be made a part of the model building is via adding some explainability constraints during model training or by approximating complex, opaque models by simpler, more transparent ones. Since inherently explainable models form a very limited class of models, we'll explore the more general methods, namely explainability via constraints and distillation, in the following sections.

Explainability via constraints

A natural extension to inherently interpretable models are models that retain some of the desired properties of the interpretable models while offering more flexibility. Monotonicity and linearity are two such properties that we will describe in more detail.

Monotonicity of prediction with certain input features can lead to models that are more interpretable and trustworthy. For example, everything else being the same, a college applicant with higher grades compared to another applicant should have a higher likelihood of getting accepted—which can't be guaranteed by models in general, leading to opaque decisions. Akin to linear models, where a positive coefficient implies nondecreasing and a negative coefficient a nonincreasing relationship, more sophisticated models can be built with monotonicity constraints injected during the design and training phase. In our work on deep lattice networks,[11] we propose model components within the framework of deep neural networks that can retain monotonicity across the layers. Intuitively, monotonicity can be propagated through the layers if the intervening nonlinear layers are monotonic (like ReLU), and the linear transformations have positive weights. Figure 6-8 illustrates this intuition.

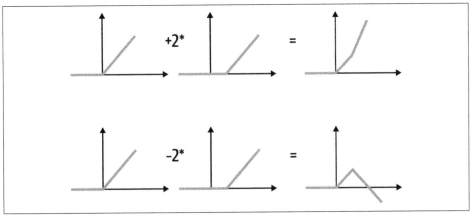

Figure 6-8. Top: a monotonicity preserving linear combination of nonlinear layer outputs. Bottom: without any constraints on the parameters, the monotonicity is not preserved.

Another way to introduce interpretability into the models is by using linear models but in a transformed space that can capture nonlinear interactions. Note that this approach would involve a postprocessing step to use an inverse transform on the transformed features to obtain an interpretation on the original features. Techniques like this have been prevalent and are often realized using kernels[12] where an input is first transformed to a different space and then a linear model is built using these transformed features. Figure 6-9 shows how points that might be linearly

---

11 Seungil You et al., "Deep Lattice Networks and Partial Monotonic Functions," *Advances in Neural Information Processing Systems* 30 (2017).

12 Bernhard Schölkopf, "The Kernel Trick for Distances," *Advances in Neural Information Processing Systems* 13 (2000).

nonseparable in their original space can become linearly separable in the transformed space, thus allowing you to build powerful yet simple models.

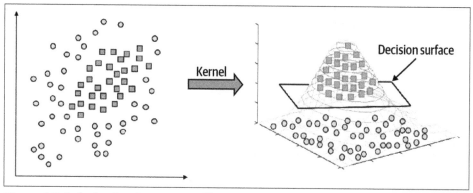

Figure 6-9. Left: the data is nonseparable, requiring more sophisticated yet opaque models for good performance. Right: kernel transformation can make the data linearly separable so an interpretable linear model can be used instead.

Therefore, the main challenge toward enforcing linearity is to come up with kernels or transformations that can make sense to an end user. For example, one such transformation for images might be encoding distance to prototypes. Let's consider a transformation to three prototype-nearness scores (horse-score, crossing-score, car-score); if an image is transformed to (0.9, 0.5, 0.001), a linear model can predict it to be a zebra, which makes for a transparent and interpretable prediction. Alvarez-Melis and Jaakkola[13] offer a formal generalization to this idea, showing how interpretable models can be built with certain constraints on transformations and composability (more general than linear combination).

Explainability via distillation

Earlier in this chapter, we discussed how simpler models like linear or tree-based models are inherently more explainable. However, they may fare poorly against the more sophisticated models in terms of performance. Model distillation is a framework that attempts to combine the performance of the complex models with the transparency of the simpler models. The central idea involves approximating the performance of a complex, opaque model called the "teacher" with that of a simpler, transparent model called the "student." Along with transparency, this approach has the added bonus of making the models smaller and consequently, faster. There are two main issues to consider here: what is the benefit of this two-tier approach

---

13 David Alvarez Melis and Tommi Jaakkola, "Towards Robust Interpretability with Self-Explaining Neural Networks," *Advances in Neural Information Processing Systems* 31 (2018), *https://oreil.ly/XxLTs*.

(complex to simple distillation) compared to directly training the simple model, and what are the general ways to build these student models?

Instead of first building a complex model (teacher), and then distilling it down to a simple model (student), a practitioner might consider directly building a simple model if transparency is the goal. While this idea is reasonable on the surface, it misses out on the rich information that the teacher model can provide to the student model. Consider a classification problem—a simple model trained using just the original training data can be thought of as an approximation to the teacher where the goal is only to match the hard labels (cat or dog) since both have access to the same information. However, with the distillation approach, soft labels (`probability(cat)`, `probability(dog)`) can be created using the teacher and provide much more fine-grained information to the student since now the data includes richer differentiation between instances of different dogs (analogously cats).

To elaborate, the general way to build student models is by augmenting the training data using the original, complex teacher model. This can be done via soft labels and predicted hard labels for classification and predicted target for regression. The student can then be built to both optimize performance on the original training set and to optimize how close it is to the teacher. Figure 6-10 shows this general framework where the original data as well as the augmented data is used to train a distilled student model. You can find more details in this foundational paper (*https://oreil.ly/1vmKs*) by Hinton et al.[14] and follow-up work (*https://oreil.ly/VvwPU*) by Frosst et al.[15]

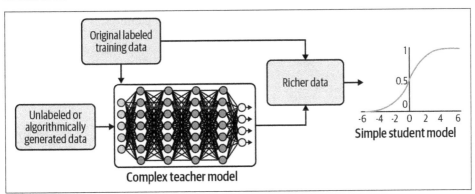

Figure 6-10. Instead of directly training a simple model from just the training data, distillation techniques can use both the training data and the augmented data from a teacher model to train a better-performing student model.

14 Geoffrey Hinton et al., "Distilling the Knowledge in a Neural Network," arXiv, 2015.

15 Nicholas Frosst et al., "Distilling a Neural Network into a Soft Decision Tree," arXiv, 2017.

Other Modalities

While you are more likely to work with datasets containing images, text, and tabular data, the explainability techniques discussed in this book are general and can be applied to other data modalities with a few extra steps. In previous chapters, we went into the details for applications of different explainability techniques to the three common modalities. In this section, we'll go over two case studies that highlight how the different techniques can be applied to other modalities.

Time-Series Data

Time-series forecasting problems are some of the most common ML use cases in the business world. Many real-world datasets have time component features, and accurate time-series forecasting can be incredibly beneficial in decision-making. However, working with time-series data is approached quite differently to how you might approach a typical supervised regression problem. With any ML task, creating features is one of the most important and time-consuming components; with time-series models, it is even more challenging because with time-series data, each feature potentially affects the prediction over different time horizons. A common approach to creating time-series is to use a sliding window where the features for a single training example are taken over a certain number of time steps and used to predict variables of interest for (potentially multiple) future time steps, as shown in Figure 6-11. In addition, these time-dependent features are often combined with static covariates such as holidays, store location, store promotions, or product information. This time dependence on features poses a unique challenge for explainability.

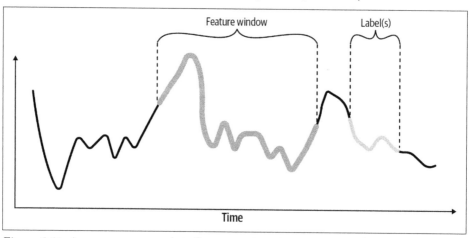

Figure 6-11. A common approach to feature engineering time-series data is to use a sliding window to create features and labels. The feature window would create the features for a single training example and its corresponding label, or labels in the case of multihorizon forecasting.

For example, suppose we wanted to build an ML model to predict customer traffic at a restaurant on any given day. In this case, the number of customers could be used as a time-series feature to capture temporal trends; but also, local ads, the weather, or special holidays are relevant features whose values depend on the time they occurred. In fact, ads and weather on a given day as well as for at least a few days in the past can affect how many people go to the restaurant. Even the future can affect traffic since a gloomy weekend forecast can motivate diners to go out on a Thursday night.

Depending on the model, techniques like Shapley values can still be used because the user can create a baseline time-series and compute how the prediction changes as features are swapped from baseline values to the given value. However, generating feature attributions can be difficult to understand since instead of n, we now have $n \cdot t$ Shapley values, where n is the number of features and t is the time horizon (past + future).

As a concrete example, let us assume we are aiming to predict the customer traffic to the restaurant on a Friday night using only the weather and advertisements and looking at the data for three days into the past, ignoring any information about the future. Now, we have six features that can affect the prediction: weather on Tuesday, Wednesday, and Thursday, as well as whether or not the restaurant was advertised on a local website on the same days. Figure 6-12 shows these features as [(False, Cloudy), (True, Rainy), (True, Sunny)]. In this case, the baseline might be [(False, Cloudy), (False, Cloudy), (False, Cloudy)].

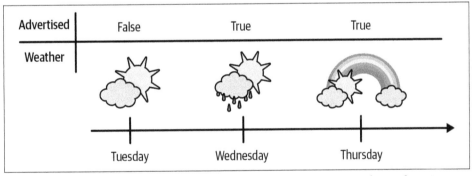

Figure 6-12. To predict the customer traffic to the restaurant on a Friday night using only the weather and advertisements and looking at the data for three days would result in six features to consider when implementing Shapley values.

Using Shapley values as is will give us fine-grained attributions on how each feature contributed on each day. While this information can be useful, it can also quickly get overwhelming and unwieldy for datasets with many features and models with long time horizons. To make sure that the explanations are more easily understandable, some postprocessing can be done. The simplest postprocessing would be aggregating the explanations by features or time.

For example, suppose our model predicts that 65 diners will come to the restaurant on Friday. Aggregating by features accumulates the Shapley values for each feature over the entire time horizon, leading to an overall attribution for an individual feature —weather contributed to 40 diners going to the restaurant whereas ads contributed to 25 diners going to the restaurant. Aggregating by time accumulates the Shapley values for each time point over all the features, leading to an overall attribution for an individual time point—Tuesday's feature information contributed to 5 diners going to the restaurant, Wednesday's feature information contributed to 30 diners, and Thursday's feature information contributed to 30 diners. Both schemes account for the 65 diners that were predicted by the model for Friday, but instead of six attributions (i.e., 3 · 2), we are down to five (i.e., 3 from aggregating by time + 2 from aggregating by features), as shown in Figure 6-13. If we were considering 20 features over 30 days, the difference would be far more drastic: 600 attributions versus 50.

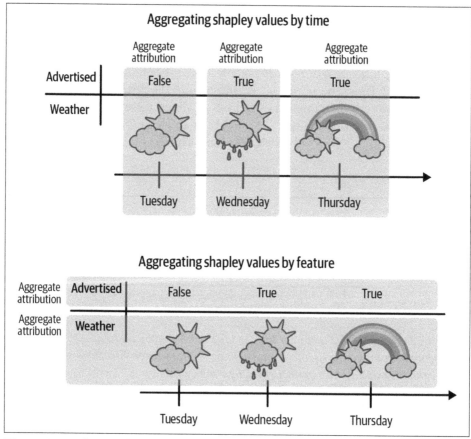

Figure 6-13. When implementing Shapley values for time-series models, one way to make explanations more easily understandable is through postprocessing, e.g., aggregating the explanations by features or by time.

This restaurant example focused on feature attribution, but similar extensions can be made, for example, for influence function-based explanations—how similar is this Thursday to other days in the past, or how would the prediction change if a specific day's data was removed from the training set.

Another approach to explaining time-series data is through attention-based models (discussed in Chapter 5). Also, AI labs out of MIT and the Harvard NLP group have released exBERT (*https://oreil.ly/A7wM0*),[16] an interactive visualization tool for exploring transformer models. However, these attention-based models are not as well equipped to handle different types of inputs such as both temporal and static features, not just language or speech. To address this challenge, a recent 2021 paper (*https://oreil.ly/ZGp1w*) introduced Temporal Fusion Transformers[17] (TFTs). TFTs are an attention-based DNN model designed for multihorizon forecasting and developed specifically to allow for more direct interpretability.

Multimodal Data

There are scenarios where the input can come from many different modalities such as medical diagnosis that can use images (X-ray), text (doctor's notes), tabular (patient information), and time-series (echocardiogram) information. Given the model-agnostic nature of several of the techniques we have discussed in the book, even models built over multimodal data can be explained with the same tools.

Let's consider a relatively simple problem of visual question answering, where given an image and a question, the model is required to predict an answer. Let's also assume we intend to use Integrated Gradients (IG), introduced in Chapter 4, as the explainability technique. We have already seen how IG can be used with images; to use it for text, we first need to transform the text from a discrete (words encoded by their IDs) to a continuous domain (words encoded by their embeddings) because IG requires gradient operations that are ill-defined for discrete domains. Once we have IG attributions for word embedding elements, they can be summed up to get the attribution for the word. The attributions for image pixels do not require any postprocessing. Figure 6-14 shows an example of this type of attribution applied to a visual question answering model with attribution at pixel and word level.[18] This can be a powerful tool for model debugging too—a model that has high attribution for uninformative words like *the* would require further scrutiny.

---

16 Benjamin Hoover et al., "exBERT: A Visual Analysis Tool to Explore Learned Representations in Transformers Models," arXiv, 2019.

17 Bryan Lim et al., "Temporal Fusion Transformers for Interpretable Multi-Horizon Time Series Forecasting," *International Journal of Forecasting* 37.4 (2021): 1748–64.

18 The code for this example can be found in the Captum tutorial on VQA models: *https://oreil.ly/7nE2e*.

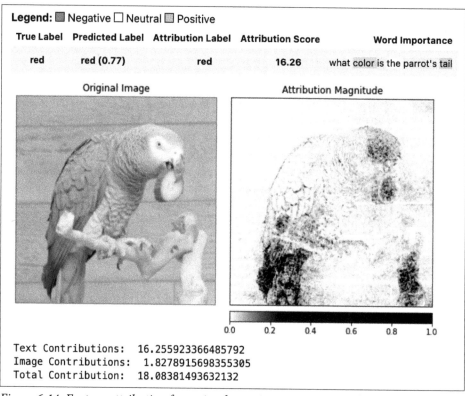

Figure 6-14. Feature attribution for a visual question answering model that takes both an image and a question (text) as inputs. The highlights show which words and which pixels contributed the most to the predicted label. Feature attributions are relative, and aggregation can be done to get the modality level attribution that yields a contribution of 16.26 from the question and 1.83 from the image. (Print readers can see the color image at https://oreil.ly/xai-6-14.)

Evaluation of Explainability Techniques

For most part, this book has focused on well-established explainability techniques that have been widely used across different applications. At this stage, you're probably wondering how these techniques compare with each other or if one technique is better than the others somehow. Unfortunately, there is no free lunch and different techniques may do better or worse depending on your dataset, your use case, and how you plan to use the resulting explanations. Just as there is no one-size-fits-all machine learning model, there is no single explainability technique that surpasses all the rest. Instead, we encourage you to view and collect these techniques as tools in a well-stocked toolkit that exists to help you analyze your model and can be utilized through your entire ML workflow (see Chapter 8).

Although you may have a bunch of explainability techniques at your disposal, the question still remains as to how you can evaluate them and which one is best to use for your use case. Evaluating a predictive machine learning model is much more straightforward; there are well-known metrics you can use like accuracy, precision/recall, mean-square error, intersection over union, and so on. However, there is a lack of consensus for how to evaluate the quality of explanations. Often, researchers have relied on showing a handful of examples to convince others of the usefulness of their proposed explanation technique, but over time more attention has been devoted to developing systematic evaluation methods. In this section, we will go over a few different approaches to evaluating explainability techniques. Even though this discussion is not exhaustive, we aim to provide you with a starting point and to create awareness for the topic.

A Theoretical Approach

With the lack of clear evaluation metrics for assessing explainability techniques, one approach is to take a "first principles" perspective, meaning with no preconceived assumptions, and define a collection of axioms that any practitioner would expect an explainability technique to have.

Axioms of Mathematics

In mathematics, axioms are statements that cannot be proven true or false. They are accepted to be self-evidently true and serve as the starting point from which the rest of the abstract theory can be developed. For example, the axiom of equality states that a number is always equal to itself. Or perhaps, in more layman's terms, "It is what it is." This seems too obvious to not be true, and it's what any reasonable person would expect. However, this statement can't formally be proven true or false, so it is accepted as true. Axioms like this form the foundation of mathematical theory, from which the proofs of all other theorems, propositions, lemmas, and conjectures follow.

An axiomatic approach defines a collection of well-understood and accepted properties (i.e., axioms) that any explainability technique *should* have. This provides an intuitive benchmark with which to judge new or existing techniques. In their 2017 paper (*https://oreil.ly/wKm1j*)[19] introducing the technique of Integrated Gradients, Sundararajan et al. also introduce a collection of fundamental axioms for qualifying feature attributions. We'll briefly discuss those axioms here because they provide a

---

19 Mukund Sundararajan et al., "Axiomatic Attribution for Deep Networks," International Conference on Machine Learning, PMLR, 2017.

nice sanity check for what we expect an explainability method should possess and, when possible, we'll compare these axioms against some of the techniques we've seen so far in the book. However, keep in mind that these axioms are just one way of framing evaluation, and just because one method doesn't satisfy one of the axioms doesn't mean it should be abandoned completely. It's very likely that it could still be a useful technique for you and for your use case.

To frame the following axioms, we'll borrow the notation from the 2017 paper. Let F represent the model's (e.g., a deep neural network) prediction for a certain class label and the $x = (x_1, x_2, \cdots, x_n)$ represent an input tensor to F. We measure attributions in the context of a baseline, so let x' denote the baseline. For example, suppose we have some input image, as in Figure 6-15, and our model predicts the class label "sulfur-crested cockatoo" with a confidence of 0.886.

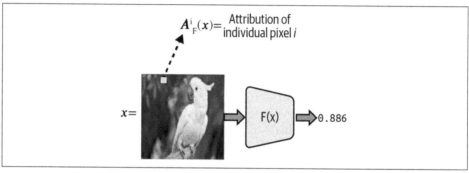

Figure 6-15. The model function F takes an input image x and maps to a value between 0 and 1, which represents the model's class prediction for that example.

The model function F maps the input image x to a probability score in $(0,1)$. If we take the baseline to be a black image, then $F(x') = 0$. The features of the model are the pixels, the individual x_i's of the image, so we take $A_F^i(x)$ to represent the feature attribution of pixel x_i of the model F at the input x with respect to the baseline x'.

Axiom of completeness

The axiom of completeness is perhaps the most straightforward. It states that for any input to the model, the total attribution must be equal to the sum of all of the feature attributions of the input. Mathematically, this means:

$$F(x) - F(x') = \sum_i A_F^i(x)$$

You can think of completeness as a sanity check that the attribution method is comprehensive in assigning attributions to features. That is to say, the attribution of a given input is "completely" accounted for across all model features. It seems like

---

a reasonable request, and many of the explainability methods we've discussed satisfy this criteria, such as Integrated Gradients, Shapley values, and Layer-Wise Relevance Propagation. However perturbation techniques, such as LIME, do not.

Axiom of sensitivity

As the name suggests, the axiom of sensitivity examines how sensitive or stable an explainability method should be to changing feature values. It states that if the baseline and input differ only by one feature, but the prediction is the same, then that feature should have zero attribution. And conversely, if the input and baseline differ by only one feature, and the prediction is different, then that feature must have nonzero attribution. For example, in Figure 6-16, the two images differ by a single pixel value, but the model prediction doesn't change. The (in)sensitivity axiom says that in this case the attribution for that feature (i.e., pixel) should be zero.

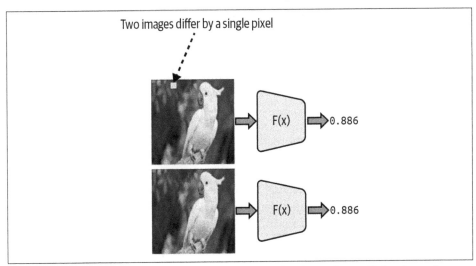

Figure 6-16. The two images differ by one feature value (a single pixel), but have the same prediction. The feature attribution for this pixel should be zero.

Mathematically, this axiom can be formulated as follows: if an input example x has only one nonzero feature and $F(x) \neq 0$ then the attribution for that feature is zero. Stated with respect to insensitivity, this axiom states that if the model function $F(x)$ does not depend on the value of a feature, as in Figure 6-16, then the attribution of that feature should be zero.

You can show that completeness implies sensitivity, so any technique that satisfies the axiom of completeness also satisfies the sensitivity axiom. Although perturbations methods of explainability do not satisfy completeness, they do satisfy sensitivity. However, methods like DeConvNets and Guided Backprop, which we discuss in Chapter 4, violate this sensitivity axiom.

Axiom of implementation invariance

The next axiom is related to the dependence on the machine learning model itself. The axiom of implementation invariance states that if two different models are functionally equivalent, meaning they compute the exact same function $F(x)$, then the attributions for all the features should be the same. In short, if the function F doesn't change between two models, then their attributions shouldn't change either. This axiom seems pretty straightforward to expect of an explainability technique. After all, why should the attributions change just because the implementation changes? So long as the final prediction is the same, that's all that should matter, right? Well, there are indeed methods that don't satisfy this criteria, such as DeepLIFT and Layer-Wise Relevance Propagation.

Axiom of linearity

The axiom of linearity says that if you can express your machine learning model as a linear combination of two other model functions, then the attributions should also be expressed in the same way. For example, if the model function F can be written as the sum of two model functions then you should expect that the attributions sum as well. Integrated Gradients and other path-based methods satisfy this axiom.

Axiom of symmetry-preserving

The last axiom is the axiom of symmetry-preserving. We say that two features are symmetric if they can be interchanged and the model function F prediction doesn't change. The axiom states that if two features are symmetric, meaning they are interchangeable without changing the value of F, then their attributions should be the same as well. This is somewhat related to the sensitivity axiom, but they're slightly different. The axiom of sensitivity says that if you change one feature value and the total attribution of the input doesn't change, then that feature must have zero attribution. Symmetry-preserving instead pertains to the model function itself. It means that there are two input variables that are symmetric. So, for any image, swapping these two pixel values wouldn't change the predicted value of F. In this case, the attributions should be the same as well.

This axiomatic approach to evaluating explainability techniques provides a reasonable sanity check and a good starting point. However, just because a certain technique fails one of these axioms doesn't mean you should discount it completely. Depending on your use case, that technique could still be beneficial to you. They simply provide one lens with which to understand the potential drawbacks or caveats of a certain method. Since these axioms were introduced, there have been a number of other studies aimed at providing a more rigorous framework for evaluating XAI techniques. Next, we'll discuss some of these empirical approaches.

Empirical Approaches

In the previous section, we looked at some of the desirable properties of an explanation technique and stated them as axioms establishing a theoretical framework. Trying to prove that your explanation method satisfies these axioms can get mathematically cumbersome and might be overkill if the aim is to quickly establish whether the method is good enough for your use case. In this section, we look at empirical approaches that can be applied to most techniques out of the box and are founded on intuition about how a technique should behave in simple scenarios.

Basic sanity checks

Basic sanity checks are the first line of investigation for the subject of evaluation. A sanity check is a quick way to weed out poor methods. A good method must necessarily pass such a check, but passing the check is not sufficient proof of correctness or good performance, since the checks are not intended to be exhaustive. With this in mind, one of the simplest questions to ask is whether an explainability technique truly does reveal something about the underlying model behavior. If the explanations don't change much with different models, the quality of the explainability technique appears rightfully suspicious. Similarly, if the data labels were changed, breaking the relationship between the model inputs and their outputs, we should expect explanations to change as well.

A sanity check–based approach (*https://oreil.ly/jprIH*)[20] has been used to evaluate saliency maps for commonly used explainability techniques, including many of the methods we've discussed in this book like Guided Backprop, Guided Grad-CAM, Grad-CAM, Integrated Gradients, and Gradient x Input. To test the sensitivity of these methods to the model weights, Adebayo et al. compare the output of each saliency method when applied to a trained model against the same saliency output for the model with randomized weights. To test for sensitivity to data, a data randomization test compares the outputs of these saliency methods for a model trained on the true dataset and for a model trained on a copy of the dataset where the labels have been randomly shuffled. As with the model parameter randomization test, you would expect that the saliency outputs would change dramatically when the labels are randomized.

Surprisingly, many of these saliency methods failed these basic sanity checks. For example, the saliency maps produced by Guided Backprop and Guided Grad-CAM were found to be not sensitive to these randomization tests. A follow-up paper (*https://oreil.ly/t19iJ*)[21] discovered some gaps in the evaluation scheme of Adebayo et al., suggesting caveats on how sensitivity should be measured and how visualization

---

20 Julius Adebayo et al., "Sanity Checks for Saliency Maps," *Advances in Neural Information Processing Systems* 31, 2018.

of the results can induce bias. These sanity checks, when done properly, can still be of value and provide one means of evaluation for an explainability technique. As a practitioner, you should be cautious when interpreting the results of both the explainability techniques and the evaluation schemes.

Faithfulness check

The next and a more challenging way to evaluate explainability techniques is to consider faithfulness of explanations to the model; that is, whether high attribution (to features or training data points) actually implies importance. In other words, an explainability technique can be considered to be revealing a model's strong reliance on a feature or training data point, if the model's performance suffers strongly when the high attribution inputs (features or training data points) are removed. However, if a technique assigns a high attribution to an input (feature or a training data point), and removing or altering that input doesn't change the model's performance significantly, the technique's attribution is less reliable.

In the paper that introduces XRAI (*https://oreil.ly/mO1Sl*),[22] a masking-based evaluation scheme is defined that captures this idea: starting with a blurry image, most-to least-salient pixels (based on the attribution) are sequentially introduced and model performance is evaluated. For a good explainability technique, we expect sharp improvement in performance at the start since the high saliency pixels are indeed the ones that would be the most useful to the model.

As a concrete example, let's consider a 5×5 image of a cat for which the model predicts "cat" with confidence 0.9. This means there are 25 pixels that can be ranked by attribution. Starting from a blurry image, we add pixels one by one based on their attribution values and notice how the prediction changes. Let's assume that the blurry image has a confidence score of 0 for the image being a cat. For a faithful technique, we would expect a big jump in confidence (say, from 0 to 0.3) when the highest attribution pixel is added, a somewhat smaller jump (e.g., from 0.3 to 0.5) for the next one, an even smaller jump (0.5 to 0.6) for the one after, and so on. This would be an insertion-based check. We can also do a deletion-based check by removing high attribution pixels one by one, and for a good technique, we should see the prediction fall sharply at the start. If the technique was poor, we should see erratic jumps with both the insertion or the deletion checks.

---

21 Mukund Sundararajan and Ankur Taly, "A Note About: Local Explanation Methods for Deep Neural Networks Lack Sensitivity to Parameter Values," arXiv, 2018.

22 Andrei Kapishnikov et al., "XRAI: Better Attributions Through Regions," Proceedings of the IEEE/CVF International Conference on Computer Vision, 2019.

Synthetic datasets

Another approach to evaluation is through synthetic datasets where the ML practitioner knows what the salient inputs are a priori. An explainability technique that can demonstrate it picks out these salient inputs is then more trustworthy than the one that picks out nonsalient inputs. For feature-based explanations, Yang, Mengjiao, and Kim provide a case study (*https://oreil.ly/EL27y*)[23] on how synthetic data can be used for evaluating explainability techniques. By taking an image patch from a specific class (say, dog) and pasting it in different backgrounds, this approach ensures that the background is never quite salient since an image can be a dog anywhere (dog on a beach, dog in a gym, dog in a ring, etc.) and a good explainability technique shouldn't attribute much relevance to the background. For example-based explanations, similar augmentations can be made by adding random data points to the training set and measuring how attribution gets assigned to these nonsalient data points.

Application specific

Using basic sanity checks, faithfulness checks and checks built using synthetic datasets can help you evaluate your explanation technique in many scenarios. However, as you might have noticed, most of these checks are built as safeguards against obvious mistakes and don't guarantee success for a technique that has passed them. Another prevalent theme of explainability evaluation is centered around real use cases and becomes most relevant for sensitive applications. If explanations are being used to facilitate cancer diagnosis, the evaluation should consider metrics like time saved, mistakes avoided, new mistakes made, etc. A technique can pass all the previous checks, but if it doesn't save doctors any time while diagnosing, it might not be a great fit for the application. Similarly, if the explanations are being used to convey understanding of a model's inner workings to an everyday user, the evaluation should consider how well the explanations align with the user's intuition (this is discussed in more depth in Chapter 7).

Evaluation of explainability techniques is an active and hotly debated topic with a consistent flux of new ideas. As these explainability techniques continue finding their way into critical or regulated applications, the question of how much trust can be placed in any technique will continue to be pertinent. Unlike areas in machine learning where the notion of ground truth is well-defined leading to clear metrics, quantifying the quality of evaluation techniques is further complicated by the fact that for real-world datasets, the ground truth is often ambiguous—is that an image of a bee because of the striped pattern or because of the presence of specific flowers? Both are valid explanations even if one corresponds more closely to human intuition. Until we have well-established evaluation methodologies, it is worthwhile to spend

---

23 Yang, Mengjiao, and Been Kim, "Benchmarking Attribution Methods with Relative Feature Importance," arXiv, 2019.

some time ensuring alignment between the technique's intended use case and the application at hand.

Summary

In this chapter, we went over some of the emerging topics in the field of explainability. Different ways of approaching the question of explainability continue to receive attention from both researchers and practitioners. With that in mind, we first discussed how attribution or saliency can be assigned to inputs other than just the data features. Specifically, we looked at attributing to training data via a notion of similarity and influence functions. We also revisited attribution to concepts that can be defined via an auxiliary input.

Next we looked at a class of explainability methods that intervene during the modeling process as opposed to the post hoc techniques that are the main area of focus for the book. You saw how constraints like linearity and monotonicity can lead to more transparent and trustworthy models. We also went over how complex models can be distilled to simpler approximate models, often by using richer data generated using the complex model. Such models are easier to understand and have been successfully used for applications like ensuring fairness.

To reinforce the point that several of the techniques discussed in this book are model and modality agnostic, we looked at a couple of examples of applying Shapley values and integrated gradient techniques to different modalities, with the former being mostly applicable out of the box for time-series and the latter applicable to mixed (image and text) modality with low-overhead pre- and postprocessing.

Lastly, we looked at the fairly nascent field of systematic evaluation of explainability techniques. Historically, hand-picked examples of a technique's good performance were taken to be sufficient evidence for the quality of a technique. However, lately, there has been a larger push toward using well-defined, independent evaluation frameworks, especially as explainability continues to be applied to sensitive domains. Ranging from basic sanity checks to faithfulness studies to methods employing synthetic data, these frameworks aim to ensure alignment between the user's expectations and the technique's performance. The goals and methodologies for evaluation are not clearly understood, and extra care is required when using XAI for critical applications. Since a significant amount of XAI usage is by decision-makers, research is also experiencing a surge in field studies involving interactions between the explainability tools and human users. We continue to explore this aspect in the next chapter.

## CHAPTER 7

Interacting with Explainable AI

Explanations cannot exist in a vacuum. They are consumed, used, and acted upon by ourselves, our colleagues, auditors, and the public to gain an understanding of why an AI acted the way it did. Without explainability (and interpretability), Machine Learning (ML) is a one-way street of information and predictions. We may see an ML do something astounding, such as translating a paragraph from one language to another, but it is rare for us to unequivocally trust technology.

Fundamentally, we are in a working relationship with every AI we use. Imagine machine learning as your coworker. Even if this coworker did an amazing job, we would find them difficult to work with if, when we asked them to perform a task, they went off to another room, returned with the answer, and then promptly left again, never answering our questions or responding to a thing we said! This silent coworker problem is what explainability tries to address by starting a two-way dialogue, as in Figure 7-1, between the ML system and its users. However, this dialogue is very limited given how novel explainability is, which makes your choices around how to construct that dialogue even more important.

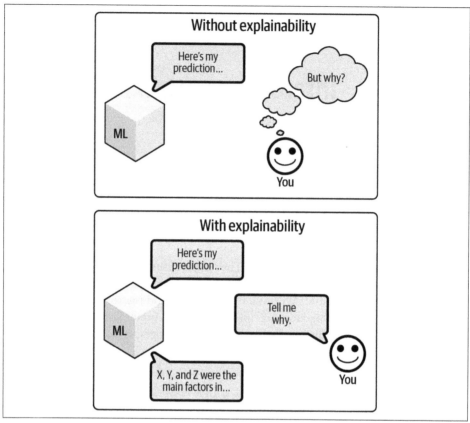

Figure 7-1. Explainability creates a dialogue between an ML and its users.

In this chapter, we will review the needs of different ML consumers and what to keep in mind when designing Explainable AI (XAI) to work best for each of these groups. We will also explore how to display explanations, and what the trade-offs are between different types of visualizations. No explanation is perfect, so we will also discuss common pitfalls in how explanations can be misinterpreted, and how to preemptively design your explainability to mitigate these issues. Finally, we will also discuss what happens after an explanation has been created and communicated, diving into the actions taken after an explanation.

Who Uses Explainability?

In Chapter 2, we discussed who consumes explanations: ML practitioners, observers, and end users. Each of these groups has a different need for explanations, and different levels of knowledge about machine learning, so we cannot treat them all the same. To better understand these groups, we can categorize them in terms of their expertise and their intent. Expertise can be in how the ML itself works, the broader environment the ML operates in, or the additional factors for the ML's input features (or inference). Intent is defined by what actions a consumer may take in reaction to receiving an explanation.

There are three common types of expertise:

Domain
> Has knowledge of the environment the ML operates in, but not necessarily how the ML itself functions. For example, a banker may understand the broader economic environment for loans.

Model inputs
> Understands or has access to additional information related to the inference inputs but may not be able to alter the inputs. While this could be the training data, it is more often the data sample used for a deployed prediction, or the dataset features in general. For example, a consumer has a deeper intrinsic understanding of their shopping preferences that informs a product recommendation system.

Machine learning
> Understands the model architecture and how the model works; however, there may be limited understanding of the dataset or implications of predictions made. For example, this could be a data scientist who was hired as a consultant to build an ML model for predicting how long it would take for robots to assemble parts in a factory, but does not have previous experience with robots, which unpredictably break down, or assembly lines, which have complex, cascading cause and effects when estimating production times.

The following are common types of intent:

Model improvement
> Based on the explanation, the user will take action to increase the quality of the model. This could include refining the training dataset, using different features, or changing the model architecture.

Build trust in the model
> Increase confidence that the model's predictions are accurate and reliable.

Verify
> Confirm that the model behaves as expected against a set of standards. For example, that a credit-rating model adheres to financial antidiscrimination regulations.[1]

---

1 This may sound analogous to the previous intent of building trust but is a distinct intent because there is no need for the model to perform well to be verified that it is working within internal and external constraints (e.g., stakeholder business requirements and industry-wide regulations).

Remediation

Understand what actions to take to alter a prediction in the future by changing the inputs to the model. For example, a consumer could remediate, in this case improve, a credit-rating prediction by reducing their debt.

Understand model behavior

Construct a simplified model in the user's mind, which can be used as a surrogate for understanding the model's performance.

Monitoring

Ongoing assessment that a model's performance remains acceptable.

An explanation consumer can have multiple simultaneous expertises and intents. In some cases, these intents can even appear contradictory. A motorist who receives a speeding ticket from an AI that tracks vehicle speeds and decides to issue tickets may simultaneously want to verify the performance of the model, and also understand what actions they could take in the future to avoid another ticket.

In practice, we have often found that people within the three main groups of explanation consumers are united by their primary expertise and needs, as shown in Table 7-1.

Table 7-1. The primary expertise and intents of explanation consumers

Consumer	Subgroup	Expertise(s)	Intent(s)
ML practitioners	Data scientist	ML	Model improvement
	ML engineer	ML	Monitoring
Observers	Business stakeholder	Domain, inputs	Trust, verify, understand
	Regulator	Domain, inputs	Verify, understand
End users	General	Inputs	Trust, remediation
	Specialist	Domain, inputs	Trust, understand

Often, as consumers become more familiar with an ML system, their expertise and intents will change. A common pattern is for data scientists to become domain experts over time, and end users, particularly in business and industries, will shift from validating a system to working to understand the model so they can anticipate and be better prepared for prediction results and common failures.

Each combination of these expertises and intents can result in a different type of explanation being more or less useful. Our advice is to think of *expertise* as the background you can assume for an explanation, and *intent* for where you want the explanation to guide the consumer toward.

Picking the Right Explanation Technique for Your Audience

The act of choosing which explanation technique is best for your audience can be difficult due to the lack of definitive guidance and vague information in the ML community. If one believes the research literature, every new technique is strictly a vast improvement over all previous explanation techniques. Conversely, there is also a corresponding number of papers demonstrating how various explanation techniques are very bad at their job. With this conflicting advice, how does one pick the right technique? By answering the following questions, you should be able to filter many possible techniques to just one or two that meet your audience's needs:

1. What needs to be explained? A single inference, a cohort of predictions, or the global behavior of the model?

2. What is the audience's expertise? Does the technique require an understanding of how ML works to interpret the results?

3. What action will they take after an explanation? Should the technique generally inform, or should it present specific details?

4. Is this ML model being used in a critical or high-risk situation? Different explanation techniques offer varying levels of guarantees and robustness.

5. How quickly do they need an explanation? The latency of generating explanations can range from milliseconds to minutes or longer.

For widely used combinations of expertise and intent, we have put together a guide of possible techniques to use. However, view these recommendations as a starting point rather than a definitive list—the best technique for your situation may vary! See Table 7-2 for a list of suggested pairings.

Table 7-2. Suggested techniques for the different expertises and intents of an ML consumer

Expertise	Intent	Explainability technique
ML	Model improvement	Sampled Shapley, Integrated Gradients, example-based, layer-based
Domain	Model monitoring	Feature attributions
	Build trust	Example-based, independent conditional expectations, distillation
	Verify	Feature attributions, concept activations, pixel attributions
Inputs	Build trust	Example-based, region-based attributions
	Verify	Partial-design plots, feature attributions
	Remediation	Example-based, concept activations

Finally, another important group of explanation consumers is other technological systems. As an example, Google has had great success in using feature attributions (*https://oreil.ly/lgWio*) to perform automated model monitoring. When abnormal drift or skew is detected in feature attributions for a newly released model, it is automatically rolled back and the previous version of the model is used. However, the topic of using explanations in an automated fashion is outside the scope of this book.

Now that you understand how XAI techniques can be used by different types of consumers and their intentions, let's turn our attention to how to visualize and present these explanations.

How to Effectively Present Explanations

Despite the whole point of explainability being to bring clarity to an ML system, explanations are often poorly presented to ML consumers. This can lead to false assumptions, misplaced confidence in an ML system, and the wrong actions being taken. Presenting explanations through a visualization, user interface, or even plain text, should serve three goals:

- Clarify what, how, and why an ML system performed the way it did.
- Accurately represent what is known in the explanation.
- Start from the ML consumer's place of understanding and build upon it.

Information visualization is an entire field of practice and research. If you want to learn more, we suggest reading *The Visual Display of Quantitative Information* by Edward Tufte (Graphics Press, 2001).

We're going to avoid the topic of explanations which themselves are interactive via UI. Although there have been research initiatives to create interactive explanations, all of these approaches are in their infancy and have not been proven to deliver at scale in the broader ML community. This comes with a caveat that we expect the future of explanations *is* interaction and collaboration, so we recommend you continue to look for opportunities in using interactive explanations.

Clarify What, How, and Why the ML Performed the Way It Did

Each explanation should provide the consumer with all the key pieces of information they need to interpret the explanation. Often, this requires additional auxiliary information to be displayed so the intent of the explanation can be understood. At a minimum, the explanation should represent:

- What is the range for a value in the explanation?

- When was the explanation generated?

- If the explanation is visual, use a recommended color scheme for good contrast in gradients, and be color-blind friendly. ColorBrewer (*https://colorbrewer2.org*) has designed and tested color palettes that are easily perceived.

- Show the predicted value(s). If it is a cohort, provide some information about how the cohort was defined.

For consumers with ML expertise, or those with an intent to verify, the explanation should also include any relevant versioning info for the dataset and model (e.g., training/validation split, randomization seed, hyperparameters, etc.) and details of the parameters chosen for the explanation technique.

We all enjoy stories, and it is natural to convey explanations through narratives. This can be a great way to convey highly technical information to a nontechnical audience. That being said, there are two risks to using narratives. First, it is easy to get swept away in trying to make the story more compelling by reaching for more impactful terms and verbiage. Second, stories almost always make use of a timeline, implying causality. In both situations, you are inadvertently conveying unfounded accuracy or certainty in the explanation to your ML consumers. Using a more journalistic style of writing, or the inverted pyramid[2] format, can be a good structure for presenting explanations as stories to users.

Accurately Represent the Explanations

The obvious goal of any explanation is to provide an accurate understanding of the model's behavior. It is equally important, but less intuitive, to be conscientious of ensuring the accuracy of the explanation itself. Raw explanations are almost always a set of numbers, and it is vital to ensure they are accurately represented when the explanation is translated into other formats (e.g., as a saliency map, bar chart, token highlighting, generated text, etc.). For example, when explaining the predictions of an image model, Integrated Gradients highlight the specific pixels that contributed to the explanation. In contrast, techniques like XRAI and LIME visualize regions that contributed to a prediction, which is less precise. Depending on your audience, either technique may be more or less appropriate. For example, a regulator seeking to verify an ML classifier for X-rays may wish to see evidence that the model was attentive to the actual X-ray scan and not ancillary, or leaked, information such as text overlaid in the X-ray image. Displaying the exact attributions of different pixels will be useful in verifying the system is behaving as expected.

---

2 The Nielsen Norman Group, one of the most respected UX research firms in the world, has an excellent article (*https://oreil.ly/n9HTD*) on the inverted pyramid.

In contrast, for a patient, it may be best to use a technique that does not mislead users into overconfidence in the accuracy of the system. For our X-ray example, we may know the system has high accuracy, but displaying exact pixel-level attributions may overcommunicate the confidence of the ML system and be counterproductive to aiding patients and medical professionals in understanding the diagnosis. In situations like these, where there is a lack of ML or domain expertise, a regional explanation technique can best convey the accuracy of the explanation, erring on the side of caution.

A common critique of explainability is that the techniques do not faithfully, or accurately, represent the actual decision-making process learned by the ML model. Many papers have been written stating that explainability should not be used due to the perceived inaccuracy of the techniques (see the Appendix for a list of suggested papers to read). However, explainability is often a necessity, not a luxury, so in many situations, you must present explanations when there is no good alternative, such as using an inherently interpretable model. It is important to not minimize the contribution of these papers to our understanding of Explainable AI, but instead view them as guides for when, and how, explainability will fail.

The majority of research on how XAI techniques fail can be grouped into two categories: the inaccuracy of the explanations, and how brittle the techniques are. The first group critiques the technical accuracy, or faithfulness, of a method to represent the model's true behavior. The second group of criticisms is focused on how robust explanations are to manipulation and noise.

Technical accuracy of explanations

Technical accuracy can be measured in several ways, such as how well the technique represents the way the model works, the numerical accuracy of the explanation value, or an independent benchmark, such as how precisely a salience map technique for an image classifier correctly outlines the shape in the image. Technical accuracy is perhaps the most utilitarian, and uncontroversial, set of research to look at when thinking about the appropriateness of a method for a given consumer. Some types of inaccuracies are mostly irrelevant to a user. For example, an end user may not expect, or be able to differentiate, between an explanation that is 90% accurate from one that is 100% accurate. This premise is what makes sampled Shapley (covered in 2 and 3) still useful, even though they represent an approximation of the true Shapley values for attributing influence to dataset features. In contrast, Grad-CAM's (Chapter 4) inaccuracy in attributing pixel influence for a multiclassification model renders it unsuitable for almost all consumers who do not have ML expertise and would understand this important exception when viewing an explainability result.

Ironically, for all the focus on evaluating the technical accuracy of explainability methods, little research has been performed on another type of accuracy aligned to our ultimate goal of having ML consumers accurately comprehend the model. We call this the *presentation efficacy*: how well the presentation of an explanation conveys information to and is understood by ML consumers. Representing an explanation with 100% efficacy means the ML consumer perfectly understood all the information conveyed by the visualization. In contrast, a presentation efficacy of 50% would mean half of the understanding was lost due to the presentation.

Consider the two explanations in Figure 7-2; both have the same underlying explanation. By using high-contrast colors, the explanation on the left has used good information visualization practices, making it easy to understand what pixels are influencing the model's classification of the bird as a cockatoo. In contrast, the explanation on the right uses the same saliency map, but rather than using a combination of high-contrast colors to represent pixel attribution, it uses white. This makes it nearly impossible to distinguish characteristics of the explanation once it is overlaid onto the original image of a white cockatoo.

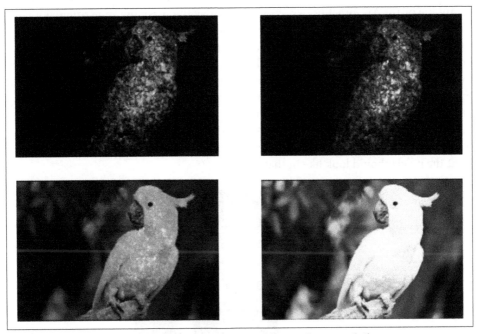

Figure 7-2. The same underlying explanation is portrayed in two different ways to illustrate how a bad visualization has very low presentation efficacy.

As of 2022, we are not aware of any research that has studied this presentation efficacy to understand topics such as thresholds for comprehension or how it may differ between types of ML consumers. In our opinion, presentation efficacy is the largest potential danger you will encounter as an ML practitioner in using, sharing, and embedding Explainable AI in your ML systems. Many Explainable AI techniques come with visualization methods that often violate core information visualization principles or, in the pursuit of aesthetics, overrepresent how accurate their explanations are.

As an example of the overrepresentation flaw, many techniques for image models mistakenly display explanation masks (heatmaps, outlines, etc.) at a higher resolution than what was generated by the technique. As these masks are often overlaid on top of the image input, the mask displays attributions to pixels that were never even seen by the model or the explanation method. Understanding how this occurs, and why it is often done, are vital to giving explainability consumers accurate explanations.

This overrepresentation comes from trying to apply an explanation mask to the original, unprocessed image used as an input to the model. Many image models crop and downsample an image to the input dimensions, often dramatically given the size of many images today compared to the common resolutions used by models (e.g., 224×224, 128×128, or 64×64 pixels). The resulting explainability mask is the same size as the input dimension (i.e., 224×224), but the designer of the explainability technique or the ML practitioner wishes to overlay the mask onto the original image, which is often at resolutions in the megapixels (e.g., more than 1024×1024). The easiest way to do this is to use an image transformation library to upsample (also known as upscale) the explanation mask using a standard image library to interpolate to the size of the original image. Modern interpolation methods are designed to "fill in the blanks" in a visually pleasing way. Figure 7-3 shows an example of upsampling on an image from the MNIST dataset using the nearest neighbors algorithm, the most basic of interpolation methods.[3] All MNIST images are purely black and white, so any gray areas in the upsampled image are approximations by the algorithm of what the pixels should look like in that region.

Figure 7-3. Upsampling an image of a 4 from the MNIST dataset to 10× its size.

---

3 Bicubic smoothing is by far the most popular technique, resulting in fuzzy-looking images. However, it is harder to see the flaws of interpolating in bicubic smoothing because our visual system naturally accommodates for images that are slightly blurry.

However, this interpolation is based on assumptions on what the new pixels should look like, rather than deriving their values from an authoritative source. As a result, upsampled explanation masks will highlight pixel attributions that never existed. Figure 7-4 shows an example of this issue. For the upscaled saliency map, erroneous attributions are introduced, resulting in light green pixels. The problem can most clearly be seen when we overlay the saliency map on top of the original image. Whereas the original pixel attribution technique showed the model as only being influenced by four pixels in a low-resolution diamond, the upscaled saliency map begins to imply that there was a fuzziness to the pixel attribution technique. This is most problematic when interesting features, such as edges or patterns, were lost in downscaling or cropping the original feature.

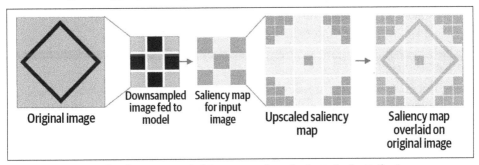

Figure 7-4. Example of an upsampled image mask and what pixel attributions were interpolated.

To avoid this problem, avoid upsampling explanation masks using interpolation. Two options, seen in Figure 7-5, are to upsample with no interpolation, which results in a disjointed but still faithful explanation mask, or to interpolate with some sort of pattern or shading to indicate "we don't know what the explanation would be for these pixels."

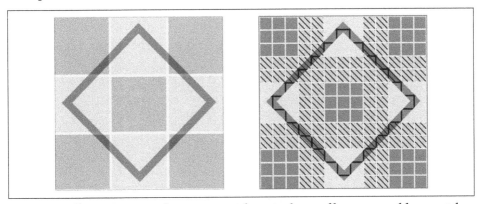

Figure 7-5. Illustrative examples, not meant for actual use, of how one could accurately show a saliency map that is resized to the original image.

Another common technical inaccuracy results from explainability techniques that do not perform per-element attributions of the input features. While this rarely occurs for structured data models, it is common to do this for feature attributions in time-series models and for region-based explanation techniques for image or text models. For example, many image explanation techniques that generate heatmap explanation masks will display a gradient to interpolate between different regions of the heatmap. This is inaccurate because the interpolation is introduced *after* the explanation has been calculated and conveys a smooth transition in model influence that may not actually exist.

A common rationale for using these gradients is that CNN models utilize a similar smoothing kernel in their convolution (downsampling) layers, so it is okay to use a similar smoothing approach in the explanation. However, the ML community has not studied the effectiveness of this claim as of the summer of 2022.

Brittleness in explanations

There is a growing body of research focused on the brittleness of different explanation techniques. *Brittleness* is the inability of a system to perform well outside of its original design parameters. For explainability, this takes the form of adversarial attacks and artificial noise injected into inputs.[4] For many techniques, it is clearly demonstrated they do not handle brittle attacks with much grace. For example, researchers were able to inject noise into an image that resulted in the image mask generated by the explanation technique spelling out different words, as shown in Figure 7-6.[5]

---

4 To the best of our knowledge, artificial perturbations of the network weights, say via retraining, and their effect on explainability techniques, has not been studied.

5 Ann-Kathrin Dombrowski et al., "Explanations Can Be Manipulated and Geometry Is to Blame," arXiv, 2019, *https://arxiv.org/abs/1906.07983*.

Figure 7-6. From the work of Dombrowski et al., the original image of a dog on the left can be imperceptibly manipulated to the image on the right to such an extent that words can be created in the explanation output.

What Are Adversarial Attacks?

In machine learning, an adversarial attack is an attempt to trick or influence a model's prediction with deceptive or manipulated data. Evasion tactics are the most common and typically involve some data modification in the form of adversarial examples; i.e., an instance with small, imperceptible changes that can fool the model into making the wrong prediction. For example, glasses or clothing that have been designed to evade facial recognition software or reflective tape that is used to trick license plate readers. These kinds of adversarial examples and attacks can pose a real problem for real-world ML systems. In 2017, scientists at MIT's LabSix, an AI research group, caused Google's image recognition model to classify a 3D-printed toy turtle modified with a slight texture as a rifle and classify a cat as guacamole.

Adversarial attacks can also take the form of model poisoning or model extraction. An extreme example of model poisoning would be when the Microsoft Twitter chatbot Tay (now defunct) was corrupted by users' input from producing light, playful conversation as intended to instead creating misogynistic and racist rants. As an example of model extraction, it's been shown that large language models (*https://arxiv.org/abs/2012.07805*)[6] like GPT-3 can actually leak details from the training data and can be prompted to return private and personally identifiable information such as names, email addresses, and phone numbers when certain manipulated keywords or phrases are sent for prediction.

In other cases, researchers have been able to demonstrate (*https://arxiv.org/abs/1902.02041*)[7] how image-based explanations can be manipulated into misexplanations through fine-tuning the model, with no significant loss in accuracy; an example is shown in Figure 7-7.

---

6 Nicholas Carlini et al., "Extracting Training Data from Large Language Models," arXiv, 2021.

7 Juyeon Heo et al., "Fooling Neural Network Interpretations via Adversarial Model Manipulation," arXiv, 2019.

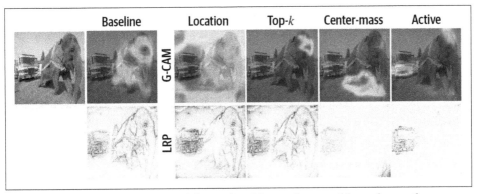

Figure 7-7. By fine-tuning the model's weights, Heo et al. were able to change the results of both Grad-CAM (Chapter 4) and LRP (Chapter 5), with no meaningful loss in the model's performance. (Print readers can see the color image at https://oreil.ly/xai-fig-7-7.)

Research into the brittleness of explainability techniques has primarily focused on image models and image-focused explanation techniques, but it is reasonable to assume many of these adversarial attacks could be adapted to other modalities. What is also not clear, as of 2022, is whether the explanation techniques are themselves performing poorly, or whether they are surfacing turmoil within the model.

While it is tempting to draw the conclusion that these explainability techniques should never be used due to their shortcomings, you should also consider how likely it is these issues may be encountered in your ML system when it is deployed in the real world. For example, how susceptible are the inputs of your model to adversarial attack? If your model draws entirely from factual internal sources, e.g., sales data or camera images on a factory floor, it is unlikely that the explanation will be exposed to adversarial attacks (or, if it is, this may be the least of your problems). Conversely, an AI that flags user comments in a forum is highly exposed to adversarial attacks, and we could expect any accompanying explanations to be vulnerable as well.

With High-Risk Systems, Ensure Explanations Do Not Overrepresent Their Validity

If your AI is being used in a high-risk system, e.g., in the medical domain or justice system, be careful to ensure your target audience does not place more emphasis on the explanation than is warranted by the technique. In such cases, we often observe that explainability is used with an intent to improve trust in the system with end users. However, these explanations are often treated as absolute truths by ML consumers and used to justify their conclusions, rather than a *probable* explanation for a model's behavior.[8]

For other, more primitive, explanation techniques such as PDP plots (discussed in Chapter 3), the risk of conveying inaccurate explanations through poor visualizations is much lower. Issues to be aware of include changing scales in the axes between explanations, which consumers may not notice, and plots that are so small they can be overinterpreted.

Build on the ML Consumer's Existing Understanding

The most useful explanations for consumers are those that build on their existing knowledge, either of the inputs, prediction, or ML model, to gain a more sophisticated understanding. To understand why this is, we must first understand a few aspects of human-computer interaction: mental models, situational awareness, and satisficing.

Mental models are very similar to ML models: they represent a framework that a person has learned that lets them quickly and efficiently reach conclusions and make decisions. Like ML, mental models often do not truly represent the actual system they model. As an example, most people's mental model of how to drive a car is that pressing the gas pedal makes the car go faster. In reality, the gas pedal controls the amount of air and fuel flowing into a car engine, which then causes a larger combustion, and in turn, causes the engine to exert more force through gears in a transmission. The gearing in this transmission allows the engine to exert more or less force depending on the speed the wheels are rotating at. While the true model of the car is more accurate, and explains why pressing a gas pedal at different speeds does not make the car accelerate the same amount, reasoning through this process every time would make driving much more onerous. Most of the time, it is sufficient to use a simpler mental model that pushing the gas pedal makes the car go faster.

---

8 An *absolute truth* explanation would be to trace an explanation throughout the entire ML's decision process/layers and annotate each weight and variable to reference its influence. It would also be absolutely incomprehensible.

For Explainable AI, the best explanations match the consumer's mental model of the ML system, or are able to help them build a sufficiently accurate mental model. It's most effective to evaluate how well the frameworks of the explanation and the mental model match each other when deciding between different families of XAI techniques. Determining user's mental models for different ML systems is done primarily through conducting user interviews and research. This is a time-consuming process that requires a trained UX researcher. Assuming your ML system is replacing an existing process, one shortcut to discovering this pairing is to ask users how they build confidence in decisions without an AI. For example, when classifying cancer in cell tissue slides, pathologists often justify their decision by referencing textbook images that represent canonical examples of cancers in cell tissue. In this case, using an example-based (or counterfactual) technique would be the best pairing for the pathologist end user, as shown by the SMILY app (*https://oreil.ly/FOSm6*) in Figure 7-8, developed by Google Health.

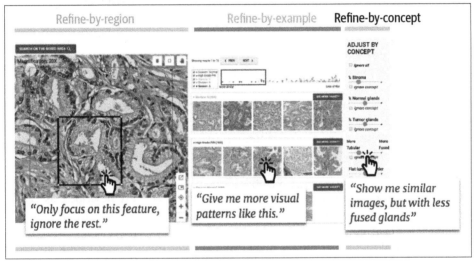

Figure 7-8. SMILY uses example-based explanations and concept explanations to help pathologists understand cell tissue slides.

Situational awareness describes how well a person understands a given scenario, and it is also a process by which people try to make decisions or arrive at conclusions when confronted with new circumstances. For ML consumers, they are often trying to improve their situational awareness when they ask the question, *Why did the ML model behave that way?*

The three steps of situational awareness are:

1. *Perceive*
   Determine what new information to gather and collect this information.

2. *Comprehend*
   Using new and existing information, build an understanding of the current situation.

3. *Project*
   With the current understanding, create assumptions about what will happen in the future. This could be which actions should be taken to change the situation, or how the situation itself will continue to evolve.

Situational awareness also heavily relies on users having a correct mental model; otherwise, it is very difficult to accurately comprehend and project, or even know what information to gather. Building situational awareness is a large field of research in its own right in human-computer interaction, so we will only briefly discuss how this pertains to ML consumers of explanations. Explanations are most influential when a person is perceiving or comprehending. As the ML practitioner, your choice of explanation technique also dictates the information available to the consumer when they are trying to gather new information about the rationale behind a prediction. Similarly, useful explanation techniques are those that best help an ML consumer comprehend the ML. Unfortunately, Explainable AI currently does little, beyond setting the stage, to help users as they project. In the future, we are looking forward to XAI that is closer to an interactive dialogue to help consumers explore different scenarios as part of improving their ability to project the future behavior of an ML model.

Satisficing is a common human behavior that might be best described as "good enough for the amount of time I've got right now." More formally, people are extremely good at deriving a generally optimal solution to a problem, doing it far faster than would be expected given the time it takes them to determine the truly optimal solution, but at the cost of relying on heuristics and stereotypes. Satisficing has been observed across all professions and, counterintuitively, as someone becomes more of an expert at their job and is faster at finding the best solution, they are no less likely to satisfice. For you, this is an important consideration of how you can expect ML consumers to interact with explanations—quickly and forming conclusions that are generally correct but may miss nuances. Anecdotally, we have seen this often arise across many model modalities and explanation techniques.

For example, consumers of feature attribution charts often summarize that features with minimal contributions (even if negative) for an individual prediction are not true for the entire dataset. For example, in a classification model, it may be that most predictions are not influenced by a feature, but for those along a decision boundary, the feature is highly influential. Another example of this approach is when one quickly assigns erroneous, semantic meaning to explanation heatmaps in images, when it is clear the model does not have the capacity for semantic representation; e.g., "clearly the model learned to recognize a cat because the cat ears and eyes are highlighted" rather than the more precise "this region of pixels contains many edges that are indicative of a cat." Satisficing is useful, and with it your ML consumers will probably arrive at the right conclusion most of the time more quickly. However, it also causes failures in the cases that may be of most interest to you and these consumers, where the model is not behaving as expected.

To counter satisficing, try to carefully curate the information presented in the explanation to the user. For example, many feature- and pixel-attribution techniques do not show negative attributions because it helps ML consumers be more focused on signals that drive the model toward the prediction (rather than away from it). It is also useful to design explanations to help answer a specific question for a consumer, rather than just being a general dashboard of the model's health.

With this discussion of mental models, situational awareness, and satisficing, it is also worth asking if explanations can be used to teach users how an ML model works. There is little research into this area of explainability, but we also expect that this would be a difficult use of explanations in their current form. By definition, the techniques we've presented in this book seek to explain a model *after* it has made a prediction, in a post hoc fashion. By asking if explainability can teach a user about how an ML model works, we are also asking if explanations could be used to create a surrogate, interpretable ML model. Whether this is feasible is still an active area of research.

Common Pitfalls in Using Explainability

In using explanations, we find there are a few common pitfalls for ML consumers. These situations occur not because there is something wrong with the explanation or ML model but come from consumers improperly understanding or using explanations. Most result from overreliance or overconfidence in the explanation technique but are also driven by how explainability results are packaged and delivered to consumers. The three most common pitfalls are assuming causality, overfitting "intent" to a model, and leveraging additional explanations in an attempt to augment the original explanation.

Helping Your Future Self Understand the Explanations You Generated Today

Once you get an explanation technique up and running, it's tempting to cash in on your hard work and generate as many explanations as you can right away. Unfortunately, you often find yourself squinting at many charts in an old Jupyter notebook or trying to explain the context for the explanation you sent along to colleagues a few months ago.

To save yourself future frustration, we've found it useful to always embed the following information in your explanations:

1. Exact technique and parameters used, e.g., was it SHAP or Captum's sampled Shapley?

2. Model version, training configuration, hyperparameter values, and dataset version, to be able to trace the source of the explanation.

3. Timestamp the explanation was generated, which is useful for knowing if the explanation is stale.

4. Input and inference values. You would be surprised how few techniques include this information in their visualizations.

Assuming Causality

Very few, if any, explanation techniques are able to establish causality in any sufficiently complex model. Techniques can only describe correlations between what influenced the model and the prediction. For example, Integrated Gradients may highlight a single pixel as highly influential in the model's prediction, but the technique does not guarantee that the pixel caused (even in part) the prediction.

At odds with explanation techniques' ability to provide correlations is the strong human desire to explain consequences due to causality. Causality is an important part of storytelling and narratives, and often you will find that consumers try to fit an explanation into a broader narrative to justify, attack, or just comprehend a model's actions. It is very difficult to work around this need for causality, and you will not get far trying to change your consumer's instinctive behavior. Instead, there are two strategies you can use to mitigate the tendency to fall back to causative descriptions:

- Language matters. Whenever introducing an explanation, whether with text, verbally, or in a presentation, be careful to not introduce or imply causation. This can be very difficult! For example, with feature attributions, it is tempting to say a particular feature caused the model to behave a certain way. Instead, try to use words like "influence" or "suggest."

- Avoid "this-then-that" narratives. Often explanations, with good intentions, try to present a logical flow of information and narrative. "This is the input to the model, then the model generated this prediction, here is the explanation" is a common narrative. Unfortunately, this narrative also implies a causal chain of reasoning from inputs to explanations. Instead, you may want to try inverting this narrative: "The model gave this prediction, which is explained by X. Additionally, here are the inputs."

Overfitting Intent to a Model

When given a sufficiently compelling explanation, consumers are tempted to extrapolate from the explanation to concepts learned by the model. Except for those focused on concepts, e.g., TCAVs, it is difficult to say that most explanation techniques are able to reveal semantic concepts the model has learned. In our earlier example of an image classifier given a prediction for a photo of a cat, it is accurate to say what pixels influenced the prediction, but it is not accurate to reach further and say, "Now we know the model has learned how to recognize cat ears." It certainly could have, but a pixel attribution technique gives explanations based on the pixels in the image, not the semantic concepts related to those pixels.

To avoid this overfitting, make explanations clear and constrained.

Overreaching for Additional Explanations

Once given a sufficient explanation, it is not unusual for ML consumers to reach for another explanation technique to augment their understanding. However, these techniques, even if good on their own, may not actually increase the power of the original explanation. For example, a common reach is for a user who has received a feature attribution explanation to try and find a counterfactual explanation to prove the validity of the feature attribution by finding a prediction for a data sample with a different value for the most influential feature and a different predicted class. The consumer may then declare this proves the influence of the top-ranked feature. While the counterfactual can enhance our understanding of the model's behavior, and even back-and-forth between looking at feature attributions and corresponding counterfactuals can tell us about different facets of the model, it is important to not treat each explanation as a validation of the other. Each explanation has its own gotchas and nuances that constrain what they can tell us about the model. Together, they may widen our understanding of the model, but may not necessarily deepen our understanding of one particular aspect.

Preventing explanation overreach is difficult because users often take matters into their own hands to find new explanations. Strongly discouraging this behavior rarely works in practice either, as the ML consumers will genuinely believe they are proactively contributing to the overall quality of the Explainable AI. Instead, to prevent overreach, you can help channel this positive energy in a productive direction by making it easy to retrieve additional explanations with the same technique, or proactively determining what techniques can be combined in advance and offering those to the user.

Summary

In this chapter, we discussed what happens after an explanation is generated by looking at how ML consumers interact with explanations. We introduced a framework of expertise and intents for ML consumers. These expertises, such as ML, domain, and inputs, combined with intents like improving, monitoring, understanding, and validating models, along with building trust in the AI and performing remediations, allow us to understand how to best match our audience with the right type of explanation. We then turned our attention to displaying explanations, highlighting best practices such as following information visualization guidelines, conveying the accuracy of an explanation, and building upon an ML consumer's existing understanding. Finally, we discussed common pitfalls that occur when users interact with explanations and identified some ways of avoiding these issues.

So you've now gotten to a point where your ML consumer has received the explanation, understood it, and is ready to go to the next step. But what is that next step? Throughout this book, we have occasionally referenced how explanations can be used to understand or improve a model. For ML practitioners, these are examples of an important part of model control and analysis. Understanding how a model works, we can analyze its behavior and make smarter choices about how to improve the model or dataset. For end users, though, this type of model analysis often is part of a larger decision support system, where they are synthesizing many competing sources of information and evaluations to decide on the best course of action. A sales forecaster at a large grocery chain may use your explanations to understand what time of year they can expect to sell the most strawberries. However, before deciding to place that order for a cargo ship full of berries, they are also likely to check the expected strawberry yield this season. For a regulator that is trying to establish confidence in your AI, and validate its predictions, this explanation may be one of many factors in an audit of the overall performance of a company's use of technology. To put it succinctly, generating, consuming, and interacting with an explanation is just the start.

## CHAPTER 8

Putting It All Together

In this book, we have given you, the ML practitioner, a framework for how to use Explainable AI (XAI) and where it can be best applied. We also gave you a toolbox of explainable techniques to apply in different scenarios, and guides for crafting responsible and beneficial interactions with explanations. In this chapter, we step back to focus on the bigger picture around Explainable AI. With the tools and capabilities that we covered in this book, how can you approach the entire ML workflow and build with explainability in mind? We also provide a preview of the upcoming AI regulations and standards that will require explainability.

Building with Explainability in Mind

Many times, explainability is approached as an afterthought to model development, an added bonus to developing your most recent top-performing model or a post hoc feature request required by your boss trying to adhere to some new regulatory constraint that's been imposed on the business. However, explainability and the goal of XAI is much more than that.

Throughout this book, we've discussed in detail a number of explainability techniques and seen how they can be applied for tabular, image, and text data. For the most part, we've explored these techniques in isolation so you, the reader, can quickly get up to speed on commonly used methods, how they work, their pros, and their cons. Of course, in practice explainability doesn't occur in isolation. You should consider these techniques as part of your ever-expanding toolkit for analysis in machine learning. This toolkit isn't restricted merely to post hoc model analysis. The true benefit of Explainable AI is that it can be applied across the entire end-to-end machine learning life cycle from collecting, preprocessing, and improving datasets to model development, deployment, and monitoring.

In this section, we'll discuss at a high level how to build more effective machine learning solutions by incorporating the methodology of explainability throughout the entire machine learning life cycle. Explainability isn't just a post hoc feature but rather a lens for viewing and improving the entire machine learning process; there are already many promising directions that XAI can be used to augment AI systems, boosting accuracy, trust, transparency, robustness, and safety.

The ML Life Cycle

Developing any machine learning solution is an iterative process, and the steps you may take from start to finish will depend heavily on your use case and, ultimately, the business goals of the project. However, most end-to-end machine learning projects follow the same basic road map, shown in Figure 8-1, at a high-level aligning along three stages: discovery, development, and deployment.

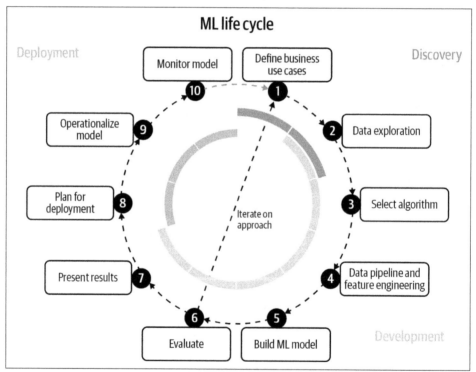

Figure 8-1. The true benefit of Explainable AI is that it can be applied across the entire machine learning life cycle from collecting, preprocessing, and improving datasets to model development, deployment, and monitoring.

Each stage is approached in turn, and there is a canonical order to the individual steps of each stage; however, there is often a healthy amount of iteration, and you may find yourself revisiting an earlier step as you gain more information from a later step, particularly between discovery and development.

Explainability through discovery

Machine learning exists as a tool to solve a problem but is often only a small component of a much bigger solution. Discovery is the initial stage of any ML project, and the first step is to define the business use case and understand how exactly ML fits into the wider solution (Step 1 of Figure 8-1). Even at this early stage, it's important to consider the role that explainability will (or will not) play in the solution as well. This decision can have ripple effects on the later choices that arise in the ML cycle, and it is important to keep sight of these requirements through each stage of the life cycle.

One thing to consider is how the model predictions will be used in the final system or how they will be presented to the end user, and how explanations may (or may not) be presented (see Chapter 7 for detailed discussion about human factors related to XAI). For example, suppose our goal is to develop a predictive diagnostic model that informs a physician of potential health outcomes for a patient. It is possible that providing model explanations alongside predictions can improve patient outcomes. For example, a 2019 study (*https://oreil.ly/i8bK0*)[1] measured doctors' ability to diagnose diabetic retinopathy from scans by comparing three settings: unassisted (no machine learning model), model predictions only, and model predictions plus XAI heatmap. They found that doctors that were assisted with deep learning model predictions alone had improved accuracy over those who were unassisted. They also found that model predictions paired with XAI heatmaps increased accuracy for those patients with diabetic retinopathy and increased sensitivity without decreasing specificity. However, there could also be unforeseen negative side effects to consider as well; e.g., surfacing explanations could lead to unwanted outcomes as well such as doctors "overrelying" on explanations, and accepting inaccurate model predictions.

Or perhaps there are legal, ethical, or regulatory concerns that are required of the final ML solution that provide additional information as to why a model makes the recommendation it does. Any machine learning project should begin with a comprehensive understanding of the business opportunity and aligning on model constraints and performance requirements for deployment. Many times, there are indirect factors related to the business use case that influence development choices that arise later, like speed of inference or model size, or the cost to obtain data for different features in a dataset. It is equally important to discuss explainability or interpretability requirements and agree on what level and type of explanations are necessary or sufficient before embarking on a new project.

---

[1] Rory Sayres et al., "Using a Deep Learning Algorithm and Integrated Gradients Explanation to Assist Grading for Diabetic Retinopathy," *Ophthalmology* 126.4 (2019): 552–64.

Step 2 of Figure 8-1 is data exploration and a deep dive into data understanding. This is also the beginning of the development portion of the ML life cycle. This is perhaps the most crucial step of designing an ML solution. Ultimately, the data guides the process, and it's necessary to understand the quality of the data that is available. From an explainability perspective, the majority of explainability techniques provide insights that are focused on the dataset and features. What are the distributions of the key features? How will missing values be handled? Are there outliers? Are any input values highly correlated? How can we augment the dataset? Is there bias in the dataset? It is important to keep in mind explainability during this stage as well. For example, as we saw in Chapter 3, when discussing explainability techniques for tabular data, some explainability techniques give misleading results when two features are highly correlated. It is important to be aware of these caveats early on.

Premodeling explainability is focused on understanding the data or any feature engineering that is used to train the machine learning model, see also the discussion in Chapter 2. This type of explainability is independent of any model and focused solely on the data. Explanations that focus solely on the dataset are often referred to as exploratory data analysis (EDA). EDA is a collection of statistical techniques and visualizations that are used to gain more insight into a dataset. EDA can take many forms, and visualization plays an important role during this step.

Commonly used tools such as Know Your Data (*https://oreil.ly/CM72I*) and Facets (*https://oreil.ly/dVhYQ*) allow you to quickly get a sense of the statistical properties of the features in your dataset such as the mean, standard deviation, range, and percentage of missing samples, as well as the feature dimensionality and presence of any outliers. Figure 8-2 shows how the Facets Overview looks when applied to the California Housing dataset. In Chapter 3, we apply many different explainability techniques to models built on this dataset. The Facets Overview gives a quick look at the feature distributions of values in the dataset. This makes it easy to uncover common issues such as unexpected feature values, missing feature values, training/serving skew, and train/test/validation set skew. With a lens of explainability in mind, this knowledge of the data distribution and data quality is important for understanding model behavior, interpreting model predictions, and exposing any biases that might exist.

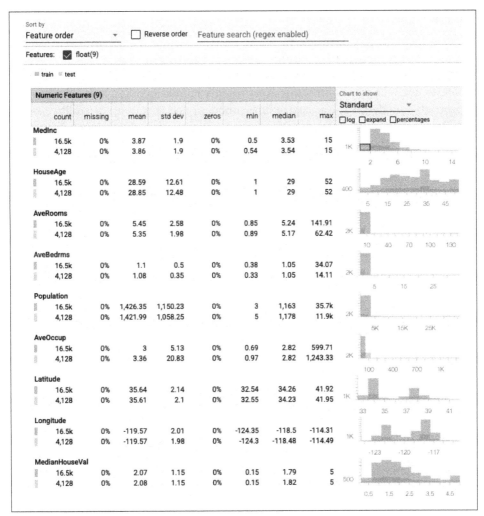

Figure 8-2. The Facets Overview of the California Housing dataset provides summary statistics for each feature and compares the training and test datasets. (Print readers can see the color image at https://oreil.ly/xai-fig-8-2.)

Explainability through development

Entering fully into the development stage, the next step in the ML life cycle (Step 3 in Figure 8-1) is model and algorithm selection. Explainability requirements play an important role in deciding which model to use, or even limit which models you may be able to use. One way to meet this explainability requirement is to employ naturally interpretable models, such as sparse linear models, decision trees, or additive models. These models inherently provide a means of inspecting the model behavior by examining the model components directly; e.g., a single rule or path in the decision tree (see "Explaining Tree-Based Models" on page 63), or the weight of a specific feature in a linear model. If you're working with tabular data, these interpretable models might perform as well or better than more complex deep neural networks, and they have the added benefit of being fully explainable. If the model meets the performance requirements in terms of your predetermined evaluation metrics and uses a reasonable number of internal components (e.g., decision paths or features), such models can provide extremely useful insights. In fact, in most cases, if an interpretable model can be used and has similar performance to a more complex one, then the interpretable model is preferable.

However, for more complex data types, like images or text, you're likely to find neural networks more performant than these more inherently interpretable models. In this case, XAI paired with a complex neural network could be the way to go. Broadly speaking, explanations that are part of the model's prediction itself are known as *intrinsic* explanations. Intrinsic explanations rely on using an interpretable model or may require modifications to the model or training loop itself, as in constrained optimization (see the discussion on constrained optimization and deep lattice in Chapter 6). Intrinsic explanations are a good example of techniques that exist halfway in between pure explainability and interpretability, so don't worry too much if you see them described as either explainability or interpretability. Many of the techniques we've described in this book (see Chapter 3 to Chapter 5) fall into the category of post hoc explainability methods, which means they are applied after model training and rely on model predictions to surface explanations. Knowing how explainability techniques work for different models and their pros and cons can have a large impact on the outcome of the model selection stage of the ML cycle.

We begin by building data pipelines and engineering features (Step 4 of Figure 8-1). Feature engineering is the process of transforming raw input data into features that are more closely aligned with the model's learning objective and expressed in a format that can be fed to the model for training. Feature engineering techniques can involve bucketizing inputs, converting between data formats, tokenizing and stemming text, creating feature embeddings (as discussed in the beginning of Chapter 5), and many others.

Using explainability to perform feature engineering and feature selection is one of the most efficient ways to understand your model's performance and identify ways to improve. Applying an explainability approach during this step can help determine if your dataset includes excessive, or even confounding, features that are not contributing to the performance of your model. Almost all of the feature-based explainability methods that we've discussed throughout Chapters 3, 4, and 5 can be used in feature selection.

To do this correctly, you should apply your preferred XAI technique first on the entire training and test datasets to generate global explanations first, before looking at individual predictions or cohorts. One thing to keep in mind is that feature-based techniques that assign a negative value for a feature does not necessarily mean that it's not important or that you should remove that feature from the model. Instead, look for features that have little (or no) absolute influence on predictions.

After identifying these low-impact features, it's then a good idea to perform a sliced analysis. *Sliced analysis* is a general term for comparing certain quantitative metrics across various cross sections of your dataset. A cross section can be formed by taking all examples with a given feature or label value. In the context of explainability, you can also create a cross section based on cohort explanations. We introduced the concept of cohort explanations in Chapter 2. Cohort explanations are aggregated explanations that are generated for a specific subset of the full dataset. Comparing and contrasting these cohorts is one method of sliced analysis.

Sliced analysis can help you understand the behavior of your model in a way that is generalized enough to lead to broad improvements in model quality but localized enough to avoid the problem of trying to boil the entire ocean. You can often use the outputs of explanations in other sliced analysis tools, or even in follow-on statistical analyses.

Document How You Selected Your Slices

When performing sliced analysis, a common regret among practitioners is that they do not extensively document the selection process for the slice, and the parameters of the analysis. This lack of information can make it difficult to compare new slices to previous slices and analyses performed much earlier in the ML workflow, for example, performance after a model has been deployed and serving predictions for a year with the original analyses done during model development.

Sliced analysis is a useful tool for feature selection because it allows you to verify that the average influence of this feature does not appear to be zero, only due to high variance between positive and negative values for different cohorts of predictions. That is, you're able to confirm that the feature importance isn't artificially low merely due to the effects of other features.

In general, when performing this kind of feature selection analysis, there is no universal attribution threshold below which a feature is meaningless to the model's behavior. It requires experimentation and exploration. These explainability techniques simply provide another powerful lens with which to analyze and understand your features. You will find that the cutoff for meaningful features varies due to the complexity of the dataset, the cost of obtaining data for that feature, and if any features are highly correlated.

Once you have identified features to remove from your model, it is important to iteratively remove one feature at a time and then revalidate your model's performance along with regenerating any global or cohort explanations. We have routinely seen that trivial features that were initially ignored by the model become very influential as other, less relevant features are removed.

What About Layer Selection?

If we can use Explainable AI to select and prune features from our dataset, it seems reasonable to assume one could also use a model-focused technique to find layers that do not contribute to the performance of the model and remove, or simplify, these layers. There has been some research in this area (see Appendix), but unfortunately, as of 2022, we have not seen any techniques emerge that are both robust and simple enough to use to justify what is often a lengthy process of setting up the technique, interpreting the findings, and iteratively trying to change the model. Instead, many other techniques for model architecture selection are more useful at this time, such as model distillation, hyperparameter tuning, and neural architecture searches.

The next steps of the development stage, Steps 5 and 6 in Figure 8-1, are focused on building and evaluating the ML model. This is another area where the power of explainability techniques really shines. Throughout this book, we have discussed how explainability can identify what is influencing a model and how it behaves. Looked at from another perspective, Explainable AI can also give you insight into a model's robustness. By identifying where a model is relying on relevant features, you can understand how well the model will be able to adapt in unforeseen circumstances. A model that arrives at the correct prediction, but relies on seemingly unrelated information, may be easily swayed to make an incorrect prediction with only slight changes to the inputs. Likewise, if you find that the model is unable to identify similar instances from your dataset via example-based explanations (discussed in Chapter 6), it likely indicates the model is brittle.

Explainability can also show where the model is overly dependent on irrelevant features. These may be the background of an image, an ancillary column in structured data, or very specific grammar in text. Any of these could reveal that the model is also vulnerable to an adversarial attack, where a desired prediction can be engineered in advance without an obvious change to the inputs.

 In general, when debugging ML models, explainability techniques are often one of the first tools practitioners reach for when they are trying to understand why a model performed poorly. It is important to recognize the value of investing in building a reusable, Explainable AI tool that allows many types of ML consumers in your organization to easily load a model, replay an interference, and receive an explanation. Investing in this tooling up front can help avoid having you, and other practitioners, having to be on call as a messenger who runs Jupyter notebook cells in order to shuttle explanations back to the interested party.

The last step of the development stage is to present results to the stakeholders and regulatory groups within the business (Step 7 of Figure 8-1). This is a critical and necessary step in the ML life cycle as it is often an important decision point for whether the ML model will make its way to production and deployment (the final stage of the ML life cycle) or not. Often this step is focused on creating numbers and visuals for initial reports that will be presented within the organization, and explainability tools provide an effective way to build confidence in the ML model predictions.

During this step, it's important to keep in mind your intended audience, and you should be cognizant of how the explanations are to be presented alongside the model results. In Chapter 7, we discussed in detail a number of aspects to keep in mind when interacting with explainability. Since the target audience during this step is the business stakeholders or end users, you'll most likely communicate to users with domain expertise and less ML experience.

Once again, example-based explanations can be used to complement a model's prediction by showing examples related to the one being predicted. There are different ways to determine "relatedness" of examples, but two types that we have found to be most useful during this step of the ML life cycle are normative examples and contrastive examples.

Normative and *contrastive examples* are examples that are closely related to the input example and whose label either agrees or differs with the model's prediction. For example, in Figure 8-3 the model predicts the label "cat" for the input image. Normative examples are examples from the training dataset that also have the label "cat," while contrastive examples are examples from the training dataset that have a different ground truth label.

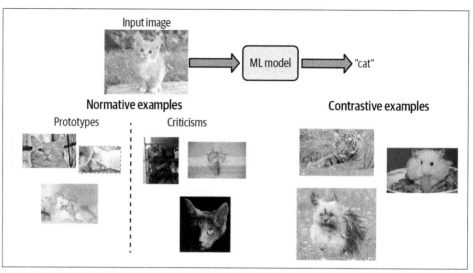

Figure 8-3. Normative examples are examples that come from the same predicted class (e.g., "cat") as the ML model, while contrastive examples are taken from a different class (e.g., "tiger," "hamster," or "dog").

One way to generate normative examples is by choosing a layer close to the model's final label layer and retrieving the k closest neighbors from the training set that have the same predicted label as the given instance. These examples are often called "prototypes." That is, these are examples in the dataset which are "close" to our given instance and share the same label. Naturally, we would expect to recognize common features between prototypes and the given instance.

To prevent reasoning errors due to overgeneralization, it is important to also present examples that differ from the norm but are still in the target class. That is, examples in the training set that share the same label as the model prediction but are unrelated to the example in question. These examples are called "criticisms." These kind of high-level, example-based explanations through prototypes and criticisms can be particularly useful to help build trust in a model's prediction.

When the model makes a prediction that is unexpected or goes against the intuition and experience of domain experts or stakeholders, example-based explanations are especially valuable. Consider, for example, a model used by a bank to assist in determining which loans to approve or deny. Suppose a business submits a new loan application and the ML model marks the application as high risk or high likelihood of defaulting. This could be based on a number of features such as the loan amount, the previous credit history of the applicant, the FICA score, or the current debt liability of the applicant, etc.

Normative examples are instances from the training dataset that share the same label. This could be historical loan applications that were also deemed too risky by human experts or underwriters, or loan applications that had been approved but later defaulted on. A prototype would be a normative example from the training dataset that is similar in some way to the given application. Perhaps they had the same FICO score or they share similar credit history as the applicant. A criticism is a normative example that is quite different from the given application in question. That is, a criticism example would have a different FICO score or debt liability, but nonetheless was also deemed too risky or ultimately defaulted. Surfacing both prototypes and diverse criticisms gives a holistic view of the model's target class and helps stakeholders identify common or diverging trends between those examples and the instance in question.

In addition to prototypes and criticisms taken from the same predictive category, contrastive examples are taken from a different class to the model's prediction, but are nonetheless closely related to the given instance. These examples allow for reasoning about related instances from different categories. In the example of the loan application model we previously discussed, a contrastive example would be a historical loan application from the training dataset that is very similar or closely related to the new loan application but whose ground truth label was "no risk" or "low risk."

Contrastive examples are similar in spirit to counterfactuals (discussed in Chapter 2), derived from real instances instead of synthetic ones and near the model's decision boundary for the predicted class. In this way, they are a more informative type of counterfactual and give insight to the model's learned representations as well as the local nature of the training data distribution.

Figure 8-4 shows an example of both normative and contrastive examples. This image was taken from the game Quick, Draw! (*https://oreil.ly/kYRo1*) introduced by Google in 2016. The game is like an AI-assisted version of Pictionary. Quick, Draw! asks the user to draw a given object, like "pool" or "truck" or "vase," while an ML model tries to guess what the user is drawing. In Figure 8-4, the user was asked to draw a scorpion. Once the neural network has had its turn guessing the image (without success, it seems), the game surfaces similar examples from the training dataset that were labeled as scorpion (on the right) as well as examples from the training dataset that were similar to the user's drawing but were not labeled as scorpion, such as a rake, a cherry, and a garden hose.

Figure 8-4. The game Quick, Draw! asks the user to draw an object while an ML model guesses the drawing. Once the user's turn is up, the game provides a comparison of normative and contrastive examples from the user's drawing.

Beyond single examples and representations, another approach to understanding model behavior is through concepts. Concepts enable reasoning about the representation of features that a model learns through training. In Chapter 6, we discussed in detail the TCAV (Testing with Concept Activation Vectors) method, which provides representable terms via sets of examples encoding the concepts of interest for a given example.

Explainability through deployment

The final stage of the ML life cycle is deployment (Steps 8–10 in Figure 8-1) and is commonly referred to as MLOps (ML operations). This stage is related to aspects of automating, monitoring, testing, managing, maintaining, and auditing machine learning models in production. It is a necessary component for any company hoping to scale the number of machine learning–driven applications within their organization.

When planning for deployment and through operationalizing the model (Steps 8 and 9 in Figure 8-1), it's important to consider what role explanations may play for the end user of the ML model. As with all things in ML, there is a trade-off between the benefit of providing explanations and the technical burden of maintaining that part of the infrastructure postproduction. Building an ML system that provides explanations alongside predictions in production will help end users of your system improve their understanding and build trust in the model. Likewise, automatically generating explanations as part of any AI governance process your organization has makes it much easier to demonstrate to stakeholders, such as business executives, regulators, and crossfunctional partners, how the model works and what influences the model. However, deploying a model that provides explanations requires additional technical investment and in some cases may be too much information for the end user who is not familiar with how to interpret those results. For ML systems that serve explanations alongside predictions to end users, the computational intensity of many techniques can prove to be a very difficult hurdle to overcome while also trying to quickly return a response in the range of tens to hundreds of milliseconds. In short, XAI can be costly, time-consuming, and potentially confusing to the end user.

We find there is often a trade-off between the XAI techniques that are most accurate and robust versus those that are computationally fast, but less valid. If you cannot find a good trade-off between the latency of your model serving explanations and the quality of the explanations, it may make sense to investigate using an inherently interpretable ML model, or to explore model extraction, which seeks to train a smaller, more interpretable model from the original model.

Deployment is not the end of a machine learning model's life cycle. Once the model goes into production, it can start to degrade, and its predictions can grow increasingly unreliable. How do you know that your model is working as expected in the real world? What if there are unexpected changes in the incoming data? Or the model no longer produces accurate or useful predictions? How will these changes be detected? These considerations are handled in the final stage, Step 10 of Figure 8-1, model monitoring.

Model monitoring and continued model evaluation provide a way to assess your model's performance over time. Traditional model monitoring focuses on detecting data skew or drift in the model's inputs or outputs using the same evaluation metrics you used during development. However, this approach treats the model itself as an opaque function, often focusing only on the inputs and outputs and when predictions start to deviate from the ground truth. This approach alone poses several challenges and lacks any actionable advice for addressing the root problem. A much more rich and detailed analysis can be obtained by monitoring feature attribution drift through incorporating XAI during model monitoring as well.

For example, feature attributions can serve as an early indicator that the model's performance may be degrading, and monitoring feature attributions over time is a useful signal for detecting drift and skew in live inputs compared to what the model was trained on. Furthermore, feature attributions provide a number of advantages over more standard skew detection algorithms.

Most skew detection algorithms are specific to the input and are most commonly only able to handle numeric and/or categorical features. Other data modalities, like time-series, or unstructured inputs, like images, are more challenging and often have to be paired with some sort of dimensionality reduction. This added complexity is error prone and can be problematic both because of loss of information through dimension reduction techniques and sensitivity implementation choices. Feature attribution methods, however, are capable of handling multiple input modalities and, since attributions are dense numeric values, they can be compared more easily across data types.

Also, monitoring based on feature attributions requires less fine-tuning to detect data skew or drift. Not all data skews are created equal, and determining the right threshold can be tricky. Alerting too often risks desensitization while alerting too infrequently risks missing important, business-impacting issues. As a result, it's often necessary to tune skew detection algorithms, depending on the skew severity's impact on the final model. As the number of features increases, this can become an increasingly challenging task. XAI provides quantification of input influence that allows thresholds to be tuned in a more informed manner and thus balance the sensitivity and specificity trade-off for better alerts.

Another direction where XAI feature attributions can assist with skew detection is in handling joint distributions. Most skew detection algorithms are developed to detect skew in the univariate distribution of a given feature. However, this misses any data shift or skew that may have occurred in the joint distribution of related features. For example, a model that has two separate features "can fly" and "bird species" that has been put into production can all of a sudden start receiving examples of "flying penguins." This would obviously constitute an outlier and be a sign of some kind of data drift or skew, but the issue could go unnoticed because individually the univariate statistics for the two features haven't changed. However, by using XAI techniques like feature attributions that take into account the joint distribution of features can catch these kinds of issues.

Lastly, and perhaps the most useful aspect of XAI techniques in model monitoring, is that they can provide actionable insights in addition to a diagnosis. Most skew detection algorithms surface outliers or alert data distributional shifts, but this can then require its own detailed analysis to determine how to address or mitigate those issues. XAI can help here as well as a means to augment the training dataset or provide an additional lens with which to better understand model features.

AI auditing often goes hand in hand with model monitoring. There are many use cases where it is advantageous to keep a detailed record of model predictions along with the corresponding model input requests and any other contextual information that may be useful. These details are useful for later diagnosis in the case of an audit.

Having model requests (i.e., instances sent to the model for prediction) and model responses (i.e., predictions) together are necessary for carrying out model monitoring, and you want to capture enough contextual information to re-create the environment exactly as is to assist in any subsequent analysis. While it may seem obvious, this can actually be quite difficult to accomplish effectively. Think, for example, of a self-driving car. This is an extremely complex system with multiple ML models in play as well as complex hardware and software requirements with onboard custom chips and real-time operating systems. In this situation, it may not be possible to re-create the environment precisely as is. However, recording some XAI outputs like attributions can be beneficial for a deeper understanding without having to re-create the exact same environment. XAI outputs can provide a high-level description of the state, which provides valuable information where a precise recreation is not possible.

More broadly, XAI plays an important role in meeting the requirements of AI regulations. Given the increased role that ML models play in our everyday lives, governments across the world are beginning to draft or introduce AI regulations that can be addressed with XAI.

AI Regulations and Explainability

Across the world, governments are beginning to draft or introduce regulations for AI. As of the summer of 2022, AI regulations have been introduced in the EU. The Digital Services Act (DSA) (*https://oreil.ly/TfYMy*) was approved by the European Parliament in July 2022 and will go into effect January 2024. The Artificial Intelligence Act (*https://oreil.ly/rXQwM*) has been proposed by the European Commission, introducing a common regulatory and legal framework applying to all types of AI. It is expected to come into effect in late 2023 or 2024. China also has several ministries drafting regulations. The first set of regulations, the New Generation Artificial Intelligence Ethics Specifications, from the Ministry of Science and Technology (*http://en.most.gov.cn*), lays out ethical norms for the use of AI in China covering areas such as the use and protection of personal information and responsible AI.

Similarly, in the US, the National Institute for Standards and Technology (NIST) has drafted recommendations for AI governance, the AI Risk Management Framework (*https://oreil.ly/Rv1Nl*). The International Standards Organization (ISO) has begun finalizing ISO 42001 (*https://oreil.ly/9DIzM*) on Artificial Intelligence, and is actively working on a draft for Explainable AI (ISO 6254 (*https://oreil.ly/Bw9Hx*)). Although individual regulations may be scoped to countries or sectors of technology, it is eventually expected the vast majority of AI employed by businesses will be subject to some form of accountability.

All of these regulations and standards have one common theme: they expect Explainable AI to have a central role in helping consumers and regulators assess how an ML behaves and whether it is adhering to regulations. So far, regulations and standards have avoided specifying exactly what type of explainability must be used, just that AI should have documentation demonstrating how the model behaves or, in real time or on request, the ML can explain its output.

This is both a blessing and a curse for ML practitioners. On the positive side, you will have the flexibility to determine which explainability techniques are the best match for your ML and use case. However, at the same time, you will likely be asked by stakeholders to demonstrate that whatever choice you made meets the regulatory standards for explainability, which are currently quite vague. In the coming years, we will likely see more clarity on the exact requirements for explainability, but we expect it will prominently feature many of the classes of techniques we have covered in this book, such as feature attributions, example-based explanations, and counterfactuals.

What to Look Forward To in Explainable AI

What most excites us about the future of explainability is how it will move from individual, narrowly focused techniques to ones that generate richer explanations with less configuration needed in advance. Broadly, there are three trends to keep an eye on in the future of Explainable AI: natural and semantic explanations, interrogative explanations, and more targeted explanations.

Natural and Semantic Explanations

We often find that many types of explanations remain too technical or abstract for nontechnical users. An array of numbers representing feature attributions isn't necessarily very helpful for these users. Instead, techniques that can either present explanations in a more natural way, perhaps via a generative text model to create fluid sentences for the explanation, or are able to generate explanations based on a semantic understanding of the model and its dataset, will be much more helpful. Imagine if instead of being presented with an array of feature attribution values for a weather prediction, a user could be told, "There is an 80% chance of rain this afternoon because the temperature has dropped significantly and humidity is above 90%."

Semantic explanations, which require an even more innate understanding of the behaviors and concepts in the ML system, will also represent a large change in how we explain AIs. For example, an explainability technique may recognize that many of the similar examples where an ML classified a dog as a cat were due to poor lighting and low resolution in the photos. Instead of trying to highlight the pixels, where, for example, poor resolution or poor lighting may result in vague pixel attributions, it could categorically identify more pervasive causes for why the model failed.

Interrogative Explanations

Today, explanations are a one-way dialogue from the ML to the consumer. It is not unusual for someone to receive an explanation and immediately have more questions (see also the discussion in Chapter 7 on the human-interaction components of building explainable ML systems and "How to Effectively Present Explanations" on page 206). However, with current methods, that often requires an ML practitioner to roll up their sleeves and implement a new type of explanatory technique or perform additional types of explanations that were not expected before. A better ecosystem of Explainable AI tools will help make this job easier but will not solve the problem.

Instead, we expect a wave of second-generation explanation AI techniques that enable a richer experience where a user can query the ML for further information about a prediction or behavior and can even guide the user in improving their understanding. Imagine this as a conversation between the consumer, perhaps a regulator, and the AI about a credit-rating ML:

Regulator: Why was this individual given a credit rating of 520?

AI: The most influential features were the high limits on the individual's credit cards, which caused the model to decrease its rating; their history of missed loan payments further drove the rating down.

Regulator: Are individuals who live in similar zip codes (often an indirect variable for race in the US) with missed loan payments penalized as much as others?

AI: No. Also, examining what the model considers to be 1,000 most similar people to this individual, there is no correlation with the zip code. Similar individuals who paid loans on time 25% more often on average had an increase of 50 points in their credit rating.

Targeted Explanations

As of 2022, there has been little work performed on assessing whether explanations follow the rule of Occam's razor: that the simplest explanation is the best. We expect that more robust explanations will be those that are more concise and targeted. For example, Local Explanations via Necessity and Sufficiency (*https://arxiv.org/abs/ 2103.14651*),[2], lays the foundation for these types of explanations by demonstrating how the minimal amount of perturbation necessary to flip a prediction provides an optimal explanation. These types of explanations will do much to address the brittleness problem described in Chapter 7, and will also take us a step further toward causal explanations.

Summary

In this chapter, we discussed how to design ML solutions with explainability in mind to build more reliable ML systems and provided a look toward the future of XAI. We've seen how Explainable AI techniques can be incorporated into each step of the ML life cycle, from discovery to development to deployment, assisting in building more robust ML solutions. We encourage you to think about XAI as a toolkit for better understanding machine learning models. We also provided a glimpse into what the future of XAI might hold and current research efforts.

Now, with these techniques and an understanding of how and where to apply them, you can improve both the models themselves and how your consumers work with them. Explainability is a rapidly changing field; we encourage you to view new

---

2 David Watson et al., "Local Explanations via Necessity and Sufficiency: Unifying Theory and Practice," arXiv, 2021.

techniques with optimism, but also give them some time to prove their worth in the rougher seas that constitute models and datasets in industry. It is also important to think responsibly about how you use explanations in high-risk settings, keeping in mind their potential to be brittle and create bias or false confidence in users. Most of all, explanations serve as a way for you to build a richer interaction with the models you work with every day.

Taxonomy, Techniques, and Further Reading

To aid you in using this book in the future, we have put together a brief review of the topics and techniques covered in this book. You can use these guides and tables as a reference in the future to help you quickly survey your options for a new problem before diving into more detail.

ML Consumers

There are three types of users who consume and interact with ML:

ML practitioners
Data scientists and ML engineers that build, develop, tune, deploy, and operationalize a model.

Observers
Business stakeholders and regulators who are not involved in the engineering of the model, but also are not using the model in deployment. They use explanations to validate model performance and build trust that a model is working as expected.

End users
Domain experts and affected users who use, or are impacted by, a model's predictions. They may have a deep understanding of the context the model operates in or may be affected by the result of a model's prediction, with little background knowledge in ML or the domain.

Taxonomy of Explainability

There are several characteristics that help define the field of explainability. These are:

Explainability versus interpretability

Although sometimes used interchangeably in industry, we define explainability as techniques that explain a model based on a prediction (or group of predictions). The technique does not need to understand how the model itself works, although it may rely on aspects of a model's architecture to generate the explanation. In contrast, interpretability can provide insights about a model's behavior without any predictions as the interpretability technique is a fundamental aspect of the model's architecture and behavior.

Data-centric versus model-centric

The technique may provide an understanding of how the dataset and its structure influence the model's prediction or describe the behavior of the model itself. For example, data-centric approaches to explainability include techniques like TracIn, influence functions, or TCAV (see "Alternate Input Attribution" on page 172). Model-centric explainability approaches are focused more on aspects of the model and model architecture itself. This would include the techniques discussed in Chapter 3, Chapter 4, and Chapter 5 in this book.

When thinking of model-centric methods, most commonly used explainability techniques can be characterized across three axes:

Intrinsic versus post hoc

Intrinsic explanations are part of a prediction. By intrinsic, we mean models that are inherently interpretable. That is, they are simple enough in structure that we can understand how the model is making predictions by simply looking at the model itself. For example, the learned weights of a linear model or the splits that are learned with a decision tree can be used to interpret why a model makes the predictions it does. Post hoc explanations are performed after a model has been trained and rely on a prediction to create the explanation. Post hoc methods involve using the trained model and data to understand why certain predictions are being made. In some cases, post hoc methods can be applied to models that have intrinsic explainability as well.

Model specific versus model agnostic

Model agnostic means the explainability method can be applied to any model while a model-specific method can only be used with certain model types. For example, the method that would only work with neural networks would be considered model specific. If an explainability method treats the trained model as an opaque model, then it would be considered model agnostic.

Local, global, and cohort explanations

A local explanation focuses only on a single prediction. A global explanation attempts to make claims about trends and behaviors for model predictions across an entire dataset. Many times, a local XAI method can be turned into a global technique by using aggregations of the local results. Thus, some techniques are useful in providing both local and global explanations. A cohort explanation is a global explanation performed on a slice of the full dataset. A slice of your dataset could be a subset defined by a single feature value. For example, let's consider a model that predicts customer churn. All users with an income over $50,000 per year could constitute a cohort. Cohort explanations can be useful to better understand why a model is not performing well for this particular subset. It can also help uncover bias in your model or indicate places where you might need to collect more data.

XAI Techniques

The techniques in this book have been arranged by use case with a focus on data modalities covering tabular (Chapter 3), image (Chapter 4), and text (Chapter 5). While some of these techniques were developed with a specific data type in mind, many of them can be applied in multiple settings. Here we break down the techniques discussed in each chapter, what you need to know about each of them, and their pros and cons.

Tabular Models

Chapter 3 focused on tabular models and the explainability techniques that are used to convey how important features were in a model's prediction. These feature-based techniques can be divided into techniques attributing influence to the feature, or demonstrating counterfactuals by changing the value of the feature to alter the prediction. See Table A-1.

Table A-1. Summary of explainable techniques applicable to tabular models

Technique	What to know	Pros	Cons
Feature permutation	Changes the value of input features to observe how the model's score changes	• Easy to implement • Intuitive	• Highly correlated features are misleading • Does not reflect the actual predictive value of a feature
Shapley values	Uses game theory to determine feature attributions	• Can be used for global, cohort, and local explanations • Intuitive	• Computationally intensive • Choosing baseline can be hard • Actual process of calculating Shapley values can be difficult to explain to stakeholders and end users

Technique	What to know	Pros	Cons
Decision tree	Explanations based directly on weights in tree nodes	• Easy to understand • Computationally trivial	• Scikit solution does not support multilabel classification
Partial dependence plots (PDPs)	Shows marginal effect of specific feature in a prediction	• Easy to implement • Can indicate a causal relationship if no feature correlation	• Assumes features are independent • Lack of values for a feature causes reliability issues
Individual conditional explanations (ICE)	Extension of PDPs to visualize feature dependence per instance	• Gives more holistic view than PDPs	• Same issues as PDPs • Visualizations can quickly become unreadable
Accumulated local effects (ALE)	Extends PDPs to account for correlated features	• Accounts for conditional dependence of correlated features • Good OSS options for visualizing	• Implementation not intuitive • Strongly correlated features can still cause issues

Image Models

Chapter 4 dived into techniques for explaining models built using image data. Many rely on generating saliency maps, new images that can be overlaid onto the original input image to demonstrate which pixels or regions in the original image most influenced the prediction. Some advanced techniques try to demonstrate the influence of different concepts learned by the model in the prediction, such as patterns or shapes. See Table A-2.

Table A-2. Summary of explainable techniques applicable to image models

Technique	What to know	Pros	Cons
Integrated Gradients (IG)	Local pixel attribution method based on sampling image along gradient of values	• Intuitive explanations • Among faster image explanation techniques	• Requires model to be differentiable • Sensitive to baseline
XRAI	Region-based attribution method based on IG	• Faster than other region-based techniques • Works best on natural images	• Only useful for image models • Less granular explanations
Grad-CAM	Popular region-based attribution method; use Grad-CAM++, if at all	• Computationally efficient	• Flawed explanations • Prone to identifying background as relevant

Technique	What to know	Pros	Cons
LIME	Primarily for classification models, pixel-based attributions	• Popular • Many visualization options	• Explanations are brittle and can be low accuracy • Prone to identifying background as relevant • Slow
Guided Backprop and Guided Grad-CAM	Build on DeConvNets, which examine the interior layers of a convolution network	• Sharper visualizations • Localize relevant regions	• Some research suggests they fail basic "sanity" checks

Text Models

Chapter 5 described how text models utilize a variety of Explainable AI methods. Most methods are not directly comparable, as they often perform best for one type of model architecture over another. See Table A-3.

Table A-3. Summary of explainable techniques applicable to text models

Technique	What to know	Pros	Cons
LIME	Perturbs input by randomly removing words, and works best with ~1K perturbations	• Easy to implement • Model agnostic	• Very sensitive parameters related to kernel width • Does not work well for highly nonlinear models
Gradient x Input	Saliency method for word tokens that allows positive and negative attributions	• Easy and fast to implement • Research indicates best performing explainability technique for transformers	• Only works for differentiable models • Should be used in conjunction with other gradient-based techniques
Layer Integrated Gradients	Variation of Integrated Gradients (IG), but focused on a single layer of the network instead of input features	• Useful for text to isolate the embedding layer • Same pros as IG	• Same cons as IG
Layer-Wise Relevance Propagation (LRP)	Accumulates influence from layers in model from head back toward inputs	• Very modular and widely usable • Good performance for text classification	• Only works with DNNs • Attributions can concentrate on only a few features

Advanced and Emerging Techniques

In Chapter 6, we presented explainability for specific types of model architectures or those that require a deeper understanding of ML. We looked at XAI techniques using example-based explanations, influence functions, and concept-based explanations, like TCAV. See Table A-4.

Table A-4. Summary of explainable techniques discussed in Chapter 6

Technique	What to know	Pros	Cons
Example-based explanations	Provide insight into model behavior by surfacing approximate nearest neighbor–based explanations for model instances	• Useful for debugging, communicating with stakeholders • Very intuitive, human-relatable representation of model behavior	• Can be difficult to scale up beyond ~1-10K examples; may need to use a cloud service • Does not offer completeness guarantees
Influence-based explanations	Influence function–based explanations measure how model predictions would change if an example was removed from the training dataset	• Useful for debugging models, detecting dataset errors • Explanations better align with intuition • Works well for small, moderately sized models	• Doesn't scale well to large models, datasets • Lacks a way to account for correlated data points • Requires twice differentiability
TCAV	Exposes learned concepts that were influential in model behavior and prediction	• Highly customizable; you can explore any concept (e.g., gender) • Works without any retraining of the ML model	• Can be difficult or expensive to curate examples of a concept • Does not perform well on shallow models • Less tested for text or tabular data

Interacting with Explainability

In Chapter 7, we laid out guidelines for how to think about presenting explanations for users and how they may interact with those explanations. We introduced the concepts of identifying the expertise and intent of the ML consumer.

Common types of expertise possessed by ML consumers include:

Domain
Knowledge of the environment the ML system operates within.

Model inputs
Has more context about the information provided to the model when it makes a prediction.

Machine learning
Understands how the model architecture and model work.

Common types of intents an ML consumer may include for using explainability techniques in the ML solution:

Model improvement
Take action to increase the quality of the model.

Verify performance
Confirm that the model behaves as expected.

Build trust

Increase confidence that the model is reliable.

Remediation

Understand what actions to take to alter a prediction.

Understand model behavior

Construct a simplified model in the user's mind, which can be used as a surrogate for understanding the model's performance.

Monitoring

Ongoing assessment that a model's performance remains acceptable.

We also presented a five-step guide for how to choose the best explanation technique for your audience and the questions you want to keep in mind when making those design decisions:

1. What needs to be explained?

2. What is their expertise?

3. What action will they take after an explanation?

4. Is this ML model being used in a critical or high-risk situation?

5. How quickly do they need an explanation?

We discussed what to keep in mind when displaying explanations to users:

Focus on clarity, accuracy

Explainability techniques should build on the user's existing understanding, and it's important to follow best practices in information visualization, such as making the visualization color-blind friendly and providing a guided experience through how information is presented to the user.

Accurately presenting an explanation to a user is critical

Unfortunately, it is easy to create a sense of false confidence in how intelligent the model may be.

Provide well-grounded explanations

An explanation that is grounded in a user's existing understanding makes it much more likely that the explanation will successfully improve the user's situational awareness of how the model works, giving users the ability to project how the model will behave in the future.

Finally, we also looked at pitfalls in interacting with Explainable AI. ML consumers are most likely to assume causality in explanations, overfit intent to a model, and overreach for additional explanations:

Assuming causality

> This is the most common and also the most dangerous. Almost no explainability technique is able to definitely establish causality for an ML model operating in the real world.

Overfitting intent

> This can also lead a user to have false confidence in the model. In this scenario, users often extrapolate from an explanation to assume the model understands concepts familiar to them. However, it is often unlikely that the ML model has actually learned these concepts, leading to a mismatch between the user's understanding of the model and its actual behavior.

Overreaching for additional explanations

> This can lead to confirmation bias as other explanations are misused to confirm existing expectations. Unfortunately, preventing explanation overreach is very difficult.

Putting It All Together

Lastly, we looked at how Explainable AI fits into the larger picture of building reliable and robust ML solutions. We discussed how the XAI techniques we've covered in this book can be applied throughout the entire ML life cycle and how to build with explainability in mind from discovery to development to deployment and production:

Discovery

> Discovery is the initial stage of any ML project, and the first step is to define the business use case and understand how exactly ML fits into the wider solution. At this early stage it's important to consider the role that explainability will (or will not) play in the solution. In this stage, premodeling explainability is an essential tool for understanding the data or any feature engineering that is used to train the machine learning model.

Development

> Explainability plays an important role in deciding which model to use or for debugging models through development. XAI methods are also a useful toolkit for understanding feature engineering and feature selection using sliced analysis. Here techniques like example-based explanations are useful for closing the loop with stakeholders.

Deployment

> This stage is related to aspects of automating, monitoring, testing, managing, maintaining, and auditing machine learning models in production. The XAI toolkit can be particularly useful when incorporated into model monitoring and skew detection algorithms and feature attribution drift.

We also looked at the emerging landscape of regulations for AI coming from the governments around the world, from the EU to the US and China. This is both a blessing and a curse: on the positive side, you will have the flexibility to determine which explainability techniques are the best match for your ML and use case. However, you will likely be asked by stakeholders to demonstrate that whatever choice you made meets the regulatory standards for explainability.

Finally, we turned an eye toward the future of XAI and what you can expect, including:

Natural and semantic explanations
> An array of numbers representing feature attributions isn't necessarily very helpful for most users. Looking ahead, techniques that can present explanations in a more natural way or are able to generate explanations based on a semantic understanding of the model and its dataset, will be much more helpful.

Interrogative explanations
> Today's explanations are a one-way dialogue; in the future, we expect to see techniques that allow for a richer experience where the user can query the ML model for further information about the prediction or behavior.

Targeted explanations
> Explanations are focused on demonstrating the minimal amount of information sufficient to slip a model's prediction, meant as a way to achieve explanations that are more concise and simpler and thus more robust.

Further Reading

Following is a list of papers that we have found influenced our thinking about how to make, evaluate, and use explanations. In each case, we have tried to list papers we think will substantively add to your knowledge and give you new ways of thinking about XAI rather than exhaustively listing all research and writing on a topic.

Explainable AI

"DARPA's Explainable AI (XAI) Program: A Retrospective" (*https://oreil.ly/H4tIi*) is a summary of lessons learned on XAI techniques by the DARPA research program into XAI from 2016 to 2021 which spanned 12 teams and studies that included over 12,000 participants in total.

NIST's "Four Principles of Explainable Artificial Intelligence" (*https://oreil.ly/AVB7D*) by Jonathon Phillips et al. has distilled many aspects of XAI into a core set of concepts that can be useful for reasoning about any XAI technique.

"Interpretable Machine Learning" (*https://oreil.ly/NSNZh*) by Christoph Molnar covers both interpretable models and gives a from-first-principles approach to teaching XAI techniques.

"The Many Shapley Values for Model Explanation" (*https://oreil.ly/NwPdx*) by Mukund Sundararajan and Amir Najmi covers the variety of Shapley value–based techniques in XAI, the theoretical basis for correctness in each approach, and introduces useful axioms for desired properties of Shapley values.

"A Unified Approach to Interpreting Model Predictions" (*https://oreil.ly/4lJHo*) by Scott Lundberg and Su-In Lee introduces how Shapley values can be used in XAI.

"The Explanation Game: Explaining Machine Learning Models with Cooperative Game Theory" (*https://oreil.ly/JzULc*) by Luke Merrick and Ankur Taly explores how subtle differences in underlying implementations, such as Shapley values, can have a disproportionate impact on the final values in explanations.

Captum's Model interpretability for PyTorch (*https://captum.ai*) is an impressive library and contains implementations of every XAI technique we discuss in this book, and then some. In addition, there are a number of excellent tutorials to get you started.

"Visualizing the Impact of Feature Attribution Baselines" (*https://oreil.ly/cwKEs*) by Pascal Sturmfels et al. gives an excellent and detailed discussion of the role and impact of baselines for attribution methods.

The Language Interpretability Tool (*https://oreil.ly/YGAxL*) is just one of a number of excellent tools out of Google's PAIR team (*https://pair.withgoogle.com*) and is an excellent platform for examining your NLP ML models through a lens of interpretability and explainability. We truly only scratched the surface of its full capabilities.

Been Kim's invited talk, "Beyond Interpretability: Developing a Language to Shape Our Relationships with AI" (*https://oreil.ly/SoUd5*) from ICMR (2022) is an excellent discussion on the role of AI explainability and interpretability and provides an invaluable perspective on how to approach and utilize this ever-expanding toolkit.

Interacting with Explainability

"Metrics for Explainable AI: Challenges and Prospects" (*https://oreil.ly/jIdNT*) by Robert R. Hoffman et al. is a thorough discussion of how users approach and evaluate the value of explanations.

"Interpreting Interpretability: Understanding Data Scientists' Use of Interpretability Tools for Machine Learning" (*https://oreil.ly/k6Drd*) by Harmanpreet Kaur et al. performs a small study on how data scientists interpret the results of SHAP, finding common themes in how participants overrelied and misunderstood the visualized results.

Technical Accuracy of XAI techniques

"The Disagreement Problem in Explainable Machine Learning: A Practitioner's Perspective" (*https://oreil.ly/FAVRn*) by Satyapriya Krishna et al. performs an exhaustive study comparing how common XAI techniques differ in their attributed feature values.

"Stop Explaining Black Box Machine Learning Models for High Stakes Decisions and Use Interpretable Models Instead" (*https://oreil.ly/ERh2j*)" by Cynthia Rudin discusses the trade-off between using opaque black boxes versus inherently interpretable models and outlines several key reasons why explainable black boxes should be avoided in high-stakes decisions in criminal justice, healthcare, and computer vision..

The pair of papers "Sanity Checks for Saliency Maps" (*https://oreil.ly/WM9Fp*) by Julius Adebayo et al. and its rebuttal, "A Note About: Local Explanation Methods for Deep Neural Networks Lack Sensitivity to Parameter Values" (*https://oreil.ly/cUkos*) by Mukund Sundararajan and Ankur Taly, gives an exhaustive comparison of different saliency map–based techniques, discusses the differences between them, and explores how parameter choices can deeply affect the resulting explanations.

Brittleness of XAI techniques

"On the Robustness of Interpretability Methods" (*https://oreil.ly/YIBAx*) by David Alvarez-Melis and Tommi S. Jaakkola introduces metrics for measuring the robustness of techniques.

"Fooling LIME and SHAP: Adversarial Attacks on Post Hoc Explanation Methods" (*https://oreil.ly/vHi5F*) by Dylan Slack et al. introduces a framework based on perturbation and repeated model analysis to effectively represent unbiased explanations for a biased model.

"On the (In)fidelity and Sensitivity for Explanations" (*https://oreil.ly/esB3q*) by Chih-Kuan Yeh et al. also examines how saliency map–based techniques are brittle to slight perturbations in the inputs, provides a theoretical explanation for these results, and shows how to strengthen techniques against these problems.

XAI for DNNs

"Understanding Deep Networks via Extremal Perturbations and Smooth Masks" (*https://oreil.ly/xAOVx*) by Ruth Fong et al. demonstrates how to use perturbation analysis for understanding the behavior of intermediate layers.

"Explaining Nonlinear Classification Decisions with Deep Taylor Decomposition" (*https://oreil.ly/ZDZzt*) by Grégoire Montavon et al. introduces a technique to explain DNNs through attributing the final output to each layer in the model.

Index

About the Authors

Michael Munn is a research software engineer at Google in the ML Solutions team. His research focuses on better understanding the mathematical foundations of machine learning and how those insights can be used to improve machine learning models at Google. Previously, he worked in the Google Cloud Advanced Solutions Lab helping customers design, implement, and deploy machine learning models at scale. Michael has a PhD in mathematics from the City University of New York. Before joining Google, he worked as a research professor.

David Pitman is a staff engineer working in Google Cloud on the AI platform, where he leads the Explainable AI team. He is also a co-organizer of PuPPy, the largest Python group in the Pacific Northwest. David has a MEng and a BS in computer science, focusing on AI and human-computer interaction, from MIT, where he was previously a research scientist.

Colophon

The animal on the cover of *Explainable AI for Practitioners* is a blue-naped parrot (*Tanygnathus lucionensis*), also known as the blue-crowned green parrot, the Luzon parrot, or the Philippine green parrot. It is found throughout the Philippines and on some neighboring islands, inhabiting wooded areas in the lowlands and foothills and nesting in tree holes.

Blue-naped parrots are named for the light blue patch of feathers that extends from the top of the crown to the nape of the neck. The rest of their plumage is primarily bright green, with darker green wings that are edged with blue and yellow-orange. They usually live in flocks of under a dozen, and they forage together, feeding on fruit, seeds, nuts, and grains. Adults reach about 12 inches long and weigh about half a pound.

Their numbers have declined as deforestation has led to habitat loss and fragmentation. They also face increasing trapping for illegal trade. Consequently, they are listed as near threatened. Many of the animals on O'Reilly covers are endangered; all of them are important to the world.

The cover illustration is by Karen Montgomery, based on an antique line engraving from *Histoire Naturelle*. The cover fonts are Gilroy Semibold and Guardian Sans. The text font is Adobe Minion Pro; the heading font is Adobe Myriad Condensed; and the code font is Dalton Maag's Ubuntu Mono.

O'REILLY®

Learn from experts.
Become one yourself.

Books | Live online courses
Instant Answers | Virtual events
Videos | Interactive learning

Get started at oreilly.com.

Lightning Source UK Ltd.
Milton Keynes UK
UKHW030755041222
413311UK00004B/14